W9-ADW-013

Columbia University Slavic Studies
A Series of the
Department of Slavic Languages, Columbia University
Ernest J. Simmons, General Editor

The Soviet Linguistic Controversy

Translated from the Soviet Press by

John V. Murra, Robert M. Hankin, and Fred Holling

King's Crown Press
New York: Morningside Heights
1951

The preparation of this work for publication
has been made possible by a grant
of the Rockefeller Foundation
to the Department of Slavic Languages
of Columbia University

King's Crown Press is an imprint established by
Columbia University Press for the purpose of
making certain scholarly material available at
minimum cost. Toward that end, the publishers
have used standardized formats incorporating
every reasonable economy that does not interfere
with legibility. The author has assumed complete
responsibility for editorial style and proofreading.

Published in Great Britain, Canada, and India
by Geoffrey Cumberlege, Oxford University Press
London, Toronto, and Bombay

MANUFACTURED IN THE UNITED STATES OF AMERICA

Foreword

In the early period of the Soviet regime the linguistic theories of N. Ya. Marr were much criticized, but of late years his teachings have been elevated to the position of scholarly dogma sanctified by an avowed Marxian content. Heresy in this respect was not easily tolerated among Soviet philologists.

However, during a recent Moscow scientific session devoted to Marr's memory (January 24-27, 1950), it became evident that some philologists had been nibbling away at an "official" linguistic apple of discord. And proof that the dogma of Marrism had at last been found wanting soon became evident when *Pravda* opened its pages to an extensive discussion, beginning with an article by Professor Arn. Chikobava in the issue of May 9th. A series of articles by leading philologists followed, climaxed by a slashing attack on Marr and his followers from the pen of J. V. Stalin (June 20th). The debate was closed in the July 4th issue of *Pravda* by another article of Stalin and final statements from various participants in the discussion.

Subsequent articles and news items have appeared in the Soviet press which indicate how far-reaching has been the application of the conclusions drawn from the controversy in the whole realm of Soviet linguistics and teaching. The Presidium of the U.S.S.R. Academy of Sciences and the Ministry of Higher Education have ordered the replacement of scientific heads tainted with Marrism in these organizations; new curricula of courses in linguistics and the history of literature in accordance with the new "line" are to be worked out; the staffs of higher schools and the dissertations of graduate students are to be examined, in order that all scientific work in these fields may be reorganized in conformity with Stalin's directives in linguistics; new courses of lectures in universities and pedagogical institutes on the results of the discussion are to be offered; Moscow State University has announced new courses to retrain teachers of linguistic disciplines in higher educational institutions; new textbooks, teaching aids, and monographs on the most important problems of linguistics will be issued; and the Linguistics Institute of the U.S.S.R. plans to publish soon two works of a theoretical nature: "Basic Problems of Linguistics in the Light of J. V. Stalin's Works" and "A Criticism of the 'Linguistic Theory' of Marr."

Further, official action on some of the major participants in the controversy has been swift. The Presidium of the U.S.S.R. Academy of Sciences has passed a decree to release Academician I. I. Meshchaninov from the post of director of the Institute of Language and Thought of the U.S.S.R. Academy of Sciences, Professor G. P. Serdyuchenko from the post of deputy director of this institute and Professor F. P. Filin from the duties of Academic Secretary of the Presidium of the U.S.S.R. Academy of Sciences. The Institute of Language and Thought and the Institute of the Russian Language of the U.S.S.R. Academy of Sciences are being amalgamated in an integrated Institute of Linguistics of the U.S.S.R. Academy of Sciences. And Academician V. V. Vinogradov has been confirmed as director of the Institute of Linguistics. Finally, the Presidium has revoked as being erroneous its decrees of July 21, 1949 and April 12, 1950.

Because of the importance that this controversy has assumed in the U.S.S.R., it was thought that a service would be rendered to American linguistic specialists and to American students of the Soviet Union in general by making available to them, in collected form, complete translations of the articles on this subject which have appeared in *Pravda*. Through the kind offices of Mr. Leo Gruliow, Editor of *The Current Digest of the Soviet Press*, permission was obtained to reprint the translations of these articles in the *Digest* (Vol. II, Nos. 18-22, 24-28), which had been edited for the *Digest* by Robert M. Hankin. An article in *Voprosy filosofii*, likewise translated in the *Digest*, has also been included. Attention is drawn to two further articles on linguistics, preceding the *Pravda* discussion, and not included here but also appearing in the *Digest* (Vol. I, Nos. 46-51). In the course of editing the *Digest* translations for the purpose of the collection, some slight corrections have been made in clarifying certain passages and in the footnotes.

The Department is deeply indebted to Miss Elizabeth Kresky, of the staff of the *Digest*, for her skillful work in editing and assembling the manuscript, and acknowledgement is gratefully paid to the Rockefeller Foundation for its financial support in the preparation of this book.

Ernest J. Simmons

Table of Contents

Scientific Session Devoted to Marr Anniversary*

By A. G. SPIRKIN

The Soviet public observed extensively the 85th anniversary of the birth and 15th anniversary of the death of N. Ya. Marr, inspired Soviet scientist and founder of the new, materialist teachings on language who brought fame to our fatherland's science through his outstanding scientific works.

Academician Marr's teaching on language, erected on the firm base of dialectical and historical materialism, constitutes a genuine, revolutionary upheaval in linguistics. The new teaching on language formulated by N. Ya. Marr, ardent patriot and true son of the party of Lenin and Stalin, is the product of the great October socialist revolution. Nikolai Yakovlevich Marr himself frequently emphasized that the new teaching on language could have developed only under conditions of the Soviet social system with its new, revolutionary world viewpoint and its solution of the national question on the basis of new principles. Academician Marr worked tirelessly for the socialist system, participating directly in national-cultural construction, carrying out the great ideas of Marx, Engels, Lenin and Stalin on the fraternal cooperation of peoples.

Since Marr's death, the materialist teaching on language which he formulated has been creatively developed by his pupils and followers.

The Soviet people profoundly revere the memory of their glorious son. Scientific sessions devoted to the memory of the inspired scientist and ardent Bolshevist patriot N. Ya. Marr have been organized in all linguistics institutes of the Soviet Union, in all academies of sciences of the union republics and higher educational institutions of our country during [the observance of] the 85th anniversary of N. Ya. Marr's birth and the 15th anniversary of his death. Scientific sessions of nationwide importance and devoted to this noteworthy date were held in Leningrad and Moscow.

The task of the scientific sessions in both Moscow and Leningrad was to sum up the work of Soviet linguistics, to subject the shortcomings which exist in this work to sharp Party criticism, and to indicate paths of future creative development of Marr's heritage in connection with profound tasks in studying the language and writing systems of the peoples of the U.S.S.R., in the field of language development.

In Moscow, the scientific session devoted to N. Ya. Marr's memory lasted from Jan. 24 to Jan. 27.

The following persons gave reports at the special session called by the N. Ya. Marr Institute of Language and Thought in Moscow on a joint resolution of the Presidium of the U.S.S.R. Academy of Sciences and representatives of institutes of the union republics working on problems of linguistics in the national republics: Academician I. I. Meshchaninov, Profs. G. P. Serdyuchenko, N. S. Chemodanov and I. M. Oshanin, Corresponding Member of the Armenian Republic Academy of Sciences Prof. A. S. Garibyan, Corresponding Member of the Azerbaidzhan Academy of Sciences M. A. Shiraliyev, Member of the Kazakh Academy of Sciences S. K. Kenesbayev, Comrade V. M. Alatyrev, D. I. Mikhalchi and others. Staff members of the Institute of Language and Thought, Institute of Philosophy of the U.S.S.R. Academy of Sciences, Moscow State University and the academies of sciences of the union republics took part in the debates. All participants stated that creative development of linguistic problems is possible only on the basis of the materialist teaching on language formulated by N. Ya. Marr which has played such a tremendous role in the development of the national languages of the peoples of the U.S.S.R. All participants unanimously demanded that a most resolute struggle be waged against attempts to resurrect reactionary, bourgeois theories of linguistics, the formal-comparative method in linguistics.

Participants in the sessions stressed in their remarks that N. Ya. Marr's works, based on the firm foundation of dialectical and historical materialism, are a most sharp ideological weapon against bourgeois, idealistic linguistics which propagandizes reactionary, racist theories.

The session was opened by A. V. Topchiyev, Chief Learned Secretary of the U.S.S.R. Academy of Sciences who called for development of Bolshevist criticism and self-criticism as making it possible to remedy existing shortcomings in linguistic work and to raise the Soviet materialist science of language to a new, higher level.

In his report "N. Ya. Marr as a Scholar and Teacher," N. Ya. Marr's closest pupil and follower Academician I. I. Meshchaninov brilliantly characterized the creative path followed by the inspired Soviet linguist. Academician Meshchaninov demonstrated on the basis of extensive specific factual material that even prior to the great October socialist revolution N. Ya. Marr adopted a very hostile attitude toward reactionary, bourgeois science. The conditions under which N. Ya. Marr worked in the pre-revolutionary university did not permit him to develop his tremendous creative talent. This talent blossomed with unusual force after the great October [revolution] when N. Ya. Marr became an active participant in cultural construction in our country.

Reforms in university teaching and reorganization of the work of an entire series of scientific institutions after the great October socialist revolution advanced N. Ya. Marr to first place in the university world and made him a most active participant in the development of a new, Soviet science. He raised archeology to the level of a genuinely scientific discipline, becoming head of the archeological commission which he reorganized into the Academy of the History of Material Culture.

Academician N. Ya. Marr created a linguistics institute in the network of academic institutions. On the basis of the Japhetic theory, N. Ya. Marr brought archeology and linguistics closer together. Archeology lost its old, treasure-hunting tendencies and became permeated with genuine historicity, while linguistics ceased to be regarded as an isolated, self-sufficient discipline. N. Ya. Marr injected a live current into the university program. Archeology and ethnography were included among the disciplines taught at the University and took on an entirely new, materialist character. Painstaking analysis of language by the method of materialist dialectics in language resulted in disclosure of a rich fund of facts of which the social historian can make extensive use.

In his lectures N. Ya. Marr spoke as a creative scientist moving ever forward toward the solution of basic questions of linguistics: what is language, how did it originate and how does it develop, on what is the connection between languages of different systems based, how are they conditioned and on what do the differences among them rest and how should one interpret the complexity of the genetical process beginning with the period when human speech was being established? These were new questions, the solution of which required

* Voprosy filosofii, No. 3, 1949 [published in April, 1950], pp. 326-327.

entirely different methodological principles than those on which bourgeois linguistics is based.

Bourgeois science furnished no answer to all these questions which faced N. Ya. Marr. N. Ya. Marr found the answers to these questions in the works of Marx, Engels, Lenin and Stalin. Language serves as a means of communication. Consequently, it was not created by an individual, but by a social environment, in the labor activity of a human collective. Changes in language do not arise of themselves; they are not fortuitous. They are socially determined. All elements of human speech are bearers of a definite social content. N. Ya. Marr demanded that the form of language be studied in connection with the determination of its social significance. He declared an implacable struggle against formalism.

N. Ya. Marr approached the solution of theoretical questions of linguistics from the tenets of Marxism-Leninism. He acknowledged language to be a phenomenon of a social character, but he did not stop at this, because even the Neo-Grammarian school does not dispute this premise. From an idealist standpoint the Neo-Grammarians asserted that language in its establishment and evolution could develop according to its own laws which have from time immemorial been inherent in it. They examined language in its evolution from the state of a primordial, proto-language. Bourgeois linguistics sketches the developmental scheme of language as an inverted pyramid with a single starting point from which, according to the scheme, came branches, causing a development from singleness [of language] to multiplicity. According to the Neo-Grammarians, language families and their proto-languages are developed in this way. How the proto-languages were formed and from what they originated is not disclosed, while even the formulation of such a question is considered unscientific. This concept is permeated with the spirit of racism and serves as justification of the imperialists' colonial policy.

In opposition to these pseudo-scientific, idealistic theories, N. Ya. Marr advanced the new, genuinely materialist theory of the origin of language. According to this theory, the dispersed clans and tribes of the primitive community could not have had a single language. Language was not created of itself but was created by the social environment which at that time did not require the development of a common speech. It developed and was perfected not of itself, not immanently, but in close connection with the development of thought. The causes determining the development of language lie outside of language, in the development of society, in social practice. Man's social-labor activity develops consciousness and language.

Concretizing Marx's references to the laws of language development, N. Ya. Marr works out the teaching on a single glottogonic process.

In his analysis of the history of language N. Ya. Marr establishes the primacy of kinetic speech and the secondary nature of vocal speech. Marr establishes the theory of functional semantics which makes possible profound penetration into history. He comes to the conclusion that gesture, kinetic language, played a leading role in that long period when the undeveloped throat of the primate had not yet been converted into the articulating voice apparatus of man.

Labor created man and also determined the origin of speech. Our voice apparatus in its present form did not develop of itself. Prolonged speech practice developed it. The original voice apparatus was different, meaning that the sound of human speech was also different originally. In complete accord with Engels, N. Ya. Marr establishes that originally man's throat issued only diffused, inarticulate sounds.

Creative labor distinguishes man from the animal. The realization that man lives in society determines both the labor act and the developing means of intercourse. Consequently, language is as ancient as consciousness. From this, N. Ya. Marr comes to the conclusion that language and thought are dialectically united and admits language to be a superstructure which is acted upon by the base through historically developing consciousness.

In studying the history of language N. Ya. Marr stands firmly on the tenets of Marxism-Leninism. On the basis of the Leninist-Stalinist definition of the nature of language as a major means of communication (Lenin), as an implement of development and struggle (Stalin), N. Ya. Marr discloses the social, class nature of language, paying particular attention to its semantics.

In adhering to the basic premises of Marxism-Leninism, N. Ya. Marr demonstrates the unity of language and thought on the basis of extensive material on the history of languages, stressing that the development of language does not represent an evolutionary process only, but is also a process of leaps, the revolutionary supplanting of one stage in the development of language and thought by another, qualitatively different stage.

N. Ya. Marr's theory of stage development of language has aided in the solution of complicated questions of glottogony.

Investigating the problem of the origin and development of language on the basis of the tenets of dialectical and historical materialism, N. Ya. Marr comes to the conclusion that the problem of the origin of language cannot be solved without studying the course of man's emergence and without disclosing the reasons determining the need for using the speech apparatus. In investigating the subsequent development of language it is essential to establish those social grounds which cause corresponding changes in language structure.

N. Ya. Marr's teaching on the origin and development of language in dependence on the development of society, on the direct connection between thought and speech, on a single glottogonic process of language development and its stage nature has played an exceptional role in the solution of theoretical problems of linguistics on the basis of the tenets of dialectical materialism.

N. Ya. Marr skillfully combined theoretical work with the completion of actual assignments imposed by the practice of socialist construction. He took active part in the complex problem of forming alphabets and orthographies, grammars and dictionaries for the languages of the peoples of the U.S.S.R., as well as the devising of writing systems for peoples who had not had them before. N. Ya. Marr derived extensive material for his theoretical work from the practice of language development in the U.S.S.R. Soviet reality gave him an opportunity to observe changes in language structure which, caused by new conditions of labor reality, disclose the social significance of language and its dependence on economic and cultural development. Peoples of the U.S.S.R. who formerly had no writing systems are obtaining their own systems of writing thanks to the new conditions created in our country by the national policy of Lenin and Stalin. Languages are developing on their own national soil, becoming enriched in vocabulary, while written literary language is becoming qualitatively different from oral, colloquial speech, and is making its demands on the present-day grammatical structure. Studying these changes in language structure, we become convinced that they are not at all fortuitous. Neither enrichment of the vocabulary nor development of grammatical structure happens by itself. It is becoming perfectly clear that the language of any given people in a given period of its historical life cannot be studied solely by itself, apart from the social life of the people. The practical work done by N. Ya. Marr in connection with introducing writing systems among peoples recently backward in their development and in connection with perfecting teaching methods, etc., has served as a motive force in the scientists' own growth. His theoretical work has practical application, and for this reason the new teaching on language becomes enriched.

Academician I. I. Meshchaninov gave special attention to N. Ya. Marr's research methods and to his exceptional teaching skill.

The Soviet linguist, says Academician Meshchaninov, sees from his own experience that theory cannot be divorced from practice, from life, that it is enriched by practice, and, in turn, practice makes very general use of the theoretical attainments of scientists who devote their energies to the socialist development of the peoples of the U.S.S.R. developing their economy and culture on the path toward communism. Like all Soviet scientists, the Soviet linguist does not lock himself up in his science laboratory; rather, he faces up to the urgent demands of socialist construction. N. Ya. Marr was a model progressive Soviet scientist, all of his work having been placed in the service of socialist construction and devoted to combatting hostile, idealist theories in linguistics. In his work he campaigned for the general Party line in the science of language. The inspired Soviet scientist trained many young people. In those young people, trained on the firm principles of materialist doctrine and consumed by the inspiring flame of Marxist-Leninist science and the desire to serve their great Motherland in every way, Marr saw the heirs of his cause. He directed the following memorable words to them: "Neither faint-hearted retreat nor conciliatory appeasment. Forward, young comrades, our replacements!"

Academician I. I. Meshchaninov concluded his report with this impassioned appeal by Academician Marr to young Soviet scientists.

Although he provided a comprehensive description of N. Ya Marr's personality as a scientist and teacher, Academician I. I. Meshchaninov did not indicate further prospects for developing the science of language and, in essence, he bypassed the unsatisfactory situation on the linguistics front, failing to disclose the reasons for this unsatisfactory situation.

Corresponding Member of the Russian Republic Academy of Pedagogical Sciences Prof. G. P. Serdyuchenko delivered a report entitled "The Creative Path of N. Ya. Marr." In his report Serdyuchenko paid particular attention to the formation of the dialectical materialist teaching of N. Ya. Marr and to some methodological questions of Marr's linguistics. The professor correctly emphasized that Marr's complete break with the old, bourgeois, Indo-European linguistics and his creation of a new materialist science of language could be realized only after victory of the great October socialist revolution, on the basis of Marxist-Leninist philosophy, Leninist-Stalinist national policy and the works of genius of J. V. Stalin. A huge role was also played by the direct personal participation of the remarkable Soviet scholar in the socialist construction. Marr's materialistic linguistics was entirely developed during the great Stalinist epoch. Solving the problem of the origin and development of national languages, Marr based himself entirely on Stalin's definitive works on the nationality question.

On the basis of the decisions of the Party conferences on the nationality question, adopted in conformity with Comrade Stalin's reports and personal directives, the work of improving and developing national cultures and languages of the peoples of the U.S.S.R. developed in our country, unprecedented in its significance and scope. It stimulated the development of many branches of Soviet science including linguistics.

During the Soviet era a broad, thorough study of the languages of the people of the U.S.S.R. has been carried out. This research has been closely associated with the fulfillment of the assignments of the Bolshevist party in regard to the improvement and development of linguistic culture and it has caused the enrichment of Soviet linguistic theory and a further flourishing of the languages themselves.

All the successes of Soviet linguistics have been due to the leadership of the great Communist Party and to its leader of genius J. V. Stalin.

Lenin's and Stalin's works on dialectical materialism as well as on the question of nationalities are of the greatest world-wide historic importance and prove an unshakable foundation for the works of Soviet linguists. They offer to our scholars a sure orientation from which to carry out a correct national policy in the work of developing spoken and written languages of the Soviet peoples and for a thorough methodological re-organization of the whole theoretical work of linguistics.

It is only on the basis of dialectical materialism that development of a truly progressive and leading science can take place at present. It is precisely dialectical materialist methodological bases that have determined the brilliant development of Michurin's biology, Pavlov's materialist physiology, the materialist physics of atomic nucleus and Marr's new linguistics. The new linguistics was formed on the basis of Marxist-Leninist materialist philosophy, of Leninist-Stalinist national policy, and the works of genius of Stalin and of the direct personal participation of N. Ya. Marr in the socialist reorganization of the country under the direction and leadership of the Bolshevist party. N. Ya. Marr wrote about this himself in his work "Language and the Present Day," and, in his report devoted to the fifteenth anniversary of the great October socialist revolution, he stressed the unqualified dependence of the successes of his new linguistics on Leninist-Stalinist national policy and on the building of socialism in the U.S.S.R.

N. Ya. Marr broke away completely from Indo-European linguistics and consciously reorganized the science of language on the basis of Marxism-Leninism. He said so himself in his speech at the Sixteenth Party Congress, in the reports "Language and the Present Day," "Marx and Problems of Language," etc. That is why all sorts of opinions that Marr was a "spontaneous" or "concealed Marxist" must be rejected because of their obvious fallacy and their endeavor to minimize the importance of the influence of the Marxist-Leninist philosophy and the guidance of the Party of Lenin and Stalin upon the outstanding scholar.

Nikolai Yakovlevich Marr is among those great Soviet scientists to whom Stalin's words about people of advanced science may be wholly applied.

N. Ya. Marr tried by all his theoretical and practical scientific activities to meet the high demands which the socialist reorganization of the country was making upon Soviet scientists. Being an untiring fighter for the social-reforming role of Soviet science, Marr by his intense activity guaranteed the domination of a fighting Soviet patriotic spirit. Being a fighting materialist, N. Ya. Marr subjected to sharp annihilating criticism all the basic propositions of the old, reactionary, idealistic linguistics, exposing their dependence on the racist ideology and colonial policy of the imperialist states.

N. Ya. Marr decisively exposed, from the Marxist-Leninist standpoint, the racist basis of reactionary, bourgeois Indo-European linguistics and untiringly led the struggle against all kinds of formulations alien to Soviet science.

Bolshevist intransigence to everything which is opposed to the spirit of Bolshevist Party ideology is a basic feature of the scientific and scientific-organizational activity of Academician Marr. He spurned the peaceful co-existence of the two opposing tendencies and was impatient with all those who attempted to combine these opposite trends. In a series of Marr's propositions and statements, Prof. Serdyuchenko shows the tremendous influence the study of Lenin's and Stalin's works had upon Marr who in his later works turns particularly often toward Lenin's teaching on unity of language and thinking. He always follows Stalin's directives on the nationality question, on national languages in the epoch of capitalism and socialism, on the single language of the future Communist society. Prof. Serdyuchenko went on to describe several methodological problems of linguistics in Marr's treatment.

Marr gives the Marxist definition of a language as a superstructural category connected in its origin with life and he spurns the bourgeois-ideologist concepts of a language as a "closed entity."

In this connection Marr points out the reflection of class differentiation and class struggle in language. He mercilessly exposes the bourgeois theory of linguistics on the non-class quality of national language in the epoch of imperialism.

N. Ya. Marr poses the problem of language origin as one of the most important in linguistics and in this he follows the classical works of Marxism. He advances the proposition of the dialectical unity of language and thought—"thinking and language are inseparable"—opposing bourgeois science, characterized by the lack of connection between the two. Applying the method of dialectical materialism, following carefully the history of language and the history of thought which are determined by the development of human society, N. Ya. Marr checked linguistic materials with the historical sources accessible to science, putting the main stress on the monuments of materialist culture.

Dwelling on the question of the primacy of gesture speech, Prof. Serdyuchenko pointed out that recently even some representatives of the new linguistics have preferred for some reason to remain silent on this recognized and solidly argued teaching of Marr's.

This was what Prof. N. F. Yakovlev in particular did in his pamphlets on the origins of language.

In agreement with Engels, Marr dates the appearance of sounds in speech from the period of creation by man of artificial work implements,although he points out that kinetic speech preceded sound and played the leading role during the first stages of language development.

Another major problem worked out by Marr was the problem of development by stages. He strove to trace the development of oral speech, of grammatical and vocabulary forms as a whole, over long historical periods, while connecting various systems of construction of spoken language with changes in public opinion, depending on the succession of social economic stages. The development of the teaching on the development of languages by stages differentiates Soviet from traditional bourgeois linguistics. The development of all languages, according to Marr, reflects the very same social laws, which results from singleness of the social-historic process. At the same time, Marr's teaching does not deny the qualitative originality of each language. Marr comes out decisively against traditional bourgeois comparativism which ignores the national originality of the languages and literatures of the world. Marr subjected to sharp criticism the comparative-formal method of bourgeois linguistics, opposing to it the paleontological, sociological method which traces the true historical development of language and thought.

The lecturer called attention to Marr's teaching on the role of hybridization in the development of languages, reflecting, in the final analysis, the social-economic union of various tribal, ethnic elements in the formation of peoples and,later, nations. Soviet linguists must, on the basis of Comrade Stalin's teaching on the formation of contemporary bourgeois and Soviet socialist nations and taking into consideration Marr's views on questions of ethnogeny, reanalyze all the literature devoted to the history of the formation and development of concrete national languages.

Marr's teaching in all its purpose is anti-imperialistic. He protests against the completely unfounded division of peoples and languages into "superior" and "inferior," into "capable" and "incapable" of development, seeing rightly the introduction into linguistics of racism and the national colonial policy of bourgeois imperialist states.

Passionately defending the Party principle in linguistics, Marr was profoundly self-critical and recognized that shortcomings were possible in his theories. However, a critical scrutiny of Marr's individual propositions on the initial development of spoken language and paleontologic analysis by elements, while contributing to the general growth of Soviet linguistics, must not cast a shadow on Marr's achievements in his creation of a new materialist linguistics. Nonetheless, some Soviet scholars (Member of the Georgian Academy of Sciences Prof. Chikobava and instructor at the Moscow State University Comrade Serebrennikov) declare that all Marr's teaching is mechanistic and oppose to it as more acceptable, reactionary, idealistic theories of various bourgeois linguists.

Prof. Serdyuchenko went on to dwell on the general state of Soviet linguistics at present, pointing out several serious shortcomings and,above all, the neglect of the Party principle in many linguistic institutes and the absence of principled Bolshevist criticism and self-criticism. Even some leaders of the N. Ya. Marr Institute of Language and Thought, says Prof. Serdyuchenko, have not only failed to consider that the reactions of the Party press and also the article by I. I. Meshchaninov in the Literaturnaya gazeta are correct in principle and demand a review of the linguistic institute's work, but have started to stifle the attempts, weak enough without this, at criticism and self-criticism. At the same time, articles in Pravda, Kultura i zhizn, Literaturnaya gazeta and local organs of different republics have reported the presence of alarming symptoms on the linguistic front of our work.

Describing the development of Marr's teaching in the national republics, Prof. Serdyuchenko pointed out that great attention is given to it in Armenia, Azerbaidzhan, Kazakhstan and other Union republics. Unfortunately, things are different in the institutes of the Georgian Academy of Science where Marr's teaching is criticized and old, definitely discarded methods used. Attempts to discredit or to ignore Marr's new linguistics,which is a brilliant example of the application of Marxism-Leninism to the study of language, repeat, in essence, similar attempts by Weismanists and Morganists to discredit and discard the materialist research of Michurin and Lysenko. The attempts to conciliate materialist linguistics with idealistic, bourgeois theories of the comparatists, immanentists, etc., are equally intolerable.

Prof. Serdyuchenko criticized several works which have lately appeared in various republics of the Union and among them Prof. Abayev's monograph which is a vivid example of the inadmissible attempts to reconcile progressive, materialist linguistics with traditional bourgeois notions.

In his report, Prof. Serdyuchenko did not content himself with presenting the basic propositions of the new linguistics but also tried to analyze the situation on the linguistics front. However, he did not succeed in showing what work had been done on several theoretical questions in the 15 years since Marr's death.

Prof. N. S. Chemodanov made a report on the subject "Academician N. Ya. Marr's Struggle Against Bourgeois Linguistics." He recalled at the beginning Comrade Zhdanov's appeal,made during the philosophic discussion, to wage an offensive against the decaying bourgeois ideology. Linguistics in capitalist countries more and more is used by the imperialistic, anti-democratic camp headed by the U.S.A. in its struggle against the camp of progress, democracy and peace headed by the Soviet Union.

Indicative in this regard is the retreat of bourgeois linguistics from genetic problems and its scorn for problems of historicity.

Hitler's fascism tried a broader use, in its own interests, of the antiquated concept of Indo-Germanic racial superiority, but failed in the attempt. Today, with the same aims, Anglo-American imperialism uses the contemporary Saussure and other neo-idealist schools for their propaganda of the notorious cosmopolitan theory of the superiority of analytical over inflected languages. This pseudo "theory" is used as a theoretical foundation for Anglo-American racism and contrasts the Western European peoples, as allegedly "chosen," to the remainder of the world and in particular to the people's democracies and the Soviet Union.

Denying national originality of individual languages, the pseudo-scientific bourgeois linguistic theories are a striking manifestation of cosmopolitanism and serve as the ideological foundation for the reactionary projects establishing a "United States of Europe," "Marshall Plan," etc.

The link between bourgeois linguistics and cosmopolitan propaganda proves what sort of filthy, selfish interests are concealed behind the abstract arguments on the structure of languages in the articles of contemporary bourgeois linguists.

Soviet materialist linguistics, founded by Marr's genius, came into existence after the October socialist revolution. It was formed and developed on the basis of the great ideas of Marx, Engels, Lenin and Stalin. The theoretical and practical achievements of Soviet linguists are indissolubly connected with the successes of the cultural revolution in our country, with the development and consolidation of national socialist cultures and the brotherly cooperation of Soviet peoples. Marr expressed this convincingly in his later works.

Marr considered the new linguistics as the fruit of the active participation of the peoples of the U.S.S.R. in revolutionary creative work. This teaching was formed on the basis of Lenin's theory of reflection and Stalin's teaching on national culture.

Marr led a decisive struggle against bourgeois pseudo-linguistics. Marr's active and untiring struggle against the alien and hostile bourgeois linguistics has kept, even today, its actual socio-political and scientific significance. He based himself on Lenin's Party principle in science and pitilessly exposed manifestations of idealism, racism and cosmopolitanism.

He exposed the racist content of the theories of the Indo-Europeanists and showed that their chauvinism was closely connected with the cosmopolitan negation of national differences.

Marr attacked every retreat from materialism, every appeasement and conciliation as shameful cowardice.

The year 1923 was the turning point in Marr's creative work. He made a final break with bourgeois linguistics in his famous declaration on Indo-European languages of the Mediterranean area and formulated his theory of development by stages as applied to Indo-European languages. The statement was made on Nov. 21, 1923. But some months earlier, in a little known letter to F. A. Braun in Leipzig, Marr had expressed the same thought in condensed form. In 1924, in his article on Japhetic theory, Marr produced a classical definition of the essence of Indo-European linguistics. He declared that it is part and parcel of the dying bourgeois society, built on oppression of the peoples of the East by a murderous colonial policy.

In 1930, N. Ya. Marr characterized the class nature of bourgeois linguistics in a report "Japhetidology in Leningrad State University," and showed its radical opposition to materialist linguistics.

Exposing the class nature of Indo-European linguistics, Marr shows that it transferred to the Indo-European peoples the theological confessional concept of chosen people.

N. Ya. Marr considered the basic flaw of bourgeois linguistics to be its divorcement from the history of material culture and other fields of science close to linguistics.

In his work "Native Speech" Marr gives a more detailed analysis of all these questions. He notes in this article "the internal decay of Indo-European linguistics" and its "idealist poverty."

Marr spoke sharply against idealism and formalism in linguistics. He showed how poor and unscientific the formalist comparative method is. He critizes this method in his article "Origin of Language," and in his work "Japhetic Chuvash on the Volga" (1926) and finally in "Language and Thought" where he calls these methods "stupid to the point of naivete."

Criticizing pitilessly bourgeois linguists Marr noted and encouraged the attempts of certain bourgeois linguists to depart from traditional idealist linguistics. He subjected to sharp criticism the linguist Meillet's pseudo-sociological theories. Marr showed the radical opposition between the new language teaching and bourgeois linguistics in his article "Japhetic Theory—Tool of Class Struggle" (1930). Marr attacked with particular violence the attempts by bourgeois linguists to consider language development as an immanent process divorced from the history of society and thought.

Marr's new teaching is our powerful weapon in the struggle against the racial Anglo-American linguistics.

The struggle against bourgeois linguistics was for Marr indissolubly linked with the struggle against the survival of formalism among Soviet linguists, against the propaganda of the backward theories of pre-revolutionary linguistics.

Prof. Chemodanov cites Marr's remarks about the Russian linguist Shakhmatov about whom Marr said that he was compelled to fetter healthy ideas with the vises of a deadening theory. Marr pointed out the class limitation of Baudouin de Courtenay. He brands D. N. Ushakov as a preacher of a "deceased science," he led a sharp struggle against the Machist Bogdanov on the question of language origin. Conducting his struggle against appeasement and conciliation, Marr attacked those linguists who refused to give up traditional concepts. He spoke about the irreconcilable antagonism between the new linguistics and Indo-European theory.

Marr considered that the new linguistics must be not only passively assimilated, but must also receive a revolutionary, creative development; for "otherwise," says Marr, "it would be merely a retreat and it could have only one fate—to serve the international bourgeoisie which has been driven into an idealistic impasse."

Exposing mercilessly bourgeois linguistics, Marr demanded the broad development of self-criticism, demanded revolutionary deductions from criticism and self-criticism and their application in actual practice.

Soviet linguists must learn from Marr the principled Bolshevist criticism and self-criticism.

Marr himself was a model of criticism and self-criticism, Prof. Chemodanov said.

Marr spoke of the significance of criticism and self-criticism in science in his remarkable report at the general session of the State Academy of the History of Material Culture in 1931.

Prof. Chemodanov declared that the contemporary state of linguistics demanded the broad development of criticism and self-criticism. We still do not have a single textbook on linguistics satisfactory by our present standards; criticism is still not sufficiently widely developed and is of a superficial and declarative nature. Creative development of the new linguistics is still inadequate. There are even open attacks against Marr's linguistics by Professors Chikobava and Akhvlidiani who preach the ideas of the neo-grammaries and immanentists. These alien tendencies have not yet received a proper rebuff.

There are erroneous propositions in V. Nikolsky's and N. Yakovlev's article published in the magazine Voprosy filosofii distorting Marr's teaching. Attempts are still being made to reinstate the comparative method, and the proto-language schemes and a political interpretation of the works of Russian pre-revolutionary idealist linguists still is tolerated in certain works.

In his conclusion Prof. Chemodanov appealed to the Soviet linguists to develop broadly criticism and self-criticism directed toward creative development of Marr's teaching, and overcoming capitalist survivals in contemporary Soviet linguistics.

It was noted by those who participated in the debates that Prof. Chemodanov's report was not self-critical. Prof.

Chemodanov failed to criticize his own works, inadequately explained the significance of Marr's new linguistics in the struggle against the most recent idealist trends in bourgeois linguistics (for instance, against reactionary, insane semantic theories, etc.)

Comrades Lysenko (Ukraine), Byelov (Voronezh) and others who spoke at the discussion criticized the heads of the Institute of Language and Thought. They noted that questions of language teaching in school were quite insufficiently treated and that theoretical work on problems of linguistics was poor.

The delegates from the Georgian Republic, Comrades Glonti and Megrelidze, and Comrade Gozalishvili, candidate of the Institute of Language and Thought, came out with sharp criticism of Professor Chikobava's views.

Comrade Megrelidze exposed the idealistic views of Prof. Chikobava. He noted justly that there were scientific forces in Georgia which could develop the science of linguistics on the basis of Marr's teaching. Comrades Megrelidze, Glonti and Gozalishvili in their speeches gave a detailed treatment of the struggle which is being waged in Georgia against the opponents of N. Ya. Marr's teaching.

M. G. Yaroshevsky and A. G. Spirkin, staff members and candidates of philosophical sciences, spoke at the conference in the name of the Institute of Philosophy.

Comrade Yaroshevsky noted that formalism was one of the basic manifestations of enemy ideology. Formalism in linguistics manifests itself primarily in severance of language from thought as a means of reflecting life. Some Soviet linguists show formalism in their understanding of the subject matter of linguistics and their interpretation of the problem of the origin of language and N. Ya. Marr's teaching on stages. Comrade Yaroshevsky sharply criticized the article, "Basic Principles of N. Ya. Marr's Materialist Teaching on Language," by Nikolsky and Yakovlev, which appeared in the magazine Voprosy filosofii. He noted that this article was a vivid instance of formalism. It distorts N. Ya. Marr's teaching on the origin of language, Marr's teaching on stages and a number of other basic principles of Marr's linguistics. The authors give a completely incorrect definition of language as consciousness in the form of sound. Such a formalistic definition has nothing to do with Lenin's reflection theory. On the one hand, it reduces language to mere sounds, ignoring all other forms of language. On the other hand, it leads to the reactionary concept of "language consciousness," which has already been criticized in Soviet linguistic literature. The morphological determination of stages contradicts the very essence of N. Ya. Marr's teaching and is theoretically defective and politically harmful. The problem of the origin of language cannot be divorced from the problem of the origin of thought. The connection between the teaching of N. Ya. Marr and the teaching of I. P. Pavlov on the second reflex system must be investigated. Language must be regarded as a reflection of reality. This is fully applicable both to semantics and syntax.

K. A. Levkovskaya (Moscow State University) criticized Prof. Chemodanov's report in her speech. She emphasized the fact that Prof. Chemodanov did not carry out the task he had set himself, did not sharply criticize contemporary bourgeois linguistics in the light of N. Ya. Marr's teaching. This, said Comrade Levkovskaya, is due to the fact that Prof. Chemodanov not only does not struggle against reactionary, bourgeois theories in his activity but, on the contrary, is under the influence of bourgeois linguistics. This has found expression in his works (in the anthology on the history of the German language and the introduction to linguistics). Comrade Levkovskaya also criticized the mistakes contained in the works of Prof. Gukhman.

Anna Movsesyan (Academy of Sciences of the Armenian Republic) delivered an interesting speech. She pointed out that the present session had seen no truly Bolshevist, uncompromising criticism of the enemies of N. Ya. Marr's new teaching on language, that the reports at the session gave the feeling of a kind of uncertainty and hesitancy with regard to those principles which N. Ya. Marr's opponents declared to be incorrect and defective. Comrade Movsesyan dwelt in detail on N. Ya. Marr's teaching concerning element analysis and affirmed that this analysis is a new, higher step in the paleontologic analysis of language. This method is the foundation of a new teaching on language and stands in basic opposition to the bourgeois formal-comparative method. Element analysis makes it possible to penetrate the true history of human language and shows us how language is formed in indissoluble unity with thought. Comrade Movsesyan noted that element analysis may not be utilized in all cases and elements may not be sought in all words. Element analysis cannot be an end in itself. It should be utilized as a tool in those cases when the linguist is confronted with the problem of investigating the extremely complicated history of the development of language, to bring out the stage stratifications in language and show the ancient interrelation of words and the reinterpretation of concepts.

The discussion on general theoretical questions was followed by reports on research work in linguistics in various republics. B. V. Gornung gave a report on the subject "The Role of Academician N. Ya. Marr in the Study of the Languages of the Peoples of the U.S.S.R." He gave a detailed account of the tremendous contribution made by N. Ya. Marr, the great Soviet linguist, to the study and development of unwritten languages, and showed his outstanding role in the upswing of the national language culture of Soviet socialist nations.

Marr personally took a leading part in linguistic work in a number of union republics (Abkhazia, Azerbaidzhan, Dagestan, Chuvashia and others). He carefully trained fighters for and propagandists of the new teaching on language. In the case of many peoples of the Soviet Union who had neither writing nor schools in their native tongue, the cultural revolution was largely connected with N. Ya. Marr's new teaching on language and with his personal, active participation in cultural construction along national lines.

The session heard a number of specialized reports and speeches devoted to the role of Academician Marr in the development of various languages of the Soviet Union.

A. S. Garibyan, Corresponding Member of the Armenian Republic Academy of Sciences, gave an extremely interesting and rich description of the work of the linguists of Soviet Armenia who are carrying out in practice the basic principles of Marr's teaching.

Prof. Garibyan spoke in his report of numerous investigations conducted by linguists of Soviet Armenia which fully bear out the correctness of Academician Marr's basic postulates regarding the formation of the Armenian language. These investigations expose the slanderous assertions of contemporary bourgeois Armenian studies concerning the degradation of the Armenian literary language. They show that the history of the development of the Armenian language is the history of the struggle of two antagonistic class languages: the dominant literary language, on one hand, and the living folk dialects on the other.

Thus, Soviet linguists, basing themselves on the teaching of N. Ya. Marr, evolved a truly scientific, Marxist history of the Armenian language.

Investigations showed that the ancient connection between the Russian and Armenian peoples had a beneficial effect on the development of the Armenian language and culture, especially after the establishment of Soviet rule in Armenia.

Thanks to the direct assistance of the great Russian language, the Armenian language received its highest development and achieved a genuine flowering. In Armenia, said Prof. Garibyan, Marr is highly regarded as a friend of the Armenian people, a fighter for the brotherhood and friendship of Caucasian peoples and a great Soviet scientist, founder of the linguistics of the fatherland.

It may be concluded with assurance from Prof. Garibyan's speech that Marr's heritage is being seriously and profoundly elaborated in every way in Armenia. Prof. Garibyan was warmly received by the participants in the session, and his interesting report made a deep impression on the audience.

Prof. B. B. Piotrovsky noted in his speech that an incorrect tendency of limiting Academician Marr's teaching to questions of linguistics has become evident only recently. This tendency is related to the linguists' striving to lock themselves up in their own ivory tower. This practice is in basic contradiction to the research methods used by N. Ya. Marr himself, who headed fruitful cooperative work by linguists, historians and archeologists. Unfortunately, there is no such cooperative work at present. In Prof. Piotrovsky's opinion, this is one of the most important reasons why such important elements of N. Ya. Marr's theory as, for example, the teaching on stages, on semantics and others are being neglected by linguists.

N. Ya. Marr's teaching on semantics is being successfully worked out by historians of material culture. The successes of Soviet archeologists and historians of material culture, Prof. Piotrovsky emphasized, is due to the fact that they are fruitfully developing N. Ya. Marr's teaching.

Comrade Byeloded (Ukrainian Republic Academy of Sciences) noted the absence of scientific connections among linguists in various national republics as a substantial defect.

Formal connections between the union and the republic academies is supplied by the Coordination Council at the Presidium of the U.S.S.R. Academy of Sciences. However, the entire connection, the entire creative contact boils down to the reviewing of the thematic plans of republic academies. Comrade Byeloded asked whether it was not advisable to set up a publication with nation-wide distribution which might reflect the investigations conducted by members of republic academies.

S. K. Kenesbayev, member of the Kazakh Republic Academy of Sciences, gave a report on the topic "N. Ya. Marr and the Development of the Kazakh Literary Language and Writing in Soviet Times." He said that the Kazakh people, resurrected by the great October [revolution], have become one of the socialist nations endowed with its own Soviet statehood and its own rich culture, national in form and socialist in content—thanks to the correct realization of the Leninist-Stalinist national policy. As a result of the historic successes attained in the years of the Soviet rule by the Kazakh people both in the economic and cultural spheres, the Kazakh language is beginning to develop rapidly. Its vocabulary, grammar and phonetics are being perfected, and standards for the literary language have been set.

The speaker noted that the Russian language has exercised and is exercising a beneficial influence on the growth and development of the Kazakh literary language. Arabic writing was a weapon of oppression in the hands of reactionary forces—the beys and the Moslem clergy.

The contemporary Kazakh alphabet and orthography are built mainly on the correct principle of completely borrowing the Russian alphabet while taking into account the phonetic peculiarities of the contemporary Kazakh language. Each phoneme has its own designation. This is precisely the kind of language construction to which N. Ya. Marr was summoning us.

Comrade Kenesbayev said that a number of measures were being taken in Kazakhstan at the present time in the field of language development, particularly toward improving and rationalizing the Kazakh alphabet and orthography, as well as terminology.

Exhaustive and deep study of the living Turkic languages in the U.S.S.R., including the Kazakh language, only started after the great October socialist revolution. Outstanding Russian scholars—N. Ya. Marr, I. I. Meshchaninov—played a leading role in the truly scientific investigation of Turkic languages. Thanks to the disinterested help of Russian scholars, linguistic personnel has been trained in the national republics in the years of Soviet rule. Textbooks and teaching aids have been devised for all types of schools in these republics. The linguists of Kazakhstan, as well as those of other national republics of the Soviet Union, devised bilingual dictionaries and made valuable investigations in the grammar, phonetics and dialects of the Kazakh language.

Comrade Amanzholov (Kazakh Republic Academy of Sciences) spoke on Prof. Kenesbayev's report. He pointed to the exceptionally interesting report of Prof. Garibyan, which testified eloquently to the enormous and fruitful work which is being done in Armenia.

Comrade Amanzholov supplemented Prof. Kenesbayev's report. He pointed to some shortcomings in the work of Kazakh linguists.

V. I. Alatyrev delivered a report on the subject "N. Ya. Marr and the Study of the Finno-Ugric Languages." He pointed to the fact that the theoretical heritage of the founder of Soviet linguistics in the investigation of Finno-Ugric languages has not yet been the object of much study. Study of this heritage [said the speaker] is, however, extremely important, because N. Ya. Marr based many of his theoretical principles on linguistic data from the Finno-Ugric language group. In contrast to the migration theory of bourgeois Finno-Ugric studies, which sought for a "proto-homeland" of the "Finno-Ugric" languages in the Sayan mountains, in the Urals, etc., N. Ya. Marr put forward the theory of the internal, local formation of Finno-Ugric, Turkic and other languages. On the basis of N. Ya. Marr's leads, the speaker asked whether the time had not come to reconsider radically our views concerning the single system of Finno-Ugric languages, and suggested that the session examine his viewpoints, that the Finno-Ugric group consists of three groups: (1) the languages of the Volga-Kama-Pechora territory; (2) the Baltic-Finnish languages; (3) the Ugric languages.

Comrade Alatyrev noted at the end of his report that Soviet Finno-Ugric scholars had done much on the basis of N. Ya. Marr's methodology propositions and methods both with respect to research on scientific grammars of individual Finno-Ugric languages and to working out questions of practical language development.

Following Comrade Alatyrev's report, comrades Perevozchikov, Maitinskaya and Kure supplemented a number of propositions in the report and made their own critical comments. Comrade Maitinskaya expressed doubt as to the reliability of the classification of Finno-Ugric languages suggested in the report. This question, Comrade Maitinskaya said, must be approached with due caution. Supplementing Comrade Alatyrev's report, Prof. Kure showed how linguistic work is being reorganized in the Estonian Republic. Comrade I. K. Vartichan (Kishinev University) gave a brief characterization of the state of linguistics work in the Moldavian Republic.

An extremely interesting question was raised by Comrade Meshcheryuk who referred to the intolerable situation in the study of the Gagauz language. The Gagauz number 100,000, the speaker said, but unfortunately they still lack a written language. The problem at present is to give this people a written language as soon as possible.

Speaking during the debates, Comrade Saidov gave a short description of language development work being done at the present time in Dagestan on the basis of N. Ya. Marr's new teaching on language.

Comrade Abdulayev (Uzbek Republic Academy of Sciences) pointed out in his speech that Uzbek linguistics was a product of the great October socialist revolution. Under the Soviet regime formerly backward peoples had been given extensive opportunities to take advantage of their national statehood. The Uzbek national literary language had taken on definitive form since the October socialist revolution. Comrade Azizov noted a number of shortcomings in the work of Uzbek linguists.

Comrade D. Ye. Mikhalchi gave a report on the subject "Academician N. Ya. Marr and the Romance Language Study," presenting a thorough description of the use made of N. Ya. Marr's teaching in research on the Romance languages.

Soviet Romance language studies cannot be considered a satisfactory sector of Soviet linguistics, said Comrade Mikhalchi. Many large problems have not only not been solved by these studies; they have not even been posed as yet. Vestiges of bourgeois methodology are inherent in such books as Prof. M. V. Sergiyevsky's "History of the French Language" which by-passes the achievements of the new teaching on language. In conclusion Comrade Mikhalchi indicated the need for training specialists in Moldavian studies, the need for whom is increasing, making it necessary again to suggest more extensive training of Romance language specialists (primarily specialists in the Moldavian and Rumanian languages) both in institutes of the Academy of Sciences and in the universities.

Corresponding Member Comrade Shiraliyev of the Azerbaidzhan Republic Academy of Sciences gave a report entitled "Academician Marr and the Development of Azerbaidzhanian Linguistics" in which he comprehensively characterized N. Ya. Marr's research on the Azerbaidzhanian language and the fruitful work now being done to develop the great Soviet scientist's heritage.

On the basis of the decrees of the Central Committee of the Soviet Union on ideological questions, Azerbaidzhan's linguists are conducting research and are thoroughly tracing the development of the modern Azerbaidzhanian language. A monograph entitled "The History of the Azerbaidzhanian Language in the Soviet Period" will be completed in 1950.

Studying the modern Azerbaidzhanian language Azerbaidzhanian linguists have completed and sent to press the first part of a scientific grammar of the Azerbaidzhanian langugae which includes vocabulary, phonetics and morphology; the second part, on syntax, will be completed in 1950.

Azerbaidzhanian linguists are also working on a six-volume dictionary of the Azerbaidzhanian language; the first volume will be sent to press in 1950.

The establishment of an institute of languages in Azerbaidzhan, the training of Azerbaidzhanian linguistic scholars, the appearance of works and monographs on various questions of Azerbaidzhanian linguistics as well as the Stalin Prize-winning Russian-Azerbaidzhanian Dictionary attest to the tremendous mobilizing force of the teaching of N. Ya. Marr who elevated linguistics in Azerbaidzhan to its due height and threw light on the further developmental course of Azerbaidzhanian linguistics.

Prof. I. M. Oshanin gave a report on the subject "N. Ya. Marr and Soviet Chinese Studies" in which he characterized in detail the tremendous significance of N. Ya. Marr's new teaching on language in research on the Chinese language. N. Ya. Marr's teaching, said Prof. Oshanin, effected a revolution in the theory and practice of studying and teaching any language, including Chinese. Prof. Oshanin stressed that our special attention to the Chinese language at the present time is dictated by important political tasks related to the brilliant victory of democratic China and by the tremendous significance which the Chinese language is now acquiring as the language of a great people who have joined the world army of fighters for peace and socialism. Prof. Oshanin pointed out that N. Ya. Marr persistently stressed the significance of the Chinese language as a superb illustration of the basic theses of the new linguistic teaching, and as a language very important for a correct formulation of the new linguistics. Prof. Oshanin reported that Marr called the Chinese language "the most cultured language of the Far East" and held that the world significance of China had not yet been sufficiently appreciated. The Chinese language is the most ancient language of the world and its study is absolutely essential if a balanced scientific presentation of the single glottogonic process is to be formulated. In studying the Chinese language Academician Marr used the paleontologic method and element analysis to do research work on Chinese root-words.

N. Ya. Marr summed up the results of his research in special works devoted to the Chinese language—"The Chinese Language and the Paleontology of Speech" and "The Ber Horse From Sea to Sea." Unfortunately, N. Ya. Marr's research on the Chinese language has not yet been made the basis for the preparation of scientific grammars of the Chinese language.

Marr foresaw the need to reform Chinese writing. This work is now being done by the people's democratic government of China.

Prof. Oshanin indicated a need to set up a Chinese language studies section in the Institute of Language and Thought.

* * *

Editors' Note [in Voprosy filosofii].— The session's work showed that on the basis of Marr's heritage a large number of Soviet linguists are performing fruitful work on studying and developing the languages and writing systems of the peoples of the U.S.S.R.

The overwhelming majority of Soviet linguists relies on the theory of linguistics based on the principles of dialectical and historical materialism.

However, the work of this session revealed the generally unsatisfactory situation in the field of linguistics.

The work of the session likewise revealed that there are major shortcomings in the field of linguistics.

The state of affairs is most unsatisfactory in the important field of the study of the Russian language. Research work and textbooks on the Russian language make entirely insufficient use of Marr's basic postulates on language.

The session also disclosed a serious lag in the theoretical sector of the linguistic front. The Institute of Language and Thought was unable to present a single report throwing light on the basic theoretical questions of Marr's teaching.

A number of theoretical reports delivered at the session did not give a sufficiently profound analysis of the ideological wealth of the teaching of the inspired Soviet scientist N. Ya. Marr.

The session was mainly commemorative in nature. The session did not reflect the creative development of N. Ya. Marr's theoretical heritage by his pupils and followers in the 15 years since the founder of materialist linguistics died. The prospects for further development of the Soviet science of language were not precisely indicated. The session did not subject to principled Bolshevist criticism the attacks on Marr made by several Soviet linguists and did not entirely expose the attempts to revise Marr's teaching and to reconcile it with idealist bourgeois linguistics.

Reports by the heads of the Institute of Language and Thought were not sufficiently self-critical. These reports, as well as the speeches by participants in the session, did not disclose the errors of the speakers themselves.

The session failed to pose the most important theoretical problems of materialist linguistics—the problem of stages in the development of language, form and content in language, language and thought, the question of the unity of the glottogonic process, the problem of relationship of the teachings of N. Ya. Marr and I. P. Pavlov and others. This lamentable fact attests that questions of the theory of linguistics are not receiving proper attention in the Institute of Language and Thought of the U.S.S.R. Academy of Sciences. The situation is particularly unsatisfactory with respect to throwing light on the major question of the relationship between theoretical research and practical work on developing the language and writing systems of the peoples of the U.S.S.R., the practical teaching of languages in educational institutions, both higher and secondary.

It is utterly inadmissible that linguists doing research on the great Russian language took no part in the session's work. It was especially important that they participate, because it is precisely in this field that a struggle against anti-Marr traditions is extremely urgent.

Many participants in the session brought up the need for close coordination of the work of linguists, historians of material culture, philosophers, ethnographers, historians and others.

By way of self-criticism, it must be admitted that Soviet philosophers, especially [in] the Institute of Philosophy of the U.S.S.R. Academy of Sciences and [on] the magazine Voprosy filosofii have not yet given real help to linguists in solving pressing problems of Soviet linguistics.

Voprosy filosofii's attempt to shed light on urgent problems of modern linguistics (the article by Comrades Nikolsky and Yakovlev in No. 1, 1949) proved unsuccessful since this article, as the newspaper Kultura i zhizn justly pointed out, contained serious errors in fact and in principle.

The question of coordinating work in the field of linguistics in the various national republics is an extremely acute one. The need has arisen for the establishment of a special agency to throw much light on the theoretical and practical work of all linguistic institutions of the Soviet Union.

The results of the session show that we must have more principled, Bolshevist criticism and self-criticism which will make it possible to end the covert and overt attacks on Marr and to raise Soviet, materialist, Marrist linguistics to a higher level.

On Certain Problems of Soviet Linguistics*

By A. CHIKOBAVA

EDITOR'S NOTE: In connection with the unsatisfactory state of Soviet linguistics, the editors [of Pravda] consider it essential to organize an open discussion in Pravda in order through criticism and self-criticism to overcome the stagnation in the development of Soviet linguistics and to give correct direction to further scientific work in this field. Arn. Chikobava's article "On certain Problems of Soviet Linguistics" is printed to promote discussion. Beginning with this issue, Pravda will devote two pages weekly to articles discussing questions of linguistics.

Soviet linguistics is called on to serve as a reliable theoretical base for the extensive language development taking place in the multinational Soviet Union. It is common knowledge what exceptional theoretical interest is evoked by scientific study of language on both the specifically historical plane (the history of a language in close relationship to the history of the culture of the people speaking it) and on the philosophical plane (language in its relation to thought). Lenin particularly noted the importance of the history of language as one of those scientific disciplines "from which the theory of cognition and the dialectic must evolve." †

"***The science of the history of society," writes Comrade Stalin, "can, despite all the complexity of phenomena of social life, become as exact a science as, for example, biology; it can become capable of utilizing the laws of social development for practical use." *

Becoming an exact science is a programmatic requirement without which not a single social science, including linguistics, can be of practical use and benefit.

Soviet linguistics can meet the requirements made upon science in the Stalin epoch if it is guided by the principles of dialectical and historical materialism, if it is built upon the fundamental statements of Marx, Engels, Lenin and Stalin regarding language, its essence, origin and development.

The discussions held in linguistic research institutions and a number of articles printed in Pravda and other publications on the situation in linguistics are clear evidence of the fact that all is not well with regard to the development of a materialist Soviet linguistic science.

It has been shown in the course of the discussion that the fundamental statements of Marx, Engels, Lenin and Stalin on language and linguistics have been replaced in the work of many linguists by Academician N. Ya. Marr's incorrect premises on linguistic theory. In case after case, lip service to Marxism-Leninism turns out in reality to be defense of N. Ya. Marr's fundamental errors.

Instead of disclosing errors and shortcomings through Bolshevist criticism and self-criticism and thereby making sure that the materialist science of language develops, nothing better has resulted from discussions held than a return to one of the fundamental premises, the erroneousness of which was admitted as far back as ten years ago. We are referring to the theory of elements and element analysis in linguistics —one of Academician N. Ya. Marr's most unfortunate generalizations. This theory was officially rejected back in 1940 by the U.S.S.R. Academy of Sciences' Institute of Language and Thought and by Academician I. I. Meshchaninov, N. Ya. Marr's closest pupil. But that was in 1940, while in 1949 Prof. G. P. Serdyuchenko, assistant director of the Institute of Language and Thought, states outright, as though summing up the discussions held, that element analysis "can be entirely applicable and useful." †

In 1946, Academician I. I. Meshchaninov, head of the U.S.S.R. Academy of Sciences' Division of Literature and

* Pravda, May 9, 1950, pp. 3-5.

[For earlier articles on linguistics, see Current Digest of the Soviet Press: I. I. Meshchaninov, "For Materialist Linguistics: The Creative Heritage of N. Ya. Marr," Vol. I, No. 16, pp. 67-69; A. V. Desnitskaya, "Linguistics in the Service of Imperialism" [an attack on American linguistics], Vol. I, No. 41, pp. 10-13; I. I. Meshchaninov, "Marr—Founder of Soviet Linguistics," Vol. I, No. 46, pp. 11-17; L. Gumilevsky, "Verbal Weeds of Foreignism," and V. Alatyrev, "A Follower of Finnish Bourgeois Linguists," Vol. I, No. 47, pp. 24-26; G. P. Serdyuchenko, "For Further Improvement in the New, Materialist Doctrine on Language," Vol. I, No. 51, pp. 8-17; "The Materialist Teaching on Language," Vol. II, No. 2, p. 53; T. P. Lomtev, "Stalin on Development of National Languages in the Epoch of Socialism," Vol. II, No. 7, pp. 3-6.

† V. I. Lenin, Philosophical Notebooks, 1947, p. 297. [Note: All works cited are either in Russian or a Russian edition unless otherwise indicated.]

* J. V. Stalin, "On Dialectical and Historical Materialism," Problems of Leninism, 11th edition, p. 544.

† "For Further Improvement of the New, Materialist Teaching on Language," Journal of the Academy of Sciences, Division of Literature and Linguistics, Vol. VIII, No. 4, 1949, p. 310.

Language, called for a decisive struggle against element analysis as a distortion of Marxist-Leninist principles in linguistics; but in 1949 he lacked the courage to declare openly that no Marxist-Leninist science of language could be created with the technique of the notorious element analysis. In 1949, Academician I. I. Meshchaninov limited himself merely to remarking in a muffled and vague way that "analysis of works in modern speech according to the four elements yields nothing."*

Meanwhile, in order to popularize materialist linguistics, the Ministry of Education's magazine Russky yazyk v shkole [Russian Language in the School] offers thousands of Russian language teachers examples of etymology of Russian words according to elements: the word "ruka" [hand] is, allegedly, composed of the two elements "ru" and "ka," each of which means "hand." The Russian word "topor" [axe] and the French word "porter" [to carry] consist, allegedly, of the very same parts, "por" and "tor" or "ter": "ruka" is an implement of labor, the axe likewise.†

Quite recently, early in 1950, the Russian Republic Ministry of Education published a pamphlet by Prof. G. P. Serdyuchenko entitled "Academician N. Ya. Marr—Founder of Soviet Materialist Linguistics" in the "Questions of Linguistics for the Teacher" series. In the pamphlet Prof. G. P. Serdyuchenko asserts, among other things, that "the problem of element analysis***requires very serious attention" (p. 60) and that "paleontologic analysis according to elements***can be fully applicable and useful" (p. 63). Having published a large edition of the above-mentioned pamphlet, the Pedagogical Textbook Publishing House characterizes it in the foreword as containing "much worthwhile material for the teacher."

Thus the Ministry of Education authoritatively recommends that teachers employ element analysis (of the ru-ka, to-por type) as being of scientific value.

This is not all. In 1949 the Ministry of Higher Education worked out a syllabus on "Introduction to Linguistics" (written by Prof. Chemodanov, edited by Prof. Serdyuchenko) which is based wholly on the incorrect premises of Academician N. Ya. Marr's linguistic theory. The syllabus says nothing about element analysis, but the postulates arrived at by element analysis are considered an achievement of Soviet materialist linguistics. This means that element analysis, examples of which are the etymologies of the words "ruka" and "topor," is being introduced in universities, pedagogical institutes and teachers' colleges as required teaching matter.

Finally, the July 21, 1949, decree of the Presidium of the U. S. S. R. Academy of Sciences openly states that N. Ya. Marr's theory is "the new materialist teaching on language, a general theory of linguistics erected on a dialectical and historical materialist base," that the principles that there is "a single [unilinear] process of language growth and [that there are] stages in the development of the world's languages" (i.e., premises internally related to the use of element analysis) constitute "a progressive revolutionary teaching."

Element analysis once forced Academician N. Ya. Marr's theory of linguistics into a blind alley. Now that element analysis has been rehabilitated, all linguistic work is arriving at an impasse.

A situation has arisen in which it is becoming impossible to do positive work on the immediate tasks of our motherland's linguistic development.

It is necessary in this connection to examine the question of what Academician N. Ya. Marr's linguistic theory represents, to what extent it is legitimate to supplant Marxism-Leninism in linguistics by Academician N. Ya. Marr's theory, and what is needed in order to develop a Soviet linguistics based on the truly scientific principles of Marxism-Leninism.

An outstanding Soviet scholar and major student of the Caucasus, Academician N. Ya. Marr is known to the general Soviet public as the author of the Japhetic theory. But even before his first research elaborating the Japhetic theory was published (in 1908), N. Ya. Marr was recognized as an authority on questions of Armenian-Georgian philology in the broad sense of the word: on language, literature, history, ethnography and archeology.

Later, Academician N. Ya. Marr, the untiring student of Japhetic languages, author of a number of valuable monographs and numerous articles on the Georgian, Chan, Svanetian, Abkhasian and Dagestanian languages as well as on the Basque and other tongues, became a scholar of world renown.

A considerable number of N. Ya. Marr's works are devoted to the struggle to create a materialist linguistics. This struggle of N. Ya. Marr against idealistic linguistics was in itself of considerable importance in strengthening young Soviet linguistic science. However, Academician N. Ya. Marr himself was, despite his efforts, unable to attain a profound understanding of the essence of Marxism-Leninism; he was unable to master the method of dialectical materialism and to apply it to linguistics. This is the reason for the serious errors and omissions in Academician N. Ya. Marr's linguistic teaching which we shall now analyse.

I.—In Academician N. Ya. Marr's Japhetic theory we must distinguish the following: (1) the teaching on Japhetic languages, their nature and origin, and (2) the general linguistic doctrine or Japhetic theory as a general teaching on language.

Our knowledge of Japhetic languages began as a theory [suggesting] the relation of Georgian to the Semitic languages. This theory passed through a number of stages of development. The decisive factor of each stage is the concept of the Japhetic languages, and what they comprise. In 1908 the Japhetic languages were the Kartvelian languages (Georgian, Megrelo-Chan and Svanetian, as well as several extinct languages of Asia Minor). In 1908 N. Ya. Marr held that the Japhetic languages are a <u>branch</u> most closely related to the Semitic branch. In 1916, the Highland Caucasian languages (Abkhasian, Adyghe and Dagestanian languages) were acknowledged to be Japhetic in addition to the Kartvelian languages. The Japhetic languages comprised [in 1916] an independent <u>family</u> of languages related to the Semitic <u>family</u>. By 1920, the scope of Japhetic languages is broadened and the following are acknowledged as Japhetic: the Basque language which had survived in the Pyrenean [Iberian] Peninsula, the extinct Etruscan language (of pre-Latin Italy), the extinct Pelasgic language (of the pre-Greek population on the Balkan Peninsula), the archaic languages of the founders of the ancient civilization of Asia Minor (Hittite, Urartic, Elamitic), etc. In the development of Academician N. Ya. Marr's Japhetic theory, the Japhetic language and those who spoke them at a given stage made up the third ethnic element in the creation of the Mediterranean culture, the third—"in time of [overall or world wide] appearance, but the first in the order of historical sequence," i.e., pre-Indo-European and pre-Semitic. Hence, objectively, the question no longer arises as to the relation of the Japhetic to the Semitic languages.

Academician N. Ya. Marr arrived at this new concept of which languages can be classified as Japhetic after many years of research on these languages. In his well-known monograph "The Japhetic Caucasus and the Third Ethnic

* I. I. Meshchaninov, "Marr—Founder of Soviet Linguistics," <u>Journal of the Academy of Sciences, Division of Literature and Linguistics</u>, Vol. VIII, No. 4, p. 295. [For a complete translation of this article, see <u>Current Digest of the Soviet Press</u>, Vol. I, No. 46, pp. 11-15.]

† See V. Malakhovsky s article "Russian Etymologies in Academician N. Ya. Marr's Research," <u>Journal of the Academy of Sciences, Division of Literature and Linguistics</u>, No. 4, 1947.

Element in the Creation of the Mediterranean Culture" (1920), N. Ya. Marr stated this with the authoritative voice of a specialist on Japhetic languages and in his passionate way, painted in broad strokes an attractive picture of the creative cultural role of Japhetic tribes and peoples.

This was also a great service of Academician N. Ya. Marr, formulator of the theory that [the various] japhetic languages, the languages of people who created one of the oldest centers of civilization in Asia Minor, were related by origin.

But such an understanding of the Japhetic languages did not last very long. Japhetic elements began to "appear" in the most diverse languages; the Japhetic languages turned out to be "related" to all languages: hence relationship by origin or genetic relationship lost all meaning.

From that time onward Japhetic languages are declared to be a stage of development; the Indo-European languages are the succeeding stage of development, the result of the transformation of the Japhetic languages; hence, genealogic classification gives way to classificition by stages. The paleontology of speech takes the place of history, and general linguistic problems are advanced concerning the nature of human speech, its inception and development. The Japhetic theory becomes a general linguistic theory, "a general teaching on language," which has of late frequently and not altogether appropriately been called "the new teaching on language."

What are the basic premises of the Japhetic theory as a general linguistic theory? Language, according to Academician N. Ya. Marr's teaching, is a superstructural category. Since language is a superstructural category, everything in it is of a class nature. Language has always been of a class nature.

Language development (glottogony) is single. This is due to the singleness of both the process and the initial material: all languages originate from four elements: (SAL, BER, YON, ROШ). [Russian Ш is equivalent to English SH.]

Analysis of any word must begin by revealing one or the other of these component elements—we are thus confronted in the analysis of any word with the beginnings of speech. The problem of the origin of language is the most basic problem of linguistics.

All languages have a single starting point: all proceed from the four elements, the difference between languages consisting merely in their [belonging to different] degrees (stages) of development.

Academician N. Ya. Marr rendered an indisputable service to Soviet linguistics by raising the question of the superstructural nature of language. Accurately characterizing language as the oldest witness to history, Academician N. Ya. Marr raises questions as to the development of language in connection with the development of thought and the evolution of technology and production. "Therefore language in general—both gesture and particularly voiced—form a superstructural category on a production and productive relations base."*

In actual fact, once the entire development of human society is conditioned by the development of productive relationships, language, that "major means of intercourse" (Lenin), "implement of struggle and development" (Stalin), must also be conditioned by these very same relationships. The history of languages abounds in facts which confirm this indisputable premise. A language's dependence on the productive base is particularly evident from the lexicon, from changes in vocabulary as well as in the meaning of words. A new object, a new phenomenon in social life insistently requires a corresponding designation in language: a new word appears, or an already existing word is used but with a new meaning.

But such a direct dependence cannot, as a rule, be traced in the structure of a word, in the structure of a sentence, in sound composition or in sound shifts: in such cases dependence is variously realized.

If the development of a [given] language structure—its phonetics, morphology, syntax or vocabulary—would uniformly, directly and simply reflect the development of production and of productive relations, one could isolate without effort in the history of any language written since ancient times at least the last three basic socio-economic periods, if not all five. However, every specialist studying the history of a given language, which includes such things as declension of nouns, conjugation of verbs or the syntactic relations of words, knows that it is impossible to isolate periods in the history of the above, which would coincide or directly reflect socio-economic eras (as well as the productive relations characteristic of a given period).

How does N. Ya. Marr's Japhetic theory explain such facts? In an extremely simplified manner. The following statements, taken as an example, are typical of N. Ya. Marr:

"Direct and oblique cases are after all passive and active 'cases,' i.e., strictly speaking, socially evaluable quantities inasmuch as at the preceding level of development by stages they were two different categories of the collective."*

In short, cases are active and passive: the direct case (the nominative) is usually active, while the oblique cases (genitive, dative, accusative—) are passive because the oblique cases are syntactically dependent (are governed by a verb or even by nouns), while the nominative case is usually syntactically independent.

According to N. Ya. Marr's theory, active and passive cases must be viewed as socially evaluable quantities: according to N. Ya. Marr, "two different categories of the collective" are reflected in active and passive cases. Thus, according to N. Ya. Marr, social relations are reflected in the grammatical dependence of words.

Such explanations cannot of course be considered Marxist or scientific.

"Language," writes Academician N. Ya. Marr, "is the same type of superstructural social value as painting or art in general."†

In our opinion, one cannot equate painting (art in general) on the one hand with language on the other as superstructural categories. Such simplification is inadmissable.

The conclusion: the posing of the problem as to the superstructural nature of language in N. Ya. Marr's Japhetic theory is correct only in a general sense because the specific traits of language as a superstructural category are obscured in N. Ya. Marr's teaching. The approach to various facts of language is not differentiated. Academician N. Ya. Marr does not even specify the questions [headings] into which the problem should be broken down.

Soviet linguistics faces much painstaking work in properly determining the components of this complex problem of disclosing the specific nature of language as a superstructural category and tracing all possible forms of language's dependence on production.

N. Ya. Marr's teaching on the class nature of language is entirely incompatible with Marxism. According to N. Ya. Marr's Japhetic theory, everything in language is of a class nature; all languages are class languages; language has always been of a class nature.

"I assert, with full awareness of my responsibility in making such a statement," writes Academician N. Ya. Marr, "[and] disagreeing fundamentally with my comrades, that there is no language which is not of a class nature, and, consequently, there is no thinking which is not of a class

* N. Ya. Marr, Contribution to the Baku Discussion on Japhetidology and Marxism, Baku, 1932, p. 25.

* N. Ya. Marr, "Japhetic Horizons on the Ukrainian Farm (1930)," Selected Works, Vol. V, pp. 239-240.

† N. Ya. Marr, "The Japhetic Theory," separate edition, 1928, p. 130; Selected Works, Vol. II, p. 107.

nature."* In another work Academician N. Ya. Marr declares: "***Japhetidology rejects the existence of non-class languages, all languages, including the national languages of Europe and the Caucasus, are, I repeat once again, of a class nature. Moreover, they are not of a class nature in the final analysis; they are of a class nature first of all. It turned out that in Armenia and Georgia each country had two national languages, both class languages, one the ancient literary feudal language and the other the so-called popular language, provided we do not now go into the different variations of this popular speech. And the remarkable thing is that the Georgian feudal language is more closely related in system to the Armenian feudal language than either of them to the popular language of its own country. The Armenian and Georgian popular languages have understandably the same relationship to their own feudal languages, being languages of a single system in many basic traits of their typology. We will, perhaps, be able to illustrate this phenomenon with examples in another instance. But the main thing is that Japhetidology holds that any approach to language study other than as class speech is unacceptable."†

According to Marr's theory, it is inadmissable to speak of a non-class language even "during the initial stages of the formation of mankind or, to be more precise, at the time when the human collective emerged from the animal world;"‡ it appears that this would mean a return to the primitive state of scientific linguistic thought—to the Indo-European theory with its proto-language and its formal teaching.

Academician N. Ya. Marr declares that his understanding of the nature of class is the only scientific, Marxist one. In N. Ya. Marr's opinion, to speak of a non-class language even during the initial stages of the formation of mankind would mean "dragging Marxism into an abyss, contrary to its social nature, contrary to its logic." N. Ya. Marr wrote in this connection: "It is impossible not only to keep silent but even to state hesitatingly the fact that there has never been a non-class language; language was of a class nature from the moment it began, it was the language of the class having control over the implements of production of those epochs, including productive [agricultural or hunting] magic."**

It is clear that such an understanding of the question of language cannot be considered a Marxist-Leninist one.

N. Ya. Marr's concept of the class nature of language has nothing to do with the Marxist-Leninist, scientific conception of "class." There were not and could not have been any classes "at the time when the human collective emerged from the animal world." Moreover, there were no classes even under the primitive-communal system when, as is known, communal ownership of the means of production constituted the basis of productive relations.

Consequently, there can be no talk of the class nature of language in a pre-class society. Moreover, even in a class society, contrary to Academician N. Ya. Marr's assertions, the existence of non-class languages cannot be disputed.

In his well-known definition of a nation Comrade Stalin has in mind just such a non-class, national language, the common knowledge of which constitutes an indispensible condition for the nation's formation.

"A nation," says Comrade Stalin, "is a historically formed, stable community of people which arose on the basis of common language, territory, economic life and psychological make-up which is manifested in a common culture."*

"Hence, a common language is one of the characteristic features of a nation," concludes Comrade Stalin.

It follows that a common language is a fact under capitalism. The bourgeois nations which Comrade Stalin has in mind in the given instance emerged in a class society, namely in the epoch of ascendant capitalism.

It is impossible to reconcile the following unproven assertion by Academician N. Ya. Marr with self-evident facts: "***There is no common national language but there is a class language. Languages of one and the same class in different countries, given an identical social structure, display greater similarity of type to each other than do languages of different classes of one and the same country or one and the same nation."†

N. Ya. Marr's bald assertion that the Georgian feudal language was closer, if only in its system, to the Armenian feudal language "than either of them to the popular language of its own country" has nothing to do with actual fact.

In a class society the class viewpoint of the speaker can manifest itself only in definite features (usually in vocabulary and style), but this does not mean at all that language is of a class nature.

The concept of a "class language" is, if one takes into account the basic function of a language, self-contradictory and scientifically inconsistent. Actually, a class language would be a language by means of which only persons of one and the same class could communicate, but which could not be used for communicating with representatives of another class of the same people or the same nation. There are no cases in the history of class societies of such self-contained classes. Accordingly, the question of class languages does not arise: there are no class languages. Nations have only national languages which are common for all classes of these nations.

Basing himself on his notion that language is unconditionally and from the very first of a class nature, N. Ya. Marr wrote: "The linguistic conclusions drawn by Japhetidology force it to state most categorically that Engels' hypothesis about the origin of classes through the break-down of the clan is in need of serious corrections."‡

If one must speak of corrections, there can be no doubt that serious corrections are needed precisely in that understanding of class which underlies such a statement. It is clear that Academician N. Ya. Marr's understanding of the nature of class is not reconcilable with a genuinely scientific, Marxist-Leninist understanding of the same concept.

According to Academician N. Ya. Marr's theory, the origin of language is conceived as follows: a gesture language is aboriginal ("manual language"); vocal speech arose much later. According to N. Ya. Marr's theory, vocal speech has existed "in general from 50,000 to 500,000 years and more, while standardized language has existed from 1,000,000 to 1,500,000 years."**

Vocal speech, according to N. Ya. Marr, originated not for purposes of communication (people spoke with their hands!), but as a "labor-magic" activity; there are only four primary words or elements; they were in the possession of the medicine men, and even these used them not as a means of communication with people (if only with other medicine men) but as a means of communicating with a totem; thus, the first words are magic both in origin (created

* N. Ya. Marr, "Language and Thought," separate edition, 1931, p. 4; Selected Works, Vol. III, pp. 90-91. Emphasis mine.—A. Ch.

† N. Ya. Marr, Contribution to the Baku Discussion, op. cit., p. 19. Emphasis mine.—A. Ch.

‡ Ibid., p. 10.

** N. Ya. Marr, Contribution to the Baku Discussion, op. cit., p. 18.

* J. V. Stalin, "Marxism and the National Question," Works, Vol. II, p. 296.

† N. Ya. Marr, Why It Is So Difficult to Become Theoretical Linguist, separate edition, Selected Works, Vol. II, p. 415.

‡ N. Ya. Marr, Actual Problems and Current Tasks of the Japhetic Theory, separate edition, 1928, Vol. III, p. 75.

** N. Ya. Marr, Language and Thought, separate edition, p. 58; Selected Works, Vol. III, p. 119.

by medicine men), and in function (they served as a magical technique). It turns out that vocal speech, the property of medicine men, originated in a class-differentiated environment; vocal speech, it seems, served as "an instrument of class struggle, as did writing later on." Academician N. Ya. Marr tells of the struggle which took place at the time when vocal speech originated "between the collective***with vocal speech," on the one hand, and "the collective without vocal speech" (i.e., with gesture language), on the other hand, until the "more powerful group with vocal speech gained the upper hand over the deaf-mutes."*

There is no need to dwell on these dubious theses. It is clear above all that in speaking of the origin of language we have in mind vocal speech which serves as a medium of communication for mankind, not mute "gesture" language which cannot properly be called speech because it is mute, wordless. Secondly, the question of the origin of speech must under no circumstances be confused with that of the origin of given individual languages. Nor should it [the origin of speech] be reduced to the determination of how many "words" there were in the beginning and which they were, let alone who possessed them and what kind of "struggle took place" over them.

The fundamental question which a theory on the origin of language must answer is: under what conditions must language have originated?

According to the teachings of Marxist classics, language arose as part of work, out of the need for communication. The primordial language was a vocal language.

Academician N. Ya. Marr's teaching on the origin and initial function of language is in sharp contradiction to the theoretical formulation of the question by the classics of Marxism. "****Language," write Marx and Engels, "originates only from demand, from persistent need to communicate with others."†

"As men developed," says Engels, "they reached the point where they needed to say something to each other. The need created an organ: the ape's undeveloped larynx was slowly transformed*** and the organs of the mouth gradually learned to pronounce one articulate sound after another."‡

The chief function of language is precisely to be a means of communication (Marx, Engels, Lenin, Stalin).

This function determines the essence of language. It is primordial. Language without this function ceases to be language. This is an indisputable premise of the science of language. However, contrary to this basic thesis of Marxism, Academician N. Ya. Marr writes: "Comrades, a most profound misunderstanding arises when the origin of language is regarded as coinciding with the appearance of voiced speech, but it is no less fundamental an error when language is supposed from the first to have had a conversational function which today is primary. Language is a magic instrument, an instrument of production in the first stages of man's development of group production; language is an instrument of production. The need and the possibility of using language as a means of communication is a very late matter; this is true of both gesture or linear***speech, as well as of spoken or vocal language."**

Thus, Academician N. Ya. Marr holds that the need for communicating could not lead to the creation of language: according to N. Ya. Marr, there was no need at first to use language as a means of communication; such a need "is a very much later development." Originally, language, according to N. Ya. Marr, was used not for communication by people, but as a magical technique.

* Ibid., p. 116.

† K. Marx and F. Engels, German Ideology, pp. 20-21

‡ F. Engels, "The Role of Labor in Man's Evolution from the Ape," Dialectics of Nature, 6th edition, 1932, p. 52.

** N. Ya. Marr, Contribution to the Baku Discussion, op. cit., p. 7. Emphasis mine.—A. Ch.

The important principle here is that Academician N. Ya Marr does not acknowledge the initial, conversational function of language in general or of vocal language in particular. Academician N. Ya. Marr rejects the origin of language as a means of communication by people, as an implement which arose from a persistent need for communication.

Academician N. Ya. Marr forgets that people in the most ancient times lived and supported themselves in hordes, in groups and not individually. Academician N. Marr does not take into consideration the fact that it was just this circumstance that brought about their need for communicating, their need to have a means of communication such as language.

And yet, under such circumstances, certain of N. Marr's followers deem it possible to assert that Academician N. Ya. Marr's theory on the origin of language is allegedly a genuine Marxist theory and is in complete accord with the principles and theses of Marxism-Leninism.

Academician N. Ya. Marr expresses himself in favor of a single common language for future mankind. This is the only matter of principle on which, it would seem, Academician N. Ya. Marr's views are in accord with the theses of Marxism-Leninism.

However, N. Ya. Marr's understanding of the question is incorrect, non-Marxist, in this instance as well. According to N. Ya. Marr, "a life of work***leads to the unity of all speech in general, provided it is preceded by a single economy and social system, and in this way sweeping away all obstacles."* Moreover, according to N. Ya. Marr, it seems that "mankind, proceeding toward economic unity and a classless community, cannot help applying artificial means, scientifically worked out, in order to accelerate this broad process."†

As is known, Marxists understand this matter differently. They hold that the process of withering away of national languages and the formation of a single common world language will take place gradually, without any "artificial means" invoked to "accelerate" this process.

The application of such "artificial means" would mean the use of coercion against nations, and this Marxism cannot permit.

Comrade Stalin says: "***The process of withering away of national differences and the merging of nations is related by Lenin not to the period of socialism's triumph in one country, but exclusively to the period after the establishment of the dictatorship of the proletariat on a world-wide scale, i.e., to the period of socialism's triumph in all countries, when the bases of a world socialist economy will already have been laid."‡

Moreover, Comrade Stalin points out with maximum clarity: "It would be wrong to think that the destruction of national differences and the withering away of national languages will take place immediately after the defeat of world imperialism, at one blow, so to speak by decree from above. There is nothing more erroneous than such a view. Attempting to bring about the merging of nations through a decree from above, through compulsion, would mean playing into the hands of the imperialists, ruining the cause of the liberation of nations, and interring the cause of organizing the cooperation and brotherhood of nations. Such a policy would be equivalent to one of assimilation."

"You are of course aware," writes Comrade Stalin, "that the policy of assimilation is unconditionally excluded from the arsenal of Marxism-Leninism because it is a policy

* N. Ya. Marr, "Concerning the Question of a Single Language," Selected Works, Vol. II, p. 397. Emphasis mine. —A. Ch.

† Ibid., p. 398. Emphasis mine.—A. Ch.

‡ J. V. Stalin, "The National Question and Leninism," Works, Vol. II, p. 346.

which is against the people, counterrevolutionary and disastrous."**

Comrade Stalin analyzes in detail the conditions of development of socialist nations, their cultures and languages, following the defeat of world imperialism.

Comrade Stalin writes: "It would be a mistake to think that the first stage of the period of world dictatorship of the proletariat will be the beginning of the withering away of nations and national languages, the beginning of the formation of a single, common language. On the contrary, the first stage, in the course of which national oppression will be finally eliminated, will be a stage of growth and flourishing for once oppressed nations and national languages, a stage of reaffirmation of the equal rights of nations, a stage of elimination of mutual national distrust, a stage of harmonizing and strengthening international bonds among nations."†

"Only during the second stage of the period of worldwide dictatorship of the proletariat, as the single world socialist economy is formed in place of a world capitalist economy—only at that stage will something in the nature of a common language begin to be formed, because only at this stage will the nations feel the need for one common international language in addition to their own national languages. This will prove a convenience in [international] relations and in economic, cultural and political cooperation. Hence, at this stage national languages and a common international language will exist side by side. It is possible that at first not one common world economic center, but several regional economic centers will be formed for different groups of nations, with a separate common language for each group of nations. Only later on would these centers combine into a single, common world center of socialist economy with a single language common to all nations."‡

This is the Marxist-Leninist understanding of the question of a future single language. It deals with the language question in intrinsic connection with the question of socialist nations and their development.

Leninist-Stalinist national policy is based of internal necessity on just such a careful attitude toward the development of socialist nations and their national languages. This policy has been formulated by Comrade Stalin as follows:

"This means that the Party supports and will support the development of the national cultures of our country's peoples, that it will encourage the strengthening of our new, socialist nations, that it will protect this cause against any and all anti-Leninist elements." **

Comrade Stalin's words are a hymn to the development of the socialist nations, their cultures and languages.

Comrade Stalin's teaching on the socialist nations and the prospects for their development is a harsh rebuff to all advocates of "artificial means" of accelerating the process of transition to a single, common language.

Such is the Marxist-Leninist understanding of the question of a single language of the future.

It is clear that Academician N. Ya. Marr's viewpoint in advocating artificial means of accelerating the process of creating a single, common language cannot be considered Marxist-Leninist.

Hence:

Posing the question of the superstructural nature of language (which is Academician N. Ya. Marr's principal service to Soviet linguistics) has unfortunately not led to a correct break-down of the problem; it has not ensured a Marxist-Leninist, scientific solution of the question of the nature of language as a superstructural category.

* Ibid., p. 347.

† Ibid., p. 348.

‡ Ibid., pp. 348-349.

** J.V. Stalin, "The National Question and Leninism," Op. cit., p. 354.

As for the class nature of language, Academician N. Ya. Marr's theory has nothing in common with the Marxist-Leninist conception either in the solution or in the formulation of this question.

Academician N. Ya. Marr's labor-magic theory of the origin of language rejects an origin coming from the need for communicating and departs radically from the basic thesis of the Marxist classics on this question.

Academician N. Ya. Marr's theory about a single language of the future, despite its seeming similarity, is in essence far removed from the Marxist-Leninist understanding of this question.

II.—A central place in Academician N. Ya. Marr's Japhetic theory is held by the palaeontology of language, with its peculiar method of element analysis. Two theoretical propositions are connected with it internally: (1) The singleness [unilinearity] of the glottogonic (language-forming) process and (2) The development of languages by stages (classification by stages of languages).

These propositions are the ones usually proclaimed as the basic achievement of Academician N. Ya. Marr's theory: a progressive, revolutionary doctrine which upsets the racist principles of bourgeois linguistics.

Is this so? This question can be answered by examining the following: what is the doctrine of stages based on? What does it affirm? Where does it lead?

Let us begin with the key factor: the paleontology of language and its method. The paleontology of language studies the most ancient conditions of human speech. In the Japhetic theory, element analysis, or the so-called four-element analysis, serves as the paleontologic method.

The formula of this analysis states:

"***All words in all languages, inasmuch as they are the product of a single creative process, consist of only four elements—each word of one or two and, more rarely, of three elements; in the vocabulary of any language there is no word which contains anything beyond these same four elements. We indicate these four elements with the Latin capitals A, B, C, D; they are the same which we indicated earlier with the tribal words (SAL, BER, YON, ROШ). They constitute the foundation of the formal paleontologic analysis of every word; without first undertaking such an analysis, without analyzing the word into the number of elements in it—one, two or more—comparison is impossible; without such analysis the comparative method is not valid."*

Marr goes on to indicate the necessity to check the results of formal four-element analysis with semantic analysis "according to the laws of speech paleontology" and later with the history of material culture and of social forms.

According to Marr, four-element analysis is an indispensable prerequisite of the comparative method: without it comparative analysis is invalid.

Element analysis is the "technique of the new linguistics." It does not exclude comparison; to the contrary, this is the new comparative technique, element comparison. What can one compare? Whatever word of whichever language: a Georgian word can be compared with a Chinese as well as a Latin one, with an Arabic as well as with a Chuvash, with a Turkish word as easily as with a Basque one: it is enough to "determine" which element (or which hybridized elements) "lies" at the origin of the word.

The question arises: do all words of all the globe's languages really have their origin in the four elements? If so—is it possible to discover these elements in today's languages? We will return to these questions below.

Let us suppose for an instant that all the words in all the globe's languages go back to four elements (SAL, BER, YON, ROШ). What follows from this? Where does the proposi-

* N. Ya. Marr, "General Course in Linguistics," Selected Works, Vol. II, p. 16, Emphasis mine.—A. Ch.

tion of a common origin in the four elements lead? If all languages come from the same four elements and all languages have a common origin—then there can be no languages which differ according to their initial linguistic material, different in their word roots.

According to N. Ya. Marr, the elements, this common initial material, explain the common origin as well as the eventual singleness [unilinearity]—given the presence of common developmental factors—of the language-forming (glottogonic) process. Without a common initial material, given the presence of common developmental factors, we would find regularities in common in the development of languages which differed in their initial material. But according to N. Ya. Marr the singleness [unilinearity] of the glottogonic process is specific inasmuch as he presupposes both a common process and [common] initial material.

But different languages do exist nonetheless: they differ in their vocabulary, they differ in word structure, they differ in sentence structure, they differ more or less in phonetic composition. This is literally a universally known fact. Where do these differences come from? If the initial material is the same, if the process of language-formation is a single one, how did the various languages arise?

Academician Marr's answer states: the various languages represent various stages of a single developmental process; differences in language are conditioned by the place which is assigned to languages of one designation or another (family of languages, system of languages) in a single language-creating (glottogonic) process.

Academician N. Ya. Marr called important segments of this single language-forming process stages of development. What causes the various stages? They express "major changes in language and thought," resulting from "major changes in productive technique"—that is the general answer.

What must the nature of these "major changes in language" be, for one to speak of a new stage? In other words: what are the criteria for the emergence of a "stage in language?" It turns out, this is unknown: no definite, concrete criteria are indicated. The closest student of N. Ya. Marr, Academician I. I. Meshchaninov writes the following in this regard:

"The problem of stages and systems was advanced on the basis of general propositions without a concrete classification of languages according to the newly proposed principle. The number of stages is not made clear, nor are the stage-defining criteria; as for systems, their details are just not worked out in the case of individual linguistic groups."*

In one of his later works Academician N. Ya. Marr tried to give the stage-defining characteristics of Japhetic languages according to syntactic criteria (word order in a sentence) and it turned out that Old Georgian in some cases differed from modern Georgian. From this Academician N. Ya. Marr concludes: the Japhetic are polystage languages.†

But that way the whole presentation of the problem changes: if at an earlier point languages were classified by stages, now [1931] stages are distinguished in [a given] language.

How many linguistic stages are represented in the extant languages? The exact number is unknown. In one of his later works Academician N. Ya. Marr tentatively classifies languages according to "period of their origin" in the following chart:

I. Language systems of the primary period:
   1. Chinese.
   2. Living Middle and far African languages.
II. Language systems of the secondary period:
   1. Finno-Urgic.
   2. Turkic.
   3. Mongolian.
III. Language systems of the tertiary period:
   1. Surviving Japhetic languages.
   2. Hamitic languages (near and far African).
IV. Language systems of the quaternary period:
   1. Semitic languages.
   2. Prometheidean or so-called Indo-European languages (Indian, Greek, and Latin). *

In this scheme languages are classified into four chronological strata according to "when they originated," "what stage of development they represent." As can be seen from the chart, development begins with the Chinese language and it ends with the Indo-European ones.

What then is the place of Japhetic languages in this scheme? Such a question is particularly fitting as these languages are the subject of Academician N. Ya. Marr's specialization. It is thus natural to expect the greatest clarity in his discussion and opinion on these languages. Japhetic languages are classified in the tertiary period—they precede Indo-European ones: the latter are nothing but the subsequent step, the Japhetic languages being the antecedent. "Indo-European languages are only a new formation of the same Japhetic languages."†

How did this new formation arise? N. Ya. Marr states: "Indo-European languages***are the result of a special, more complex, stage of hybridization called forth by an upheaval in the community depending upon new productive forms apparently connected with the discovery of metals and their widespread use in the economy." ‡

In this statement of N. Ya. Marr we find at least two contradictions. According to N. Ya. Marr, "The discovery of metals and their widespread use in the economy" called forth a new stage in the development of the speech of the particular peoples.

But even two thousand years B.C., when nobody had even heard of Indo-European languages in the Mediterranean area, the Japhetic peoples were the creators of metallurgy, as is generally known and emphasized by N. Ya. Marr himself. If this be so, the Japhetic languages more than any others should have found themselves on the "quaternary" step of development. But it doesn't work out that way for Academician N. Ya. Marr; the Indo-European languages turn out to be the new stage of development. This is the first contradiction.

Let us go on: According to N. Marr, the Japhetic languages became transformed into Indo-European, but they nevertheless continue to exist; they get stuck in that stage in which they were before their transformation into Indo-European. This is the second contradiction. Either one or the other: Either the Japhetic languages became transformed and if so cannot be at a previous stage of development; or they got stuck at an earlier stage and then one cannot talk of transformation.

Parent and offspring can exist side by side in world of living beings; the parents do not disappear with the birth of the son. But in language there can be no coexistence of the newly developed language and of the one through whose metamorphosis the new tongue arose. (Vulgar Latin does not coexist with Italian, which originated from it.)

In touching the question of language displacement in the process of linguistic growth, Academician N. Ya. Marr states:

"The languages of the whole world are products of a single glottogonic process. Depending on the date of their first appearance, they belong to one system or another. These succeed each other and the obsolete systems are character-

* I.I. Meshchaninov, The Problem of Classification of Languages in the Light of the New Linguistics, 1935, p. 31.

† See N. Ya. Marr, "The Japhetic Languages," Large Soviet Encyclopedia, Vol. LXV.

* N. Ya. Marr, "Why It Is So Hard to Become a Theoretical Linguist," Selected Works, Vol. II, p. 405.

† N. Ya. Marr, "The Ibero-Etrusco-Italian Hybrid Tribal Environment in the Formation of Indo-European Languages," Selected Works, Vol. I, p. 187.

‡ N. Ya. Marr, "The Indo-European Languages of the Mediterranean Area," Selected Works, Vol. I, p. 185.

istic of people who have fallen away from [the main line of] the over-all world development. It does not matter that the world economy and social organization eventually involve them again into the cycle of global life—they go along the new historical path of their higher cultural development with a language belonging to a system set apart from over-all growth or with a language of an obsolete system. In some cases, people got thoroughly stuck, economically and socially, on a given level of human development."*

The meaning of this quotation amounts to the following: in the process of a single language-forming, some language systems (groups, families) are replaced by others; the replaced systems are obsolete; such obsolete systems characterize peoples "who have fallen away from the overall world development."

Such languages (the obsolete ones) get stuck at a given stage; they can go no further, even if the peoples speaking such languages get eventually "involved" again in world economy, social organization and life; they will have to remain content with a language of an obsolete system; it is with such a language that they will have to follow "the new historical path of high cultural development."

All this—at best; at its worst one might get "stuck" not only linguistically, but also economically and socially on a given "level of human development."

Briefly stated, exclusion from "world movement" interrupts the development of a language, but its eventual re-integration into this universal movement does not renew development; therefore, the base influences the superstructure only in specific periods.

This means that the sentence passed on the "obsolete languages" which have fallen out of the world movement is definitive; languages "get fastened" at certain levels of the single glottogonic process—history has indicated hard and fast limits for them.

The first, second and third periods of the stage-chart of Academician N. Ya. Marr are full of just such obsolete languages, fallen away from world movement. It is only through such freezing at given stages that one can explain, according to N. Ya. Marr, the fact that we are confronted today with both Chinese (a language of the primary period) and Indo-European languages (quaternary period); languages at all four stages exist side by side.

"Not only the so-called Indo-European and Semitic languages," writes N. Ya. Marr, "but also Turkic, Mongolian ***Ugro-Finnic***Chinese, African, Oceanian as well as Australian***native American languages, all turned out to be incontrovertibly related to one degree or another. The differences between them are due to the fact that the archaic language systems abandoned the language-creating center and their chief features were preserved almost in petrified fashion at given stages of the development of human voiced language. These stages had already been traversed by all other [language systems] which had then moved ahead."†

This is how the single process of language-formation and the interrelations of the various languages within this single process are conceived in N. Ya. Marr's theory.

In distinction from Academician N. Ya. Marr's classification by stages, the genealogic classification, worked out on the basis of a Marxist comparative and historical analysis, groups languages according to origin, along genealogic principles. It presupposes diversified initial phonetic materials in varying linguistic groups. For example: the [Russian] word for number "three" [tri] is in Latin "tres," in old Indian "trayas." In this case the Russian, Latin and old Indian have a common initial material, a common root. On the other hand, the Georgian word for "tri" is "sam-i," the Turkish "uch;" the Georgian "sami" cannot be genetically connected with either Turkish "uch," or Latin "Tres": these are different roots. They cannot be compared: Georgian is not related to either the Indo-European languages or Turkish.

Related languages form a group, a so-called "family of languages." Thus for example the Hittite-Iberian family (including the living Ibero-Caucasian languages), the Indo-European or the Semitic family*** The Chinese language and the Siamese and Tibetan tongues form a similarly independent genealogic unit.

Academician N. Ya. Marr speaks of languages related through "contact": but one cannot explain the presence of common roots in Latin, Russian and old Indian through contact. On the other hand, the "contact" of Basque with ancient Latin and modern Romance language for at least 2,000 years did not make Basque related to Spanish or French.

In a genealogic classification, the various language families are placed, if one may express it this way, side by side, each with its independent origin, a concrete linguistic individuality and a separate historical path of development.

This, of course, does not imply the isolated existence of given languages or the absence of influence and interaction up to and including hybridization between languages, both related and unrelated. This also undoubtedly implies the presence of general regularities in language growth conditioned by similar processes in the development of the socio-economic life of peoples. The disclosure of these general regularities in the development of language is one of the fundamental problems of general linguistics.

The theory of Academician N. Ya. Marr denies that there could be different language origins because of the [common] initial material. By deriving all languages from four elements, Academician N. Ya. Marr has deprived languages of their individuality by reducing the whole wealth of human speech forms to these four aboriginal elements. The theory of Academician N. Ya. Marr affirms the exclusive superiority of Indo-European and Semitic languages: no other languages have reached that level on which we find the Indo-European languages—all others froze at more or less earlier, archaic levels.

Of course, some languages can preserve more archaic traits than others but an archaic level does not become a lower level, insofar as these languages start with different initial material and insofar as they are not denied the capacity for development.

But a more archaic level becomes a lower level of development if one affirms that all languages derive from the same elements and the archaic tongues are proclaimed to be forever stuck at ancient levels of development, incapable of further growth. As a matter of fact, science knows of no living languages incapable of development and cannot conceive of it in principle. No matter how archaic Academician N. Ya. Marr thought the Chinese language to be, the latter as a living language has developed, undoubtedly is developing now and will develop and thrive in coordination with the socio-economic development of China, despite the philosophy of stages of Academician N. Ya. Marr.

In arguing for the singleness of the glottogonic process, Academician N. Ya. Marr proclaimed the genealogic classification to be a racial one and on the lips of some followers of the Japhetic theory it becomes a racist one.

Meanwhile it is just Academician N. Ya. Marr's classification by stages, which denies certain languages the capacity for development, that objectively helps racism.

It may be remarked that these deficiencies are part of the classification by stages and of the glottogonic process in their present condition, inasmuch as "the classification by stages has not been fully worked out, the number of stages is ill-defined and diagnostic criteria of the stages have not been revealed."

In one of his works dated 1931, Academician N. Ya. Marr actually does state that not only the whole population of the

* N. Ya. Marr, "Language," Selected Works, Vol. II, p. 135.

† N. Ya. Marr, "Why It Is So Difficult to Become a Theoretical Linguist," Selected Works, Vol. II, p. 411. Emphasis mine. —A. Ch.

European, Asiatic and African Mediterranean spoke Japhetic languages, but also that of America, Polynesia and Australia; it is thus affirmed that Japhetic languages are at the base of all other languages.* Therefore, according to the new version and contradicting the old version of the same classification by stages, the Japhetic languages belong to an earlier stage, not only than the Indo-European languages, but earlier too than all the others.

The possibility of such diverse interpretations of the place occupied in the classification by stages by the languages most intensely studied by Academician N. Ya. Marr, the Japhetic ones, indicates that classification by stages as a more or less definite theory simply does not exist in Academician N. Ya. Marr's work.

And what of the problem-statement, the principle involved, the basic idea of such a classification? Is this principle in Academician N. Ya. Marr's theory a progressive, scientifically valuable one?

By embracing [all] languages in a single glottogonic process, Academician N. Ya. Marr denies these languages the chance to develop.

According to the theory of Academician N. Ya. Marr, the whole glottogonic process consists of languages (systems of languages) frozen in their development; languages (systems of languages) illustrate "the development" of a single glottogonic process but do not develop themselves.

If the question is put this way, in Academician N. Ya. Marr's theory the classification of languages by stages and the corresponding glottogonic process are devoid of historicity and are thus necessarily metaphysical and unscientific.

A scientific, materialist understanding of the concept of stages is possible only if the stages are revealed in the development of each language system, in the development of each language.

Therefore an investigation based on stages cannot replace historical investigation: the study of stages must be based on the results of the specific history of specific languages; therefore one cannot replace genealogic classification with a classification by stages.

III. The center of gravity of Academician N. Ya. Marr's theory rests on his teaching about elements. As we have had an opportunity to be convinced, the common initial material [the four elements] predetermines the thesis of development by stages and the singleness of the glottogonic process. All words in all languages on earth are derived from four elements (SAL, BER, YON, ROШ); any word of any language might contain one of these elements (or a hybrid of them); these elements must be found, because no comparison is valid without them.

Thus, the primordial nature of the four elements is not a harmless hypothesis about something that could have existed at one time; no, it is an implement of analysis without which no comparison can be made, without which research on languages is impossible.

Academician N. Ya. Marr frequently emphasized the especial importance of paleontologic element analysis.

"The Japhetic theory, the new linguistic teaching, makes unqualified use in its research of two absolutely firmly established techniques. One of them is a special research chart, an analytic alphabet; the other is analysis according to the four linguistic elements."†

The significance of element analysis is stressed in even more definite terms in another statement where Academician N. Ya. Marr states outright that access to the history of thought "is provided by the paleontology of speech, on the basis of the four linguistic elements" and that "once this new implement of research was mastered, hitherto unsuspected relationships were discovered between individual languages, scattered over all of Africa, Europe and Asia."*

How is four-element analysis carried out? What is the basis of the teaching on elements?

Four-element analysis is based on "a table of regular variations of the four elements."†

According to this table, one can trace the following to the element SAL: zal, tsal, tal, dal, gal; tkal, dgal, tskal, dzgal, etc. The other three elements have similarly numerous variants.

In what languages and at what point in time can one observe the sound "s" shifting to sounds t, d, ts, dz, k, d, etc.? Neither a language nor a time can be pointed out. These changes are outside of time and universal. Hence, element analysis is not limited either in time or by language: one can compare a Russian word with an Arabic word, a Hittite with a Turkish, Latin, Finnish, etc. Four-element analysis is a means for arbitrarily breaking down and arbitrarily comparing any words and their parts in any language—analysis according to elements is a universal skeleton key.

Using the elements, N. Ya. Marr is able to compare the Russian iz-rek-at [to utter, pronounce], the Armenian dzain "voice," the Georgian ena "language," the Svanetian rakv "he said," the Lezghian chanapa "to call" and the English "tongue."

Thanks to element analysis, N. Ya. Marr "establishes" the linguistic community of the words: "Japheth," "Prometheus" and "Karapet."‡

Megrelian dikha "earth," Georgian dug-s "is boiling," and Russian dukh [spirit] are compared according to elements. But what connection is there here in meaning? Megrelian dikha, it appears, "denoted" "not only the earth as firmament, but also the heavens as firmament; and through sky and sun, it also means fire (compare: Georgian dug-s "is boiling"); further: the heavens as a totem acquired the meaning "dukh" [spirit]."** This is according to the norms of "pre-logical thought": element paleontology of speech as well as the paleontology of thought, in which logical norms have no meaning, support one another and make the impossible possible.

Special attention should be given to one example of element analysis. The Georgian word "mukha" ("oak") is recognized to be made up of two elements: "mu" (the BER element) and "kha" (the SAL element). Academician N. Ya. Marr "links" the first element "mu" to the Chinese mu ("tree"), the Mordvinian pu ("tree"), the Georgian pur-i ("grain" [or "bread"]), the Greek bal-an-os ("acorn"), the Megrelian ko—bal-i ("grain" [or "bread"]). But he links the second element "kha" to the Georgian words: khe ("tree"), tke ("forest"), etc.††

Thus, one and the same element "mu" and its variants (pu, pur, bal, etc.) signify: tree—acorn—grain [or bread]. Conclusion: at one time mankind lived on acorns. A conclusion vital for the history of culture is derived from a seemingly innocuous comparison of the Georgian with the Chinese, Greek and other languages. Meanwhile, all this is based on element analysis of the words: mukha, puri, balanos, kobal-i, etc. A sense (semantic) cluster: tree—acorn—grain [or bread], with all its conclusions regarding the his-

* N. Ya. Marr, "The Japhetic Languages," op. cit.

† N. Ya. Marr, "[Contributions] to a Semantic Paleontology in Non-Japhetic Language Systems," 1931, Selected Works, Vol. II, p. 256.

* N. Ya. Marr, "The Japhetic Theory's Language Policy and the Udmurt Language," 1931, Selected Works, Vol. I, p. 288. Emphasis mine. —A. Ch.

† N. Ya. Marr, "General Course in Linguistics," op. cit., p. 96.

‡ N. Ya. Marr, "[Contributions] to a Semantic Paleontology," op. cit., p. 256.

** N. Ya. Marr, "Language and Thought," separate edition, 1931, p. 42; Selected Works, Vol. III, pp. 113-114.

†† N. Ya. Marr, "The Chinese Language and the Paleontology of Speech," 1926, Selected Works, Vol. IV, pp. 104-106.

tory of culture, is created by element analysis contrary to the facts of the history of the Georgian word "mukha": the root in question does not break down into "mu" and "kha," and neither "mu" nor "kha" can be linked to the roots signifying "tree" or "grain," according to either the modern or the historical rules of the Georgian language. We are not competent to judge whether the human organism could exist on acorns; it seems there is only one variety of oak which produces edible acorns. We will limit ourselves to pointing out that when investigated impartially the Georgian word "mukha" offers no evidence whatsoever in favor of the element analysis carried out [above].

Academician N. Ya. Marr has "arrived at" many of the conclusions so attractive to the outside observer by way of similar element analysis.

Academician N. Ya. Marr demands that element analysis be checked with semantic analysis (analysis according to meaning), "according to the laws of speech paleontology," and also with the data from the history of material culture.

But how can the semantic laws of the paleontology of speech define the results of formal paleontological analysis when one is dealing with the era of "pre-logical thought?"

The norms of pre-logical thought can hardly limit the arbitrary operations of element analysis; as for data from the history of material culture, for Academician N. Ya. Marr they themselves are based on conclusions drawn from element analysis. In short, paleontological element analysis is not only the indispensable, but also the decisive factor in conducting paleontological research on human speech, according to Academician N. Ya. Marr's theory.

Where, when and by whom has it been proved that all words of all languages on earth go back to the four elements (SAL, BER, YON, ROШ)?

Nowhere has anyone ever proved this.

Naturally, the elements did not appear accidentally in Academician N. Ya. Marr's theory—they are the names of tribes. Academician N. Ya. Marr devoted special attention to these names in the last stages [of his] study of the history of the Japhetic languages: the greater the number of languages which turned out to be Japhetic, the more limited became the historically checked material available for comparison and the more often tribal names began to figure as the favorite basis for comparison. Academician N. Ya. Marr saw the most ancient lexical material in the names of the tribes. Thus, he arrived spontaneously at the elements, at the most ancient tribal names (at first 12, later four).

A chance fact was elevated to the norm. Naturally, Academician N. Ya. Marr was unable to justify logically the four elements. To frequent and irksome questions as to why there were just four elements Academician N. Ya. Marr gave evasive answers. The last variant of the explanation reads: "Some things do not have to be proved; they can be shown*** Observation shows that there are only four elements. Why, I do not know." *

This means: <u>an unprovable theorem is proclaimed an axiom</u>.

A theory which uses paleontologic four-element analysis as a technique of linguistic research is not only not a Marxist-Leninist theory of language; it cannot even become one. It is impossible to proceed from the teaching about four elements to dialectical materialism. To declare that element analysis and the theses relating to it are attainments of Soviet linguistics means to discredit the materialist science of language.

Insisting on relations through elements, Academician N. Ya. Marr denies the kinship of languages in terms of origin; advancing his classification by stages, he describes the genealogic classification as being based on race; according to him, it classifies languages according to races. Subsequently, the "racial" classification is branded as racist.

The genealogic classification of languages is not related to division by races, much less to racism, either in fact or in logic. Genealogic classification of languages gives no reason for the pseudo-scientific reactionary racist assertions of the Gobineau-Chamberlins and their contemporary Anglo-American followers.

The existence of related languages having a common origin, (common initial language material), grouped in their respective families of languages, and the emergence of these languages in the process of differentiation of a common linguistic equipment is an irrefutable fact which is to be explained rather than denied.

The same common origin unites groups of related languages inside one or another linguistic family. For example, the Slavic, Germanic, Romance, Iranian and others within the Indo-European family; the Kartvelian languages within the Ibero-Caucasian ones; the Finnish within the Finno-Ugrian, etc.

Slavic, Germanic, Romance and other similar groups of languages are genealogical concepts. These concepts are legitimate as the concept of a linguistic family.

In his polemic with Dühring, Engels wrote:

"***The matter and form of the native language become intelligible only when one traces its emergence and gradual development. This is impossible if one neglects, first, its own obsolete forms and, second, the related languages, living and dead."*

Should Marxist-Leninist linguistics reject such kinship between languages based on common origin and therefore the genealogic classification? No, it should not. These theses are incompatible with the metaphysical classification by stages of Academician N. Ya. Marr but are quite legitimate from the point of view of Marxist-Leninist principles.

Marxist-Leninist linguistics considers the formation of new languages in the process of differentiation a regular [normal, natural phenomenon]. At the same time it in no way denies the hybridization of languages (the process of integration). Hybridization has its regularities; it is <u>one</u> of the processes [observed], but not the <u>only one</u>.

The paleontology of language, which studies the most ancient forms of human speech, is in principle indisputable as a deepening of historical perspective, but not as a technique which replaces or abolishes the history of language and the comparative historical method when understood in a Marxist sense.

Marxist-Leninist linguistics does not repudiate comparison: neither the comparison of common roots in related languages, nor the typological comparison of languages of different origin.

The techniques of such comparison must eliminate chance, they must establish regularities: the formulas of regular sound correspondences, established in the process of comparison are a reliable checking technique of the comparative historical analysis. For example, Megrelian dja "tree" cannot be traced to Georgian khe "tree"; the word which legitimately corresponds to it is the Georgian dzel-i "log," "stake." Such a technique of analysis is justified by research experience.

The genealogic classification of languages is established through a comparative historical analysis: not knowing the history of [given] languages, one cannot determine their place in a genealogic classification. The genealogic classification is a product of historical linguistics.

The classification of languages by stages in N. Ya. Marr's theory is a rejection of the genealogic classification just as element analysis is a rejection of the comparative historical analysis.

Arguing with Dühring, Engels refers flatteringly to historical linguistics, [which was] created through the application

* N. Ya. Marr, <u>Contribution to the Baku Discussion</u>, <u>op. cit.</u>, p. 44.

* F. Engels, <u>Anti-Duhring</u>, 1950 edition, p. 303.

of the comparative historical method.

"***Once Mr. Dühring," writes Engels, "strikes all contemporary historical grammar from his study plan, all he has left for his linguistic studies is the old fashioned*** technical grammar with all its casuistry and arbitrariness, which is conditioned by the absence of a historical foundation. ***It is obvious that we are dealing with a philologist who never heard anything about historical linguistics, which has undergone such powerful and fruitful development in the last 60 years. Hence Mr. Dühring is searching for "the highly instructional elements" of linguistics not in [the works of] Bopp, Grimm and Dietz but in [the works of] the late lamented Heyse and Becker."*

Comparative historical analysis is used by Engels in his works, for instance, in the book "The Origin of the Family, Private Property and the State" where he compares the words meaning "clan" in related languages, Latin, Greek, Old Indian, Gothic, etc.†

Whatever has been achieved of a positive, factually reliable nature in the historical study of Indo-European, Semitic, Ibero-Caucasian, Uralo-Altaic languages, all that is factually accurate in Academician N. Ya. Marr's own Japhetic theory, is due to the use of the techniques of such comparative historical analysis.

Obviously, such an analysis is not omnipotent; its methodology has not been worked out in all essential factors. In particular, the establishment of phonetic regularities faces great difficulties, especially when dealing with mixed (hybrid) languages. But this means that comparative historical analysis needs to be perfected but not to be replaced with the arbitrary element analysis.

A Marxist-Leninist history of languages must be built on rigorously checked, accurately established facts.

The facts of the history of languages must be illuminated with the method of materialist dialectics; this is the only method of Soviet science in general and of linguistics in particular. Only such a history of languages will be truly scientific. Soviet language history, materialist language history, stands in opposition to all idealist language history—be it a Vosslerite understanding where the spirit appears as the cause of change, be it a positivist interpretation in which Durkheim's psychologizing sociology appears as a basis of linguistics (Meillet), or where linguistics is proclaimed a part of social psychology (de Saussure).

The dividing line between bourgeois, idealist linguistics on one hand, and Soviet, materialist linguistics on the other must naturally be defined by contrasting idealism with Marxist materialism.

In N. Ya. Marr's Japhetic theory there is no genuine critique of the fundamental bases of idealist linguistics. While taking up arms in declaratory fashion against idealism in general, Academician N. Ya. Marr does not say a word about psychologism—that basic source of idealism in the most influential trends of Indo-European studies (Paul's neogrammarian orientation, de Saussure and Meillet's French sociologism). Vossler's militant idealism goes completely unnoticed. The question of formalism in grammar and the means to overcome it are left untouched.

Essentially, there is no real struggle with concrete idealist tendencies in Academician N. Ya. Marr's Japhetic theory. This is, after all, understandable, inasmuch as the struggle in N. Ya. Marr's Japhetic theory is carried forth in the name of element analysis, in the name of classification by stages and inasmuch as Academician N. Ya. Marr himself could not rise to a correct understanding of Marxism-Leninism.

Rooted in element analysis, the Japhetic theory of N. Ya. Marr has not found and is not finding any application in the cultural development of the peoples of the Soviet Union. All the positive things that are being done in this connection (preparations of grammars, dictionaries, be they for school use or historical in nature, the elaboration of rules for the literary language, etc.) are being done despite the linguistic theory of Academician N. Ya. Marr, for the simple reason that in solving the many problems indicated we cannot expect any help from element analysis.

* * *

Our critical analysis was limited to only the fundamental theses of Academician N. Ya. Marr's theory of general linguistics.

Of course it would be incorrect to equate the linguistic heritage of Academician N. Ya. Marr with the element speech paleontology. It would be unjust to consider the paleontology of speech the most substantive accomplishment of almost a half century of N. Ya. Marr's untiring and creative scientific work.

Academician N. Ya. Marr is valuable to Soviet linguistics not because of element speech paleontology, but despite this paleontology. Utilizing comparative historical analysis, which he himself unfortunately later rejected, Academician N. Ya. Marr elevated to high scientific significance the study of Ibero-Caucasian (Japhetic) languages. He disclosed their extremely rich history as well as the enormous significance in the cultural history of mankind of the people who spoke these languages.

But Academician N. Ya. Marr's theoretical formulation of a general linguistics contains serious mistakes. Without overcoming these mistakes the growth and strengthening of a materialist linguistics is impossible. If ever criticism and self-criticism were needed, it is just in this area [of general linguistics].

Soviet linguistic science is confronted with problems of enormous responsibility. To solve them it is essential to re-examine critically the linguistic heritage of Academician N. Ya. Marr, and, what is most important, to re-organize scientific work in the field of the study of language in order to work out a system of Soviet linguistics based on the principles of Marxism.

* Ibid., pp. 303-4.

† F. Engels, The Origin of the Family, Private Property and the State, Chapter III, "The Iroquois Clan," 1950 edition, p. 86.

For a Creative Development of Academician N.Ya. Marr's Heritage*

By I. MESHCHANINOV

The discussion initiated by Pravda and devoted to basic questions of Soviet linguistics is of exceptional importance for the further development of linguistics here in our Soviet Union. Struggling with the pseudoscientific theories of bourgeois idealist linguistics, Soviet scholars are developing a genuine science of language, a materialist linguistics, on the principles of dialectical and historical materialism.

In the work to come we must follow this fundamental trend accurately and not stray from the correctly charted course.

The trend is clearly indicated in the works of the classics of Marxism-Leninism, in the works of Marx, Engels, Lenin and Stalin. The wide circles of Soviet linguists are aware that the first of linguists to struggle determinedly for the penetration of the basic tenets of Marxist philosophy in the science of language was Academician N. Ya. Marr. And now the question arises: should we proceed by developing his creative heritage or should we renounce it and build anew a materialist linguistics?

In the solution of this problem, I disagree radically with Prof. A. S. Chikobava, whose article initiated the discussion.

Prof. A. S. Chikobava, a major specialist and expert on Caucasian languages, laid stress mainly on the incorrect and incomplete theses in the works of Marr. He does not deny the merits of N. Ya. Marr. Prof. A. S. Chikobava acknowledges Marr as a very great expert on Georgian and Armenian philology. Yet such a statement places in the foreground the prerevolutionary works of Marr. The Soviet period of Marr's work, characterized by what is most important for us—the works of a mature Soviet scholar—is evaluated only negatively. Only his individual erroneous statements are emphasized, so that all positive aspects of his works remain undisclosed. An impression is thereby created that Prof. A. S. Chikobava is not inclined to recommend the post-October works of Marr and wants to proceed independently of them. He thus rejects the creative heritage of a very great Soviet linguist.

It is difficult to agree with such a state of affairs. Without denying the existence of a number of erroneous statements made by Marr, I think that it is not they which characterize the basic postulates of Marr. These erroneous theories should be set aside, but one does not simultaneously eliminate the whole of Marr's creative path. Precisely the reverse. I submit that to build a truly Marxist linguistic science without Marr is unacceptable for us.

An Evaluation of the Present-Day Situation in Soviet Linguistics.

Recently a number of articles have appeared in the Soviet press which remark on the alarming situation in linguistics. The absolutely correct indications of the Soviet press served as the basis for a discussion of the problems which relate to the future trend of linguistic research. The Presidium of the Academy of Sciences of the U. S. S. R. acknowledged the necessity of adopting a series of measures for eliminating the indicated shortcomings and on July 21, 1949, issued a special declaration about present-day conditions in Soviet linguistics and about the measures designed to improve linguistic work in the Academy of Sciences.

The fundamental shortcomings indicated by the press and diagnosed by linguists' conferences consist in the lag of work in linguistic theory behind the practical tasks of the cultural and linguistic development of the peoples of the Soviet Union. Projects of a purely applied nature were undertaken and show positive results, but certainly not on the scale required by socialist construction, which has raised the economic and cultural levels of many peoples who were persecuted and stagnating under the Tsarist regime. The coordination of these projects with research on theory is far from assured.

The completely inadequate development of that progressive materialist study of language elaborated by Academician N. Ya. Marr on the basis of the Marxist-Leninist methodology is another cause of this lag. There has been almost no popularization or introduction of the principles of Soviet linguistics into teaching practice. As a consequence of inadequate scientific and organizational activity by Academician N. Ya. Marr's students and followers it also became apparent that even here, in the Soviet Union, one can still find today reflections of bourgeois, idealist theories in the works of individual linguists. The formal comparative method and the reactionary hypothesis of a proto-language have not yet been shaken off. The study of linguistic processes in complete isolation from [the study of] social development, the history of peoples and nations continues. One can observe the influence of linguistic theories popular now in the West, which reflect the imperialist policies of the Anglo-American bloc and so on. The decisive struggle with these deficiencies in research and particularly with propositions inimical to Soviet linguistics brings to the foreground as an especially urgent task not the repudiation but, on the contrary, the creative development of N. Ya. Marr's teaching about language in its basic pronouncements which introduce the Marxist method in the scientific work of linguists.

The Materialist Bases of N. Ya. Marr's Teaching About Languages.

N. Ya. Marr was the first of Soviet linguists resolutely to set about introducing the method of historical and dialectical materialism into linguistic research work. He gradually developed and clarified this new linguistic approach, which he named the Japhetic theory. In his latest works he called it materialist linguistics. N. Ya. Marr frequently emphasized that the approach he was elaborating introduced a method in linguistics which had not been used [before] in this scientific discipline, to which the basic propositions of Marxism-Leninism had until then been alien.

In a work dated 1931, "Linguistic Policy of the Japhetic Theory and the Udmurt Language," N. Ya. Marr clearly formulated the main proposition of his researches in the following words: "The materialist method of the Japhetic theory is the method of historical and dialectical materialism, that is, the selfsame Marxist method. It has been rendered specific through studies of linguistic materials and

*Pravda, May 16, 1950, pp. 3-4.

related data, not only of speech in general, but also of material and social culture."*

Consequently, Marr's materialist doctrine of language does not create any new method but applies the method established and developed by the doctrine of Marx, Engels, Lenin and Stalin. Marr set himself such a task. Where he unwaveringly follows this aim, he establishes and persistently develops through research the basic principles of materialist linguistics.

Thus N. Ya. Marr examines linguistic processes in their social context. Therefore he indissolubly connects the history of a given people's language with the history of this people and thereby emerges in sharp contradiction with the premises of bourgeois linguistics still prevailing in the West, where languages are studied in both their contemporary and their historical manifestations as an independent and spontaneously developing category. N. Ya. Marr strikes a decisive blow at such propositions of bourgeois linquistics and one after another upsets all the best known premises of idealist linguistics. N. Ya. Marr refuses to see the operation of chance in the changes of linguistic forms. N. Ya. Marr affirms that, since a language cannot develop by itself, all observable structural shifts and partial changes in grammatical forms observable in it have their explanation in sociological forms.

The demand made of the linguist is therefore the following: he should study grammatical form not only in itself, but also in its social significance. This demand, alien and unacceptable to bourgeois linguistics is presented by N. Ya. Marr as indispensable to the Soviet linguist. He considers inadmissible the examination of only the formal aspect [of grammatical forms] without comprehending it, that is, without a clear idea of what social function it fulfills. This is why N. Ya. Marr insists categorically on the recognition of the fallacy of a narrowly formal approach to the language under investigation. This is just the approach characteristic of all bourgeois linguistic schools, new and old.

N. Ya. Marr affirms that linguistic form cannot be understood without considering its content and its social significance. No words and none of the grammatical forms arise spontaneously, because language is a product of the social environment and the latter also conditions whatever changes occur. This is a radical rejection of the basic premises of the leading personality of contemporary linguistics, F. de Saussure, who draws a sharp distinction between external and internal linguistics. Such separation is typical of formal language study. Questions dealing with how language arose, how and by whom it is developed (external linguistics) do not interest the bourgeois scholar. For a Soviet linguist, who sees in language the major means of communication, a weapon for development and struggle, such an approach to language is totally unacceptable. One of Marx's merits consists in being first among linguists to educate his students and followers in a spirit critical of the obsolete views of foreign science.

Of no less significance is N. Ya. Marr's assertion that language is a superstructural phenomenon, subordinate in its genesis and development to the material conditions of the [socio-economic] base which it reflects. It therefore becomes through its grammatical structure and the semantics of its vocabulary a first class historical source. In his investigations, N. Ya. Marr approaches his materials as a historian and from this vantage point analyzes the formative periods of given languages even though they may be of various epochs and different peoples.

He follows through the effect of hybridization of separate languages which results eventually in a new qualitative formation, a new language. If a nation be neither a racial nor a tribal, but a historically elaborated community of people, then its language is similarly a historically developed entity without which the national community is unthinkable. N. Ya. Marr denies the existence of languages which are not basically hybridized. Correspondingly he also affirms that national languages and their predecessors cannot be racial. N. Ya. Marr protests decisively and firmly against racial characterizations of language and thereby refutes racist theory in linguistics. Here he acts in his capacity as a historian who takes into account the history of the development of social forms.

As early as 1924, in his work "The Indo-European Languages of the Mediterranean Region," N. Ya. Marr insisted that "the Indo-European family of languages does not exist as racially separate. Nowhere did Indo-European languages of the Mediterranean region appear with any special linguistic material which could be traced back to any racially unique family of languages. Still less could it be traced to any racially unique proto-language*** The Indo-European languages form a special family, but not a racial one. They are the offspring of a special, more complex level of hybridization provoked by a social upheaval conditioned by new productive forces connected, apparently, with the discovery of metals and their widespread use in the economy.*****

This refusal of N. Ya. Marr to follow the proto-language theory which still prevailed in bourgeois linguistics is exceptionally significant for the further development of linguistic science. By connecting the history of language with the developmental history of human society, N. Ya. Marr could not but arrive at the conclusion that the proposition broadly accepted in science that languages moved from singleness to plurality was erroneous. The several isolated small tribes dispersed over enormous territories could not, according to N. Ya. Marr, have a common language. More powerful linguistic masses developed only later, under favorable social conditions which corresponded to new social formations.

The rejection of the proto-language is the beginning of materialist linguistics. "Language and Society" becomes the basic problem in N. Ya. Marr's work. If each nation and each people represents a mixture of various [ethnic] ingredients, then its language, too, is similarly an historically blended phenomenon. Thus the main task of Soviet linguistics becomes the tracing of a complex blending process resulting in qualitatively new languages and not the search for their single aboriginal source.

From its very genesis the historic process of language development is viewed by N. Ya. Marr as consisting not only in the hybridization of different languages, but also in changes occurring inside a given language. He thus traces both external and internal factors. N. Ya. Marr affirms that "language is a social phenomenon and is socially acquired*** No language could appear without the formation of social groups and their need for organized communication, without concerting voiced symbols and meanings. Without one another and without their mutual blending, no language could have arisen. Least of all could any language have developed further. In this sense, the more words many contemporary languages have in common, the more visible and easily ascertainable are their formal connections over large territories and the more grounds there are for affirming that these common phenomena are their latest component elements. Their growth in individual languages is the result of very late and frequently repeated hybridization."†

By establishing the social significance of any grammatical form, N. Ya. Marr gives an answer to the question preoccupying all linguists: how can one explain the simi-

*N. Ya. Marr. Selected Works, Vol. I, p. 276.

*Ibid., p. 276.

†N. Ya. Marr, "Why It Is So Hard to Become a Theoretical Linguist," 1929, Selected Works, Vol. II, p. 399.

larities observable in a number of languages, similarities which make it possible to classify them into a single system, or according to the old terminology, a "family," if one rejects the proto-language? The question is frequently asked, how does one explain the "kinship" of such languages as the Romance, the Germanic, etc., and on what can one base tracing them back to a common family of Indo-European languages? In the above-mentioned work, N. Ya. Marr gives the required answer in a few words: "Kinship is due to social convergence, lack of kinship to social divergence."*

Therefore, the kinship of languages is not an aboriginal condition referring to prehistoric eras of the proto-language. N. Ya. Marr's opinions on this subject are precise and unhesitating: "We deny not only the existence of a single aboriginal homeland of specific languages*** We also deny the existence of any proto-languages, in the case of particular groupings of human speech such as Indo-European and Semitic or in the case of more limited clusters found inside the Indo-European circle, such as Slavic, Germanic, Romance*** Only a mind torn from existing material reality can hold that the kinship of the Russian and German languages is to be traced to a common ancestral tongue, or that French and Spanish have a common origin which permits, if you please, the reconstruction of a proto-Romance language, without even mentioning that most scientifically invented common proto-Indo-European tongue."† The primary [aboriginal] character of the prehistoric source is denied by N. Ya. Marr in all his works after 1924. Yet he does not deny the closeness of certain languages, clustered in groups; he gives it a different explanation.

From these propositions stated by N. Ya. Marr, one can draw the following conclusions: if Romance languages, including French and Spanish, arose from the blending of several other languages and reveal numerous common features, then in these converging so-called Romance languages similar components participated in the same way in which they participated in the formation of the respective peoples, later nations. Thus are created the historically formed similarities between languages which are classified by groups. To these external characteristics are added internal ones — because once a language is formed its developmental process continues, by no means spontaneously, but drawing from the same social soil. Therefore the convergence of languages according to a number of external criteria must be viewed as a historic formation.

In this direction, N. Ya. Marr's conclusions not only disagree radically with the bases of bourgeois linguistics, but also offer entirely new criteria for comparative work which are alien to bourgeois science. The formalism reigning in foreign linguistics, which rests on a scheme of proto-languages, must necessarily concentrate its attention on manifestations of similarity, without which the whole evolutionary theory of the development of language falls apart. But Marr, who examines language and its developed systems as the product of the history of human society, submits to analysis not only the similarities, but also the divergences. What is more, he pays no less attention to the latter than to the former. In the very divergences of particular grammatical structures he can establish their unifying elements that can be found both in the concepts which assume various forms in different languages, as well as in the formation of words and their syntactic combinations. He reveals the norms of functioning consciousness.

The turning point from a comparative grammar to one worked out on the facts provided by the paleontology of speech was precipated by intensification of the historical approach in dealing with the most diverse languages, whose number grew and grew. Along with paleontology, emphasis was placed increasingly on the study of material culture, economy and social organization as factors in the creation and development of speech (cf. the preface to "A Classified Bibliography of Printed Works on Japhetidology" (1926) [in Russian]). In his own words, N. Ya. Marr "takes into account in his analysis not only the formally similar manifestations of various languages, but the dissimilar ones as well. By analyzing their functions he reveals the very content of each linguistic fact and, first of all, of words. He thus establishes a sense connection between languages outside the so-called families and their imaginary proto-languages and also connects the nature of voiced speech in general with its social function." The Japhetic theory "is based for its direct origin and source of developmental growth***not on the physiological prerequisities of the technical aspect of language, i.e., only the formally recognized sounds, but on a phenomenon which is social in its origin— the hybridization of languages owing to increasingly close communication and the unification of the economy."* This is what N. Ya. Marr bases his historical approach to language on.

N. Ya. Marr considers that linguistics has no right to limit its investigations to given periods of already developed speech. He indicates that with such a scientific approach the structure of a language under study receives inadequate attention, a structure in which archaic forms survive from a distant past. Bourgeois linguistics also goes back to the distant past, but, being divorced from genuine history, it reconstructs various proto-linguistic blueprints through wholly artificial means. In lieu of such blueprints N. Ya. Marr offers his understanding of the genesis of human speech based on the paleontology of language. This proposal is not based on theoretical considerations of an idealist nature, but on vast linguistic materials and the developmental history of social forms and material production.

Attributing special significance to the semantics of words, N. Ya. Marr traces out in detail semantic correspondences and ascertains cases of polar contradictions in the meanings of a single stem. Thus, using the data of Japhetic languages he finds that a single stem includes such contradictory meanings as light and dark, beginning and end. The explanation of this phenomenon is based on the primary plural meanings of the root and on the acquisition by the word of a new meaning while preserving the old, which arose under different conditions of social usage. N. Ya. Marr dedicates a whole series of works to this kind of semantic similarities based on the unity of opposites. (See "On Semantic Paleontology in the Languages of Non-Japhetic Systems" (1931); "Impersonal, Defective***Verbs" (1932); "Language and Writing" (1930); etc.)

Recognizing the social base as most important in the development of language, N. Ya. Marr emphasizes those categories of speech which are most saturated with definitive meanings. Such a formulation of the work is alien to bourgeois linguistics with its self-sufficient formalism. In sharp contradiction with the main orientation of bourgeois linguistics, N. Ya. Marr concentrated his attack on this aspect of linguistic culture, on a sensible utilization of language's resources. As a result he gave a completely new meaning to linguistic structure, which could not be achieved by the old linguistic school. Examining in detail the semantics of a word, N. Ya. Marr observes that the word contains a complete lexical content, whose general meaning becomes precise in its specific usage only in the structure of the sentence. N. Ya. Marr takes into account that the word could not appear outside speech. Therefore his attention is given not only to the meaning of a word but also to the meaning of the grammatical form which the word obtains in the structure of a sentence. From this N. Ya. Marr's

*N. Ya. Marr, Selected Works, Vol. IV, p. 3.

†N. Ya. Marr, "From Pyrenean Guria," 1928, Selected Works, Vol. IV, p. 3.

*N. Ya. Marr, "Japhetidology at the Leningrad State University," 1930, Selected Works, Vol. 1, p. 257.

interest shifts to the sentence itself. From this stems also the raising of the question about the mutual interrelations of parts of speech and parts of sentences. N. Ya. Marr attributes special significance to the study of syntactic structure, which does not receive adequate consideration from bourgeois linguists.

Speaking genetically, N. Ya. Marr assigns the formation of parts of speech to later periods. He considers that sentences ust earlier have been broken up into their component parts so that the words which make up the sentences could have acquired their morphological indices which characterize the parts of speech formed later. In tracing the process of the formation of parts of speech and summarizing his earlier statements, N. Ya. Marr writes: "***parts of the sentence of an already developed thought mechanism became transformed into parts of speech. In their turn the latter became ideologically crystallized as self-contained units, assuming the form not only of their basic meaning-function (which had already acquired a single designation) but also their auxiliary function in the structure of speech."*

N. Ya. Marr's conclusions emerge from his understanding of language as a phenomenon of a social nature, conditioned by the conscious working activity of man. This is why the reflection of actual reality in man's consciousness is made the basis of the research work of the Soviet linguist. In this connection, N. Ya. Marr's interest in the relationships between language and thought appear in sharp contrast to bourgeois linguistics. Marr starts with a statement from the classics of Marxism-Leninism: "Men, in developing their material productivity and their material communication, change their thinking and the products of this thinking along with changes in this reality." "Language is the most direct realization of thought."† This outlook permeated all of N. Ya. Marr's work during the last decade of his life. In his words, "the linguist's shying away from expressing opinions about thought is the heritage of European bourgeois linguistics. It hangs like a curse over all our institutions, and over the organization of research and teaching, not only in languages. The old doctrine on language correctly rejected thought as a subject within its scope, for it studied speech without thought. It contained laws on phonetics—sound phenomena, but it had no laws on semantics—laws on the meaning of speech, and later of parts of speech including even the word. The meanings of words were given no ideological basis whatsoever."‡

A wonderful confirmation of N. Ya. Marr's views can be found in the languages of the peoples of the Soviet Union. They are united through a common socialist content, while simultaneously continuing to develop their national forms. The latter get saturated with new content which leads to their contradictory state. Their old linguistic forms acquire new meaning, and either change their form or are replaced by another. These postulates about the dialectic unity of language and thought which were worked out in detail by N. Ya. Marr on the basis of materialist philosophy, not only differ radically from all the notions of foreign bourgeois formalism, but also demolish their pseudo-historical and idealist conceptions. If one separates language from thought and considers the latter a field apart, outside the domain of linguistic research, then it is obvious that all that is left to the science of language is the formal aspect. N. Ya. Marr firmly objects to this narrowly defined formalism which permeates the entire bourgeois school.

The Study of Contemporary Living Languages.

As a linguist-historian, N. Ya. Marr does not neglect studies in linguistic structure of contemporary languages. On the contrary, it is precisely in living speech that he finds source material also for his historical researches. His ideas [on this topic] are formulated with exhaustive completeness in a report published in 1931 called "Linguistic Policy of the Japhetic Theory and the Udmurt Language." He affirms in that report that "the new science according to Japhetic theory was developed from the study of living languages independent of any racist mirages, independent of any feudal and bourgeois class and national barriers and vicious prejudices, independent of the imperialist nuances of any language and independent of any social class preferences for dead languages."*

N. Ya. Marr assigns special significance to the study of living languages. He sees in them rich material which develops before the very eye of the investigator. Here one can observe the processes at work in language which change its formal aspects and those causes which condition the process. The languages of our Union are particularly illustrative of this context, as it is only here, thanks to the Leninist-Stalinist national policy, that the languages of even the smallest ethnic groups receive all the necessary aid for further development. Many of these were until recently quite backward in economy and customs, having no schools nor written language. Education in the native language, periodicals, the radio, the appearance of literature and development of the economy and way of life all clearly indicate the source which propels the linguistic structure to higher levels of development.

The Soviet linguist has received for observation such linguistic material as is not available to any foreign student of language, particularly not to those who are still under the oppression of imperialist policy. The abundance and variety of linguistic structures of the peoples of the U.S.S.R. have unfolded wide horizons for the serious scientific work of the Soviet scholar.

In sharp contrast to bourgeois linguistics, by connecting the history of language with social history, N. Ya. Marr not only penetrates far into the historical process, but, in examining present-day realities, touches also on the question of a future single language. Here, too, it is not language per se which is basic, but a language undergoing major changes which occur in the social base conditioning the development of language. In commenting on a single future language, N. Ya. Marr also quotes J. V. Stalin's words: "As an example," says Marr, "I will quote from a speech by Comrade Stalin dealing with the withering away of national languages and their coalescence into a single, common tongue*** The indicated portion of Comrade Stalin's speech says: '*** the question of the dying out of the national languages and their merging in a single, common language is not an internal question of state; it is not a question of the victory of socialism in one country, but an international matter, dependent on the victory of socialism on an international scale*** Lenin meant it when he stated that national differences will remain long after the victory of proletarian dictatorship on an international scale.' "† The quotation was used in a report by N. Ya. Marr, "The Linguistic Policy of Japhetic Theory and the Udmurt Language" (1931).

The Creative Path of N. Ya. Marr.

N. Ya. Marr did not work out the principles of materialist linguistics straight off. They were elaborated by intensive research, through the accumulation of fresh materials and the planning of investigations based on the principles of Marxism-Leninism.

N. Ya. Marr was clearly aware of the internal struggle which he had to wage with himself; a struggle with the old scientific propositions inculcated in him by his schooling,

*N. Ya. Marr, "The Japhetic Languages," 1931, Selected Works, Vol. I, p. 297.

†K. Marx and F. Engels, Works, Vol. IV, pp. 17, 434.

‡N. Ya. Marr, "Language and Thought," Selected Works, Vol. III, p. 103.

*N. Ya. Marr, Selected Works, Vol. I. pp. 274-5.

†Ibid., p. 274.

‡Ibid., p. 228.

from which he was becoming free. He saw that his students would also "face great difficulties in acquiring not only the new methods, but also knowledge and more knowledge, concrete knowledge for a competently waged scientific struggle with the obsolete ideology of the old school in oneself."* He also submitted his own works to critical revision, having noted in them some substantial errors. He warns that his works, primarily those dated before 1924, needed revision and particularly the basic premises of "The Japhetic Caucasus and the Tertiary Ethnic Element in the Creation of the Mediterranean Culture" which were theoretically incorrect. He admits "many questions have since changed so much not only in the answers, but even in the way they are posed, that the explanations given are diametrically contradictory*** It is clear," continues N. Ya. Marr, "that one cannot remain content with the reading of a given Japhetidological work***without taking into account that which has been complemented, complicated, refined or corrected, changed or deleted in later works, at later stages of the theory's development."† In this same 1926 work, N. Ya. Marr does not hide the fact that his newly created linguistic theory "has been freeing itself with difficulty only these last [few] years from the swaddling clothes of bourgeois thinking and its corresponding methodology in scientific work."‡

One must therefore keep in mind that the radical transformation in the phrasing of scientific theory, mentioned by N. Ya. Marr, took place only in the last 15 years of his life. During the 30 preceding years of scientific endeavor (counting from 1888, date of his first printed paper) N. Ya. Marr was not familiar with the works of Marxist-Leninist classics. This explains the fruitlessness of his efforts to go beyond the hampering theories of the neo-grammarians, with whom he could not agree even then. Such prerevolutionary, narrowly philological works are considered by Professor A. S. Chikobava to be particularly to the credit of N. Ya. Marr.

Only after the great October socialist revolution, however, did N. Ya. Marr see clearly the dead end reached in the work of the linguistic school which nurtured him and consequently in his own work. Marr did not conceal the difficulties which lay in his path and frequently noted in his own work the premises inculcated by the school which had trained him and which were hindering progress. The only way out of this complex situation led to familiarization with Marxism-Leninism. N. Ya. Marr starts on this path. But even here his old views come into conflict with the new ones and this leads to partial failures, the assumption of positions which Marr himself had to reject later.

One finds some printed statements which are not repeated by N. Ya. Marr in his later works, and which he replaces with new ones. Nonetheless, dealing self-critically with his own works, Marr most often corrects his own mistakes. An excellent example will be found in Marr's attitude toward his own, already mentioned, report "The Japhetic Caucasus and the Tertiary Ethnic Element in the Creation of Mediterranean Culture" (1920). This report, which provoked exceptional interest and is extremely significant for the wealth of the material collected and its analysis, was based on an incorrect premise which reduced the rising Mediterranean culture to the migrations of Japhetic tribes, moving from the Ararat valley along the northern and southern shores of the Mediterranean. Japhetic tribes turned out to be a cultural proto-people and the Mediterranean region an aboriginal cultural center. Three years later, N. Ya. Marr inclosed a preface to the German translation of the same report, in which he expressed doubts as to the correctness of the basic premises of the report and in 1926, as we have already seen above, he warns the reader about the need to be critical in using this work, and as for all of his earlier works, he suggests that "it is better not to look into them."*

The university lectures on "The Japhetic Theory; a Course in General Linguistics" found themselves in a similar situation. They were given in 1927 in the city of Baku and thus widely known under the name of the "Baku Course." These lectures, being the only work giving an over-all view of Japhetic theory and its basic premises, became the foundation for the teaching of [linguistics] courses in universities. Sold out in a very short time, they had to be reissued. While including detailed descriptions of sound [-change] laws and correspondences established by Marr, the lectures also contained in their other sections a presentation which did not always correspond to the tenets of a materialist science of language and the author himself did not give his consent to the reprinting of this work in 1931, finding a radical revision indispensable. One should point out here that through the fault of N. Ya. Marr's students, the "Baku Course," which the author had refused to reprint as obsolete, is included without any qualifications in the list of texts recommended to the students.

Erroneous and Still Uncorrected Theses of N. Ya. Marr.

Some of N. Ya. Marr's conclusions did not bear out his correct premise that in linguistics one should thoroughly follow the method of historical and dialectical materialism, as, for example, the elaboration of a family tree based on a morphological classification of languages, published in the "Baku Course" (1928), in which he classifies as the highest link in the contemporary condition of languages the inflected structure of Indo-European. Below it and preceding it one finds, one after another, the inflected Semitic languages, before them the agglutinating Turkic ones, and below those the ergative Japhetic and beneath them all the amorphous languages. As a result we get a structure in many ways similar to the usual morphological classification which is by no means alien to the bourgeois linguistic school.

There are also cases of incorrect use being made of completely true propositions of N. Ya. Marr. Thus, his insistence that the study of form and content be inseparable brought his attention to the semantics of words and sentences. Starting from this, N. Ya. Marr could and actually did reach the conclusion of an auxiliary meaning to morphologic indicators, but Marr's students deduced from it the need for the complete exclusion of morphology from the ranks of independent divisions of grammar (my work "General Linguistics," 1940). What is being forgotten here is the already quoted statement of N. Ya. Marr that the parts of speech once arisen "began in their turn to develop ideologically as independent units..."†

An absolutely correct recognition of language as a phenomenon of a superstructural kind and the indication that in the classification by stages of the language-forming process it is indispensable to take into account the social factor and its changes served as a justification for mechanically juxtaposing social eras with the division of languages by stages, which means the identification of the base with the superstructure (a series of my articles at the end of the '20s).

The inadequate clarity and the unfinished nature of some of N. Ya. Marr's theses get combined with not always successful attempts by his followers to give them the necessary explanation. But even in N. Ya. Marr's own work there are statements which do not correspond to the main line he himself elaborated. Some of his conclusions, as we saw, were refuted in print by N. Ya. Marr [himself], others he rejected and did not repeat in later works but without mentioning in print their theoretical incorrectness. There are also statements which N. Ya. Marr did not have the chance to correct.

*Ibid, p.228.
†Ibid., pp. 224, 226.
‡Ibid., p. 222.

*N. Ya. Marr, Preface to "Classified Bibliography," Selected Works, Vol. I, p. 224.
†N. Ya. Marr, Selected Works, Vol. I, p. 297.

N. Ya. Marr left without refutation such statements to be found in his works of the 1920s as the ascription of a class nature to the most ancient periods of voiced speech among the tribes of the primitive community. Statements of this kind are strewn through numerous works. They can be found in the preface to the "Classified Bibliography" (1926): "But at the same time, the tribe itself which spoke a voiced language turned out to be, insofar as its so-called natural speech was concerned, a class phenomenon."* The same topic is discussed in a 1928 paper, "The Present-Day Problems and Current Tasks of Japhetic Theory," where one is reminded of "such serious sociological problems as that of class differentiation in primitive social organization which I (meaning N. Ya. Marr—I. M.) would only conditionally call a horde, even if a primitive horde."† Even in his report on "Language and Thought," read in 1931, he mentions the obstinate struggle through which the voiced language, due to its technical possibilities, outgrew gesture speech and later became "conversational speech, but again [belonging] to the dominant stratum." ‡ In the same year, 1931, in a report on "Linguistic Policy of the Japhetic Theory and the Udmurt Language" one finds a chapter with the heading "On the Road of Pre-Clan Class Differentiation of the Totemic Community."**

In continuing to affirm the class nature of nascent voiced speech, N. Ya. Marr gives it a special meaning, different from contemporary speech through gestures (manual language). In relation to this, voiced language receives a magic content, and medicine men are described as a ruling class. In developing the same thought in his article "On the Origin of Language" (1926) N. Ya. Marr comes to the conclusion that "the use of the first voiced language could not but be a magical technique: particular words could not fail to be regarded as sorcery. It was prized and kept in secret, as to this day the special magic hunters' vocabulary is kept secret."†† Further on, N. Ya. Marr speaks of the transition of "oral language into wider usage out of the hands of the class which owned it, through the blending of various primitive tribes."‡‡ From here also stems another conclusion—about the labor-magic content of the first voiced language. Later N. Ya. Marr goes on to the establishment of cosmic thinking. In 1931 in his report "Linguistic Policy of the Japhetic Theory and the Udmurt Language" he returns to the same theme and outlines three stages of thought, namely: (1) the totemic one, with linear (manual) labor-magic speech; (2) the cosmic stage, with a social superstructural world: totems, later sky, sun, land, water, etc.; (3) the technological one. Here N. Ya. Marr connects labor-magic content with manual speech and assigns to it totemic thinking.

N. Ya. Marr does not reject his older understanding of totem even in his Large Soviet Encyclopaedia article "The Japhetic Languages" (1931). His understanding of totem is as a collective "master-owner," the naming of which gave rise to pronouns, as expressing the self-naming of the totem (its substitutes) and therefore of the oldest human collective (clan, tribe). This is why N. Ya. Marr considers tribal names to be totemic.

In the thesis of a totemic society and the role of magic and medicine man in the creation and development of voiced speech, N. Ya. Marr abandons the study of language in its conditioning by a genuine social factor, an action involving productive labor, that is [he abandons] just what he insists on in his basic premises of a materialist science of language. The recognition of the act of labor as a labor-magic act led easily to separation from social background. As a result, thought, which develops language, began to be considered as cosmic and microcosmic. What is more, this world view was ascribed to the initial periods of development of human speech.

*Ibid., Vol. I, p. 226.
†Ibid., Vol. III, p. 75.
‡Ibid., p. 109.
**Ibid., Vol. V, p. 487.
††Ibid., Vol. II, p. 204.
‡‡Ibid.

Such erroneous conclusions penetrated into the works of N. Ya. Marr and have kept their place in his printed works. There are also unsuccessful attempts to elaborate a classification by stages, as, for example, those included in a 1929 paper "The Present Day Problems and Current Tasks of Japhetic Theory": "The shifts in thought," says N. Ya. Marr, "are three systems of constructing voiced speech, which emerge in the aggregate from the joining of various economic systems and their corresponding social structures: (1) primitive communism, with a synthetic structure of speech*** (2) a social structure based on the appearance of the various types of economy and social division of labor*** a linguistic structure divisible into parts of speech [such as] clauses within the sentence and other parts within the clause *** (3) an estate or class society, with technical division of labor, [and] with a morphology of an inflected kind"* The mixing up evidenced here of syntactic with morphological criteria, the assignment of synthetic languages to the primitive community and of inflected ones to the class society could confuse the followers of N. Ya. Marr and lead them to erroneous conclusions, including those which were mentioned above.

One can also find occasional mistakes in the etymology of words in N. Ya. Marr's works. One can sense a certain exaggeration in the historical evaluation of the cultural importance of the Mediterranean and so on. But all of these erroneous places, an occasional [display of] enthusiasm for the leading role of the Japhetides, etc., are an extraneous element, the elimination of which will reveal the true stature of N. Ya. Marr, a very great Soviet scholar, who laid the foundations of a materialist science of language and dealt a shattering blow to the scholastic concepts of the bourgeois linguistic school. To isolate in N. Ya. Marr's works the enthusiasms which have led to confusing propositions and conclusions becomes a task of the first magnitude. They are relatively easy to isolate as they obviously contradict his own basic works, which introduced in linguistics the method of historical and dialectical materialism. N. Ya. Marr was sincerely and firmly on his way to the latter. The elimination of these erroneous theses and schemes will reveal the real Marr, the builder of a materialist linguistics, who laid the foundations for its later development. The works of N. Ya. Marr will retain their exceptional significance and vital strength in growing Soviet science. The basic contributions of N. Ya. Marr will stand clearly outlined.

Problems Requiring Refinement and Additional Work.

The treatment of certain theses which have great significance for linguistic investigation was left unfinished by Marr. This causes serious difficulties for his students and followers who until now have not been able to overcome the obstacles which have arisen in their scientific work. There are statements in Marr which were left incomplete or in need of certain refinement. Among the latter is his paleontologic analysis, which remains basic for Soviet linguistics and separates his propositions radically from those of bourgeois science. Evolutionism is contrasted with transitions by jumps, by steps, in Marr's terminology, from one qualitative condition to the other. But the actual content of paleontologic analysis did not receive a single interpretation from N. Ya. Marr's followers. Here one can mention analysis with the four linguistic elements, that is [an analysis] according to those primary words—the roots of voiced speech, isolated by Marr, who described them as archaic

*Ibid., Vol. III, p. 71.

totemic tribal names, the basis of all eventual linguistic word building.

Some of N. Ya. Marr's followers and particularly his opponents completely reject element analysis (Prof. A. S. Chikobava). Some of Marr's students consider such analysis unsuitable for periods of developed speech, which [according to them] have worked out more complicated stem structures. These students pass over in silence the question of the existence of these elements, in their Marrist sense, in the structure of language during its most archaic periods of its development (Academician I. I. Meshchaninov). Some statements exist, tending to view four-element analysis as unsuitable, given the [possibilities of] etymologic break-down of contemporary speech, yet admitting at the same time the value of Marr's discovery which established the most archaic types of break-down of the aboriginal diffuse sound [-making] (Academician L. V. Shcherba). Some linguists recognize the usefulness of element analysis even in historically known languages. They think it possible to apply element analysis in explaining certain archaic words, particularly ethnic and toponymic terms in those cases when their surviving stems cannot be clearly etymologized along with the rest of the given language's words (Professor F. I. Filin). Demands are also made that element analysis be applied in all cases, with wide and refined utilization in the lexical analysis of languages of various periods, including the contemporary (I. D. Dmitriyev-Kelda).

Actually, even in his latest works N. Ya. Marr did not relinquish element analysis. And yet the actual concept of a linguistic element remained inexact. Originally N. Ya. Marr identified the four elements with the self-designations of four Japhetic tribes (SAL, BER, YON, ROШ); later he added to the content of element a totemic significance. In his last works Marr suggested a new explanation of linguistic element pointing to its inseparable connection between its formal and its ideological aspect. Even if this latest instruction remained unclarified, paleontologic analysis, which traces qualitative changes in language, nevertheless makes it possible, even without element analysis, to approach the developmental history of different languages through the use of their own data, but taking into account the qualitative changes occurring in the process of internal development of the language. This remains inaccessible to the formal comparative historical method, which is based on evolutionism.

And yet the historical path of language formation in the process of blending of ancient tribes and peoples was revealed by N. Ya. Marr through paleontologic analysis (qualitative changes in language). And if particular etymologies are doubtfully traced, a significant number of them give splendid results when applied to the correct illumination of the history of word-creating development. The refinement in understanding and significance of paleontologic analysis stands before the followers of N. Ya. Marr as a task demanding the earliest consideration.

Closely connected in N. Ya. Marr's thinking with paleontologic analysis is the teaching that language grew by stages. N. Ya. Marr paid exceptional attention to this question. Even if his several attempts to present a classification of languages by stages and their temporal arrangement were not successful and were not repeated in his later works, still he never gave up the problem of development by stages. The best developed scheme of such temporal arrangement side by side with a classification of [particular] languages by stages can be found in the report "Why It Is So Hard to Become a Theoretical Linguist," presented in 1928, the same year that the "Baku Course" was published.

Although N. Ya. Marr is no longer in complete agreement with the latter and replaced the family tree presented in his university lectures with a chart of the development by stages of voiced speech, still certain propositions are presented in both works which coincide in their final analysis. The new distribution according to periods which he presents is of some interest. It consists in the following: (1) languages of the system of the primary period, monosyllabic and polysemantic (plural meanings): Chinese, African and other languages belong here; (2) languages of the system of the secondary period, such as Finno-Ugric, Turkic, Mongolian; (3) languages of the system of the tertiary period, namely, Japhetic and Hamitic; (4) languages of the system of the quaternary period—Semitic and Indo-European.*

In presenting the distribution of languages according to the four periods in lieu of the family tree, N. Ya. Marr does it with reservations: "In rejecting the family tree*** which we ourselves had elaborated***we have only had time to outline the data for the drawing of a life-like graphic diagram, but have not presented the diagram itself, leaving its completion for a later time as it is a purely technical problem*** The question, therefore, is not whether or not it is possible to present a truly life-like image in a family tree or some other diagram of the mutual interrelations of languages. It is obvious that such a life-like portrait cannot be obtained if one isolates the linguistic superstructure, as language in its entirety is a creation of the human community, a reflection not only of its thought but also of its social organization and economy—a reflection [seen] in the techniques and structure of speech, as well as in its semantics.

The defect of the schemes presented above is that they were elaborated according to formal morphological criteria, which are the same ones used in the classifications of the bourgeois school (amorphousness—agglutination—inflection and later—Marr did not say this—the analytical structure). Meanwhile N. Ya. Marr demanded the use of not only formal paleontology of speech, but ideological as well. (Ibid.)

In one of his latest works ("Japhetic Languages," Large Soviet Encyclopedia, 1931) N. Ya. Marr returns again to the question of a classification by stages. It is Japhetic languages which are involved. They are classified as a system "similar to Prometheidean (Indo-European), Semitic and other languages."‡ Marr characterizes the Japhetic languages as belonging to a single system according to ideological criteria, but variegated according to form assumed and number. Japhetic languages, "each with its own peculiarities, represent collectively through their system a definite stage of development in human speech."** This stage "is discernible in clearest fashion through the syntax, a structure of speech as thought in the system of symbols which reveals it."†† This time it turns out that not morphology but syntax is used as a criterion of a stage, which is at the same time a system (family). But syntax is not the only diagnostic trait of the Japhetic stage (which is also a system). It turns out it is only the most revealing ("primarily.") One can ask: is it so for all stages or only for the Japhetic one? Nor does N. Ya. Marr give an answer to the following: and how about the other systems (Indo-European, Finno-Ugric, Turkic, etc.)? Are they also a stage? If not—why not, and if yes, according to what criteria?

In relation to all that has been said one must come to the conclusion that the problem of language classification by stages and the temporal arrangement of these stages still remains unsolved. Still this refers only to the plan itself and not to the basic proposition.

The problem of arrangement by stages and the teaching in paleontologic analysis completely crush the classification elaborated by bourgeois science which classifies languages according to families with their aboriginal proto-language. Thereby one also decisively rejects in linguistic work the

*Ibid., Vol. II, p. 405.

†N. Ya. Marr, "Why It Is So Hard to Become a Theoretical Linguist," Selected Works, Vol. II, p. 421.

‡N. Ya. Marr, Selected Works, Vol. I, p. 295.

**Ibid.

††Ibid.

formal comparative-historical method. Basing itself on similarities, mostly of phonetic and morphological kind, bourgeois science bases its formal comparative method on proto-linguistic forms. The rejection of the proto-language destroys the whole scheme. Thereby the path is open to the comparative juxtaposition of languages belonging to different systems and also to their full-scale juxtaposition, that is, not only according to similarities establishing "kinship," but also according to divergences, which reveal that uniqueness which is peculiar to each language and which sets it aside in the mass of other languages.

The historical approach to language, which starts not from an alleged, artificially constructed proto-language, but from a genuine source, that is the history of language and the history of peoples, makes it possible to apply widely paleontologic analysis by using the extremely rich data of the languages in our Union, which are extremely variegated in their grammatical structure. To do this we used a refinement of our understanding of the paleontologic approach to the study of contemporary languages, independent of the four element analysis. At the same time it will be possible to give a correct appreciation to the comparative-paleontologic method mentioned by Marr. Here, too, the student of language cannot carry on without the help of the historian-social scientists (philosopher, social historian, ethnographer) and the historian of material culture (archeologist). N. Ya. Marr always insisted on such scientific cooperation.

For a satisfactory answer to these as yet not definitely answered questions it is necessary first of all to gather together the very definite statements by N. Ya. Marr—which are, however, widely distributed through various papers—about the unity of language and thought and about the social basis of the language-forming process: language and society, the singleness of the language-forming process, form and content, and then—grammatical and meaning categories.

Freed of occasional erroneous theses, N. Ya. Marr's propositions which remain valid and correspond accurately to the statements of the Marxist-Leninist classics about language and society's development, will form the foundation of the further development of materialist linguistics.

Marr's Significance for the Further Development of Soviet Linguistics.

The main body of N. Ya. Marr's propositions, which correspond to the premises of materialist philosophy, reveals the true countenance of the originator of materialist linguistics, a major and first-rate Soviet scholar, who decisively and finally destroyed the idealist bourgeois science of language. He was first among linguists to approach language as a superstructure on a material base. He was the first to recognize linguistic categories as having social significance and insisted this quality be taken into account in all research work. He smashed formalism in linguistics and brought the form of language into close coordination with its sense content.

The students and followers of N. Ya. Marr must come together and with their own experience prove the whole erroneousness of those points of view, which occasionally still reveal themselves in the research of Soviet linguists. To these ends one must intensify the critical examination not only of the old but particularly the new idealist premises and the works of bourgeois linguists founded on them. The criticism directed at them by N. Ya. Marr is awaiting its continuation, thereby strengthening the position of Soviet linguistics and helping the hesitating to become firmer in the struggle for a materialist science of language.

The students and followers of N. Ya. Marr must be particularly vigilant in carrying out their own investigations, developing criticism and improving their self-critical approach to their own works. And there are in them a number of shortcomings. Thus, in a dictionary of linguistic terminology by L. I. Zhirkov, published under my editorship, mention is made of proto-language. The placing of this term into the dictionary is fully justified as the term exists in linguistic literature, but in the article itself there is no appropriate criticism of proto-language theory. This confuses the Soviet reader and the student. Incorrect theses can be found in N. Ya. Marr's followers' [works] such as my own and those of V. I. Abayev, A. V. Desnitskaya, M. M. Gukhman, N. V. Yakovlev and others. Occasionally, Soviet scholars present their thoughts with insufficient clarity, use the excessively ponderous terminology of the scientific investigator, abuse foreign terminology and introduce their own new terms copied from these foreign ones (Professor S. D. Katsnelson, L. R. Zinder) and confusing to the reader. The presentation must be scientific but accessible. For the dissemination of the new science of language this assumes special significance.

The inadequacies found must be eliminated promptly through the appropriate criticism, book reviews and self-critical corrections. Increase in vigilance toward one's own work and toward the work of one's comrades will bring the necessary corrections, so important particularly because Soviet linguistics is now widely spread over the whole Union. The work of the linguists is increasing. Locally, in the republics and regions, new linguistic centers are being organized which watch carefully for the guiding line in the works of the capital's scientific institutions. Thus their work becomes particularly responsible.

Let us hope that the followers of the materialist science of language, whose number is constantly growing, will straighten out the line of their investigations, and that those claiming their readiness to join them will confirm it through their scientific work.

The Scientific Positions of Professor A. S. Chikobava.

Still one should not deny the existence of a series of statements openly inimical to the materialist science initiated by N. Ya. Marr. The positive aspects of this science are hushed up and it is proclaimed to be wholly vulgar materialist.

Such points of view are shared by the great expert on Caucasian languages, A. S. Chikobava. His text on general linguistics which was published in Georgian is extremely significant from this point of view. In contradicting Marr, he leans toward the bourgeois science Marr refuted. N. Ya. Marr destroyed the proto-language theory, but A. S. Chikobava admits that related languages have their origin in one language, represent the differentiation of a single language, which must be called the stem-language (Vol. I, p. 212). In developing this same thought, A. S. Chikobava affirms that those languages are now called related which originate from a single language and represent the result of development of the dialects of a given language. This one language is the stem-language. Such stem-languages are suggested for each family (an Indo-European stem-language, a Semitic one, etc.), for each linguistic branch (a Romance stem-language, a Slavic stem-language, a Germanic stem-language, etc.). The conclusion as to the existence of a stem-language is derived from the presence of clearly defined, concretely related languages (Vol. II, p. 203). The kinship [manifested by] a real language is reason to believe that the proto-language presumed once to have existed—actually did exist.

Thus A. S. Chikobava does not admit the hybridization of languages and their qualitative transformations. The emphasis is on evolutionary development. In abandoning N. Ya. Marr he leans wholly in the direction of bourgeois linguistics and while abiding by the proto-language scheme, he thereby preserves the formal-comparative method built on it.

N. Ya. Marr in emphasizing the social background in the origin and development of languages, in approaching language as real consciousness, categorically objects to the sign theory in linguistics, while A. S. Chikobava ignoring even

V. I. Lenin's critique of the sign theory, endorses it wholeheartedly. He admits that language is a system of signs, utilized by a given language community as a means of communication (Vol. II, p. 144). Here A. S. Chikobava joins not with N. Ya. Marr but with the architect of the new bourgeois science of language, F. de Saussure, almost repeating his words: "language as defined by us, is a homogeneous phenomenon: it is a system of signs***" "language is a system of signs***"*

In fully disagreeing with N. Ya. Marr, A. S. Chikobava does not take into account the special social significance of language, as real consciousness, and in conclusion denies the class nature of language. "Language," says A. S. Chikobava, "is a weapon in the class struggle, but this does not yet mean that language is of a class nature*** The rifle held in the hands of the Tsarist policeman was a weapon to defend the monarch and the bourgeoisie. The same rifle in the hands of a worker on the barricades served the working class, being thus a weapon to overthrow the monarchy: the rifle is a weapon of class struggle in a literal, direct, not a figurative sense, a weapon of actual struggle (in the physical content of this word). Is this rifle, this gun, of class nature? If yes, what class does it belong to? To none, and therefore to all classes, or better yet, outside class. Whatever the rifle represents in the struggle on the barricades, the same applies to language in a class society, under conditions of class struggle." (Vol. II, p. 182.) A. S. Chikobava lost sight of the irrelevancy of his comparisons: language—the direct realization of thought—is compared with a rifle.

In all statements of a similar kind one can perceive an obvious unwillingness to take into account the enormous achievements of N. Ya. Marr and to embark on the path of these achievements. Efforts are made to find one's own path with attempts made to develop some other materialist science of language. The result was the repetition of the basic theses of bourgeois linguistics, precisely against which Marr struggled decisively, thus assuring the penetration into linguistics of the methods of materialist philosophy. The works of A. S. Chikobava, directed against the basic conceptions of N. Ya. Marr simply confirm the correctness of the path selected by Marr.

The Most Immediate Tasks of Soviet Linguistics.

Soviet linguistics must proceed on this path, the path of historical and dialectical materialism, utilizing widely the works of N. Ya. Marr and continuing to develop his basic, correctly stated premises. There is a lot of work still to be done in this direction.

In order to guarantee the correct development of the materialist science of language it is desirable to present in a special monograph the statements about language in the classics of Marxism-Leninism: Marx, Engels, Lenin, Stalin.

Through separate scientific monographs one should indicate the true countenance of N. Ya. Marr—the initiator of the materialist science of language; his statements should be freed from erroneous deviations from the correct path he had undertaken and particular attention should be given to his basic statements on language and society, language and thought: these two leading ideas, to which all other can be traced.

One should allow time for the occasional statements by N. Ya. Marr which remain still not worked through and therefore should devote special monographic investigations to such problems as: paleontologic analysis, the singleness of the glottogonic process, the initial periods in the formation of human speech, the problem of stages, the comparative-paleontologic method and so on.

It is indispensable to provide university students with texts on introduction to linguistics and on general linguistics, elaborated on the main bases of the materialist science of language and thus guarantee the correct approach to the rearing of young cadres of Soviet linguists.

The selected works of N. Ya. Marr should be issued in ten volumes with the corresponding commentaries, placing the papers in their chronological order, indicating the prerevolutionary and the Soviet periods and thus helping the reader capture the changing stream of the author's thought. Taking into account the fundamental prescription by N. Ya. Marr about the complex nature of the work, approaching language in its real social background, this collection should not only include the linguistic papers of N. Ya. Marr but also the archeological and ethnographic ones. Marr must also be shown as a civic worker. At the same time it is necessary [to issue] also a one-volume, annotated edition of the selected work of N. Ya. Marr, especially recommended to students and candidates for degrees.

In order broadly to acquaint the Soviet intelligentsia with the new science of language it is desirable to issue a series of popularizing monographs and articles about N. Ya. Marr's creative path and about the basic theses of the materialist science of language.

To assure the further development of materialist linguistics and the struggle in its favor it is indispensable to intensify the critique of the basic conceptions of bourgeois linguistics and of the individual statements of that school's leading scholars as well as of Soviet scholars in whose work the premises of bourgeois science have not yet been completely overcome.

One must encourage criticism and self-criticism among N. Ya. Marr's own followers and the persons who have stated their readiness to go over to the positions of materialist science. Undoubtedly this will help the rapid transition of their investigations to the correct, scientific path.

It is indispensable to utilize the wealth of linguistic data available in the Soviet Union. A more intensive study of the languages of the peoples of the U.S.S.R. will enrich linguistic science. Attention is centered not only on their grammatical structure, distinguished by great variability, but particularly on the process of their development as national languages of socialist society.

One must strengthen contacts with local workers, sharing with them the experience of scientific investigations, directed toward the strengthening of materialist linguistics.

We face a critical survey of existing school texts (particularly grammars) in certain languages. Taking into account the experience of teaching practice and a more thorough elaboration of the ways and means of compiling grammars, which still are repetitions of the older varieties, it will be possible to approach the point of figuring out a basic plan of their elaboration using the principles of a materialist science of language.

*F. de Saussure, A Course on General Linguistics, 1933, pp. 39-40.

The Paths of Development of Soviet Linguistics*

By N. CHEMODANOV

The open discussion of problems of Soviet linguistics now taking place on the pages of Pravda is a great event in the science of language. The need for the discussion and its timeliness are obvious. The linguistic discussions which have taken place during the last two years in Moscow, Leningrad and other cities have been of little use to Soviet language study. Critical discussion of a number of books and articles has been too general in nature. It has lacked creative analysis of the basic problems in linguistics. There has been one-sided praise in the evaluation of N. Ya. Marr's theory with no indication of its substantial inadequacies.

The article published in Pravda by Prof. Arn. Chikobava "On Certain Problems of Soviet Linguistics" is the first boldly to pose the question and contains a number of correct theses. Seen as a whole, however, it is, in my opinion, undoubtedly erroneous. One can in no way agree with Prof. Chikobava that the stagnation which exists in Soviet linguistics is to be explained by the wide popularity of N. Ya. Marr's theory with Soviet linguists. Prof. Chikobava evaluates N. Ya. Marr's theory and his role in Soviet linguistics in a prejudiced, onesided and therefore incorrect fashion. Trying to reject this theory, as allegedly the chief impediment in the way of linguistic study, Prof. Chikobava is in essence trying to return to a bygone day in science, to restore comparative historical linguistics, to direct Soviet linguistics onto a path alien to Marxism-Leninism. I think that this harsh but fair evaluation of the article will be shared not only by many linguists, but also by archeologists, ethnographers and historians, because Prof. Chikobava's conception is in opposition to the development not only of linguistics, but also of other sciences.

None of the Soviet linguists viewing the subject with any seriousness has affirmed or affirms that N. Ya. Marr's theory, taken as a whole, is free of erroneous theses. Only the blind can think this. In any case, N. Ya. Marr himself did not think so.

In 1930 he said: "*** The Marxist elaboration of Japhetic linguistics can stand improvement and correction."† At the same time N. Ya. Marr clearly understood the enormous role played in the development of his theory by Marxism-Leninism.

"***The new science of language," he indicated in 1933 "***is the fruit of active participation in the revolutionary creativity of the U.S.S.R., extending science to a Leninist understanding of the theory of cognition, to Stalin's accurate definition of national culture, including language and its technique."‡

It was of course not hard for Prof. Chikobava to collect a number of erroneous or even contradictory statements on one subject or another in N. Ya. Marr's work. But one should not forget that in working out his theory N. Ya. Marr frequently reexamined statements made earlier and recognized the erroneousness of some of the terms he used. For example, this is what N. Ya. Marr said in 1932 during the Baku discussion about the term "class", which he had applied to primitive society: "***you are thinking of the Marxist meaning of class. But of course I am not referring to the present-day meaning of class when I say 'class' *** I am looking for a term and no one can find it for us. Whenever there is a collective organization, founded not on blood, then I use the term 'class,' do you see **** I took this term 'class' and used it with a different meaning; why not use it?"* This is the real situation, and not the desire to oppose my 'classes' to classes in the interpretation given them by Marxism."*

One must evaluate the theory of N. Ya. Marr not from the point of view of some isolated unsuccessful formulation, but in its essence, in relation to the progressive role which it played and is playing in the development of materialist linguistics. In the history of native and foreign linguistics, N. Ya. Marr is the most progressive scholar. His theory is so far the best produced in the development of science by this branch of knowledge and therefore any attempt to nullify the significance of N. Ya. Marr objectively delays the forward march of science.

What are then, in essence, the linguistic views of N. Ya. Marr which are either concealed or presented in a false light by Prof. Chikobava?

The cardinal question in all philosophy, as Engels wrote, is the question of the relation of thought to being. As is known, in their attitude to this philosophers have divided themselves into two large camps—the camp of materialism and the camp of idealism. This problem remains fundamental for linguistics also. It is in regard to this that Marx and Engels say in "The German Ideology" "***neither thought nor language forms a kingdom by itself***they are only manifestations of real life."†

N. Ya. Marr was the first linguist fully to comprehend this thesis of Marxism-Leninism and to use it in the investigation of linguistic materials. In all his works, both on general and specific questions in research on lexical or grammatical phenomena, N. Ya. Marr constantly concretized this thesis. This turned out to be possible only because he analyzed language not as pure form, not as bare technique, but as practical "real consciousness," "the immediate reality of thought."** ‡

In this connection N. Ya. Marr emphasized that language is not only sound, but also content and thought. He considered the problem of language and thought the most important problem in linguistics. The practical conclusion drawn from this theoretical thesis was to pay special attention to the study of vocabulary and syntax, that is, those aspects of language in which the contents [of language] are most directly revealed.

While accurately separating content from technique in speech, N. Ya. Marr sharply emphasized the social basis of language. Prof. Chikobava considers it as a special merit of N. Ya. Marr that he raised the question of language's superstructural nature. But, in his opinion, N. Ya. Marr solved this problem incorrectly. Prof. Chikobava considers N. Ya. Marr's conception of the class nature of language as completely incompatible with Marxism.

*Pravda, May 23, 1950, p. 3

†N.Ya. Marr, Selected Works, Vol. I, p. 267, Col. 2

‡N.Ya. Marr, Contribution to the History of the Caucasus According to Linguistic Data, Tiflis, 1933, p. 12.

*N.Ya. Marr, Contribution to the Baku Discussion on Japhetidology and Marxism, Baku, 1932, p. 39.

†K. Marx and F. Engels, Works, Vol. IV, p. 435.

‡Ibid., pp. 20, 434.

In reality it is precisely the views of Prof. Chikobava himself which are incompatible with Marxism. In affirming the non-class nature of language he is trying to nullify the Marxist-Leninist teaching on language as a social superstructure. Here Prof. Chikobava's point of view contradicts the clear statements of Marx and Engels on the subject.

Exposing the class nature, hypocrisy and falseness of bourgeois terminology, Marx and Engels wrote in "German Ideology:"

"The bourgeois can easily prove on the basis of his own language the identity of mercantile and individual relationships, or even of general human relationships, because this language is itself a product of the bourgeoisie and hence, both in reality and in language, buying and selling relationships have become the basis of all other relationships."*

In his work "The Condition of the Working Class in England," Engels writes even more vividly about the reflection in language of social ideology and class contradictions. Indicating that "the shameful slavery in which money keeps the bourgeois***has left its imprint even on language," that "The spirit of petty trade penetrates all language;" Engels emphasized: "there is nothing surprising in the fact that in the course of time the English working-class has become a completely different people than the English bourgeoisie***. Workers speak a different dialect, have different ideas and points of view, different mores and moral principles, a different religion and politics from the bourgeoisie." †

Confirming the non-class nature of national languages, Prof. Chikobava ignores Lenin's statement that there are two nations in each modern nation, two cultures in every national culture under the bourgeois system, and Stalin's teaching on the class nature of bourgeois nations. If, as Comrade Stalin says, "the bourgeoisie and its nationalistic parties were and remain at this period the main guiding force of such nations,"‡ then this cannot but be reflected in language.

One could cite numerous facts to show that Prof. Chikobava is wrong. In his well-known work "The French Language Before and After the Revolution," in the subtitle of which were deliberately placed the words: "Outlines on the History of the Origin of the Modern Bourgeoisie," Paul Lafargue provides a very accurate picture of the reflection of the class struggle in the French language, beginning with the Middle Ages.

Under different historical conditions class distinctions in language appear in different ways. In medieval England, the feudal exploiters for centuries spoke French, while the exploited people used Anglo-Saxon dialects. And didn't knightly poetry in feudal Germany reflect the class language of the knights? Finally, if one examines the history of the development of Russian, didn't class contradictions determine the differences in the speech of the nobility, the democratic intelligentsia drawn from various classes and of the peasantry in the 19th century?

Linked indissolubly with the concept of language as a superstructural phenomenon is N. Ya. Marr's thesis of the singleness of the language-forming (glottogonic) process. This singleness was understood primarily by N. Ya. Marr as a reflection in language of the singleness of the historical process:

"Language is a device of communication which arose in the process of work or, more accurately, in the process of creating human culture, that is, the economy, community and Weltanschauung*** Language has reflected in itself all paths and steps in the development of material and superstructural culture, the perfecting of its productive techniques and all the twists of the community's thinking connected with such a materially-initiated progress*** **

Thus singleness in the development of languages is not viewed by N. Ya. Marr as Prof. Chikobava portrays it, but as singleness of regularities which are manifested in each separate language. This uniformity of regularities can express itself both in the meaning of words and also in grammatical structure. For example, the Russian word gorod [town], indicating, strictly speaking, a fenced-in place, has its parallels, let us say, with the English town, related in its root to the German Zaun (fence). On the other hand, the process of development of parts of speech in languages, having no historical connection whatever, reveals very frequently similar traits, for example in the origin of adjectives from names.

In establishing such general principles in the development of languages, N. Ya. Marr did not deny the need to study the history of given languages and the peculiarities of their development. To this one should add that the thesis of the developmental singleness of languages does not eliminate the question of the existence of certain linguistic clusters—the so-called "families of languages."

Prof. Chikobava, however, distorting and diluting N. Ya. Marr's theory, incorrectly affirms that the basis of the doctrine of a single language-forming process and of otner most important theses in Marr's theory is the hypothcsis of four primary linguistic elements.

The following should be said on the question of the four elements. Where the problem of the origin of language is concerned, the hypothesis of in'tal sound-and-meanings complexes presented by N. Ya. Marr is quite legitimate. In his time, Engels himself wrote: "*** in the process of development, they reached the point where they met the need to say something to each other. This need created its own organ: the undifferentiated larynx of the ape slowly but surely became transformed through greater and greater modulation, while the organs of the mouth gradually learned to pronounce one articulate sound after another."†

Thus, in the early stages of man's development his actual physical structure, limited and to a certain degree, determined the sound nature of aboriginal speech. Nevertheless, too much time has elapsed since and the quality of sounds pronounced by man has changed drastically.

The actual composition of the initial linguistic elements and their number are a different matter. One should note that N. Ya. Marr always emphasized that human speech began not with isolated sounds but with meaningful complexes. From the very beginning this determined the qualitative difference between the sound aspect of human speech and the cries of animals.

Another aspect of the question is the use of four element analysis in linguistic investigations. The fact is that no Soviet linguist used the technique of element analysis after N. Ya. Marr's death. More than that, Academician I. I. Meshchaninov has repeatedly indicated that an analysis of words in contemporary speech with the four elements gave no results. One should not forget, however, that the paleontologic investigations of N. Ya. Marr, based on element analysis, have revealed such incontrovertible semantic regularities as the functional semantics of the word. Consequently, the principle of element analysis cannot be simply eliminated from science, if for no other reason than that the phonetic cognates thus revealed are no more dubious than the phonetic laws of traditional comparative phonetics for which Prof. Chikobava fought so [vigorously].

Most intimately connected with the singleness of the language-forming process is the development of language by stages. Prof. Chikobava correctly calls attention to the

---

*Ibid., p. 210.
†Ibid., Vol. III, pp. 554, 415.
‡J. V. Stalin, Works, Vol. XI, p. 388.

*N. Ya. Marr, Selected Works, Vol. II, p. 127.
†K. Marx and F. Engels, Selected Works, 1948, Vol. II, p. 73.

fact that this problem was only stated by N. Ya. Marr, but not resolved. But the most important theoretical aspect of this problem consists not in N. Ya. Marr's desire to decide which language is better and which worse—as affirmed by Prof. Chikobava—but in phrasing the problem in terms of two [alternative] forms of linguistic development: an evolutionary and a revolutionary one. If language is conditioned in its development by society's development, it cannot avoid undergoing qualitative changes (by stages). This is essentially what N. Ya. Marr's theory about development by stages consists in.

But Prof. Chikobava tries to prove that N. Ya. Marr belittled certain languages like Chinese, which allegedly froze on definite levels of development. In reality, N. Ya. Marr is talking only about the fact that some languages are more ancient, others more recent in [the date of] their appearance. N. Ya. Marr by no means denied the development of languages. Prof. Chikobava will be unable to prove that N. Ya. Marr, who devoted all his life to combatting the racial concepts of bourgeois science and rose against "Indo-European conceit," denied any language the capacity for development. This contradicts not only the spirit but also the letter of N. Ya. Marr's theories.

It would be incorrect to think that the theory of N. Ya. Marr reduces merely to declarative statements about the necessity of applying the main ideas of dialectical and historical materialism to language. The works of N. Ya. Marr and his followers dealing with specific problems and languages represent an enormous and concrete contribution to science. N. Ya. Marr worked out anew the place of semantics in the science of language. The fundamental investigations of N. Ya. Marr, I. I. Meshchaninov and others of problems of syntax represent a most valuable contribution to science. The theory of the origin of parts of speech, advanced and elaborated by N. Ya. Marr and I. I. Meshchaninov, is a great accomplishment of Soviet science. One cannot forego mention also of the scores of research studies on languages of the peoples of the Soviet Union as well as on German, Chinese and other languages—studies which represent the concrete realization of N. Ya. Marr's ideas.

The statements above, of course, do not mean that there are no erroneous and controversial theses in N. Ya. Marr's theory. Such theses include: the derivation of language from labor-magic action; statements about the role of medicine men in the development of voiced speech; the dubious outline of the development of thought (cosmic or totemic, technological, etc.), which must be evaluated by philosophers; a certain simplification in the discussion of relationships between language and society and certain mechanistic elements connected with this.

But one should not conclude from this that N. Ya. Marr's theory must be rejected as was done by Prof. Chikobava. Something different is called for. Soviet linguists must advance materialist linguistics, starting from a Marxist-Leninist Weltanschauung, emphasizing the strong parts of N. Ya. Marr's theories, elaborating questions not raised or only sketched by this theory, but at the same time overcoming its weak aspects and incorrect theses.

What then does Prof. Chikobava propose as the way out of the unsatisfactory state in which Soviet linguistics finds itself?

Prof. Chikobava's prescription is quite simple and, one must say, not new: it is to reinstate the traditional, so-called comparative linguistics with its protolanguage theory and its comparative-historical method and to admit these premises of traditional science to be Marxist. Although Prof. Chikobava does not use the term "protolanguage," which has become so odious in our science, what else could his "common origin of related languages," "common initial material of language families," etc., mean? It must be openly stated (leaving aside temporarily the political ins and outs of the protolanguage theory) that such outlines of language development radically contradict not only all data collected by Soviet linguistics during the last 20-30 years, but also the data available to archeology, ethnography and historical science as a whole.

For example, what is this Indo-European protolanguage of which Prof. Chikobava speaks between the lines?

It seems convincing to Prof. Chikobava that the comparison of such words as Russian <u>tri</u> [three] with Latin <u>tres</u> and such, establishes the <u>reality</u> of Indo-European <u>languages</u>. But he knows very well that the number of such roots common to most Indo-European languages is very small, that they form only an extremely thin stratum on the surface.

A. Meillet, dean of bourgeois comparative linguists, looks on the Indo-European protolanguage as the language of an ancient people who possessed a single language in addition to a common culture and physical and spiritual make-up in ancient, prehistoric times. The extent to which such notions are contrary to history can be seen, for example, from the fact that such an admittedly Indo-European language as Hittite existed as long ago as 1,500 years B.C. The protolanguage state of the Indo-European languages must, obviously, be moved back to some even more ancient time. Such a conception of ethnic unity in such a distant epoch contradicts the definition of ancient society provided by historical materialism, which teaches that that stage in the development of human society is characterized by ethnic units of small size and instability.

The works of Soviet historians like Tretyakov on the history of the Eastern Slavs and other peoples clearly indicate how complicated is the process of formation of tribes and peoples and what an enormous role is played in this by diffusion, which Prof. Chikobava recognizes only as a special case in language-formation. The processes of formation and development of language in preclass society must obviously have gone on parallel to the ethnogenetic process and reflected it.

On the other hand, the protolanguage scheme of language development is incompatible with Comrade Stalin's doctrine on the formation of modern bourgeois nations resulting from the blending of the most diverse ethnic elements.

The "theory" of a protolanguage cannot be accepted by Soviet linguistics because it is a concept which is clearly contradictory to the only true scheme of historical development, that of Marxism-Leninism.

Soviet linguistics cannot return to the comparative historical method either. N. Ya. Marr's qualification of this method as simple-minded was not an idle one. This method is inseparably connected with protolinguistic schemes and is incapable of revealing the whole complexity of linguistic similarities and divergences in their social causation. The times of Bopp, Grimm and Vostokov have passed in science and there is no need for us to return to them. In addition, Prof. Chikobava forgets that Marx and Engels, while giving due credit in the 50's to the 70's of the last century to the accomplishments of comparative-historical linguistics, at the same time, indicated more than once the limited nature of its representatives. The best testimony to this fact is Engel's work "The Frankish Period" where Engels decisively objects to the traditional classification of German dialects, elaborated on the basis of the comparative-historical method and the comparativist outline of linguistic development.

The path of further development for Soviet linguistics traced by Prof. Chikobava cannot satisfy us. It seems indisputable to us that the further development of Soviet materialist linguistics on a Marxist-Leninist base is possible only by taking into account all that is positive in N. Ya. Marr's work.

However, successful forward movement also rests upon the overcoming of the weak and erroneous aspects of this prominent Soviet linguist's theory. It is most important at present that the work continue on the basis of analysis of the vast concrete materials [available] and not on the level of scholastic generalities. Concrete investigations of contemporary languages and their history in connection with the history of peoples speaking these languages and the posing of the problems of the formation of languages and dialects on a specific historical level will help Soviet linguists to bring [their] science out of the unsatisfactory condition in which it finds itself. Soviet linguists should raise problems more boldly and should not be afraid to advance controversial theses, even where these contradict the points of view of recognized authorities in this field of knowledge.

On N.Ya. Marr's Research Methods*

By B. SEREBRENNIKOV

In the linguistic theory of Academician N. Ya. Marr one can distinguish three component parts: (1) a formal recognition of the fundamental importance of Marxist principles for a scientific Soviet linguistics; (2) the subsequent development and concretization of these principles by N. Ya. Marr himself; (3) research methods emerging organically from certain initial theoretical assertions.

The first component part of this theory, of course, cannot be the object of criticism. Of special interest is that part of N. Ya. Marr's work in which he tries to establish his theoretical propositions on the enormous body of data from dozens of languages of different systems. This is interesting, as it permits an evaluation as to how accurately and thoroughly N. Ya. Marr understood the basic outline of the Marxist dialectical method and how correct his methods of scientific inquiry were.

In an article [called] "Marx and the Problems of Language," N. Ya. Marr himself described his method in the following way: "Marx and Engels even then created the only historical method, without which there is no way of carrying out a significant historical investigation. They discovered in the history of language changes levels of linguistic and societal developments which at the time seemed improbable. Marx and Engels themselves did not present their views fully or without qualification, but the new science [of language] more than fully confirms these changes by excavating in language itself the strata of the various social formations. We call these strata 'stages.'

"[The new science] continues to confirm thoroughly Marx's theses by defining these stages more accurately through the development of the new technique of speech analysis, [called speech] paleontology, which reveals by stages of an epoch the levels of development of any language or languages, independent of nationality and race, independent of whether the language be Eastern or Western, Asiatic or European and so on and so forth."†

In deciding to face such a major task, N. Ya. Marr, like any serious scholar, was naturally interested in the use of facts which could create an unshakeable base for his theoretical concepts.

But the ascertaining of facts demanded in turn a method of scientific inquiry and tangible investigative tactics deriving from the nature of the method itself.

Since Marxism is unthinkable without the dialectical method, we are fully entitled to expect that N. Ya. Marr would most thoroughly figure out the multiple ties of a given linguistic phenomenon with other linguistic phenomena by utilizing all possible direct and indirect historical, linguistic, ethnographic, and archeological evidence. We may expect that he will study each linguistic phenomenon in its movement and development by tracing out in the most detailed way those often barely perceptible quantitative changes which lead to revolutionary transformations of a language system. He should also determine those contradictions attendant on its development.

However, direct acquaintance with N. Ya. Marr's linguistic works frequently makes for disappointment.

The wide scope of Marr's research thinking turns out, in a vast majority of cases, to be bound in the iron ring of a rather small number of basic theoretical theses, into which a vast body of linguistic material is stuffed as into a Procrustean bed.

Let us attempt to get acquainted in somewhat more detail with these initial theoretical theses. The first thesis: all the wealth of human speech descends from four original elements.

What do these four elements represent?

N. Ya. Marr himself says the following on this topic in his work "A General Course in the Study of Language."

"The four elements, which arose along with the other arts in the evolution of the work process, which was magic, did not have originally, nor for a long time could they have, any lexical meaning, as there were as yet no voiced words since there was no voiced speech. The significance of the work process, magic, in relation to the names elements, is that they [the elements] were worked out, not, of course, in the pronunciation of the versions (SAL, BER, YON, ROШ) selected and analyzed by us, but in a pronunciation still to be established for each of them, a complex and total pronunciation, a genuine archetype***"*

This quotation indicates that the true phonetic nature of the four elements was completely unknown to N. Ya. Marr himself since their true pronunciation was still to be ascertained.

Knowing nothing about the nature of these elements, N. Ya. Marr nevertheless affirms that the four elements were originally inherent in any human group's [speech] and from the first were to be found together.

Thus the four-element theory was from the very beginning built literally on thin air.

Why did these four elements have to exist in any human group's [speech]?

N. Ya. Marr answers this question comparatively simply. Voiced human speech is preceded by kinetic or gesture language and appears only considerably later. Following Engels, N. Ya. Marr affirms that voiced speech arose in the process of work. However, he introduces into Engel's work theory a correction to the effect that work originally was not simply work but was always accompanied by magical action, or, as N. Ya. Marr puts it, was a labor-magic action.

As can be seen from the explanation of N. Ya. Marr

*Pravda, May 23, 1950, pp. 3-4.

†N. Ya. Marr, Selected Works, Vol. II, p. 455.

*Ibid., p. 89.

himself, the four elements were originally yells. "Technically we envisage these early elements of the work process [and] the magical action as yells, developing the vocal chords and the organs of speech generally through repitition."*

But where did this magical number four come from? From N. Ya. Marr's further explanations we learn that the number four was determined by the nature of magical action: "The number of elements (the fourfold magical prerequisite of voiced speech) can thus be explained first of all in the technique of magical play-acting, and in this sense one should pay attention to the role of the number in the inseparably participant elements of a given magical play-acting, dancing and singing with music and, in general, the epic prototype."†

Thus the four elements are four original yells, accompanying the elements of labor-magic activity, which of necessity existed together and were inherent in any human group.

What happened in the later development of voiced speech?

The four elements, which originally served as a device for addressing magic forces, turned into words with tangible meaning. The meanings of one and the same element became differentiated depending on different regional conditions and the type of economy. Languages were hybridized, and from one-element words there arose two-element words. N. Ya. Marr ascribes enormous importance to language hybridization. Here emerges his second theoretical affirmation: all languages are mixed, hybridized.

[The number of] elements could increase also through the formation of a whole series of varieties or derivatives from one element. In this connection, one notes with astonishment that N. Ya. Marr can cite a whole table of such variants although he never ascertained the original pronunciation of the elements.

One should note that the thesis of the original four elements served only as a starting point for N. Ya. Marr's hypothesis. His element analysis is actually built on this table of variants.

The theses of the four original elements, inherent in all languages in the world, and of the hybrid nature of all languages, allowed N. Ya. Marr to compare words of the most different languages, independent of system and geographic location.

But that which is erroneous from the very beginning cannot but lead to greater error in the future.

The absence of solid ground beneath the theory of the four elements cast doubt on the correctness of the element variants themselves, which greatly reduced the value of the results achieved with their aid. How can one talk of variants zal, shor, shur, tal, etc., as derived from element A if it is unknown what element A consisted of?

But the main danger did not lie here. N. Ya. Marr engaged in the comparison of that which sounded alike at a given moment in different languages, ignoring completely the real history of each separate concrete language. He apparently forgot that each word in contemporary languages is in its outward form only an upper layer resting on other, historically obsolete layers which frequently differ radically in their outward manifestations from later conditions. That which is alike today may not have been alike in antiquity.

Where such scorn for the history of the word can lead can be seen from the following examples. In the article "Language," N. Ya. Marr finds a common element "bor" in the Russian word "bor" [pine grove] and Latin "arbor"—tree. However, N. Ya. Marr, unwarrantably regarding the established history of words as sheer phantasy of the Indo-Europeanists, obviously did not take into account the fact that Latin "arbor" once sounded as "arbos," as is clearly indicated by the nature of the stem ending in "s," which, under the influence of the rhotacism of intervocalic "s" in oblique cases, became final "r" in the nominative also. Consequently, we are here dealing with element "bos" and not "bor." Firmly established sound correspondences allow us to connect "arbor" with the stem of the old Indian verb "ardkhami" which means "to grow, to prosper," on the basis of the correspondence dkh—b (cf. Latin "verbum"—word, and Lithuanian "vardas"—name or German "Wort"—word). Thus the "bor" element used in the [Marrian] comparison showed a more ancient form "dkhos."

In trying to prove that the name "acorn" could be transferred through community of function as an object of consumption [food] to the word "bread," N. Ya. Marr juxtaposes the Greek word "balanos" —acorn and the Latin "panis"—bread, tracing them to the original "palan." But he disregards the fact that Greek "balanos" has a precise phonetic correspondence as well as meaning correspondence with the Latin word "glans" (stem "gland") and the Russian "zhelud" (ancient "gelond"). Consequently, the Greek "b" developed historically from the postpalatal labialized "g," and Latin "panis" once had the form "pastnis" (cf. its diminutive "pastillum"—small bread, cookie). Thus on historical analysis these words turn out to be absolutely incomparable.

In his article "The Hottentots—Mediterraneans," N. Ya. Marr tries to prove the common element composition of such words as Chuvash "pus"—head, Basque "buru"—head and Latin "i-pse"—self. But did he know that element "se" in Latin "ipse" represents an archaic prenominal stem "so," while "p" is another prenominal stem? Therefore, that which in the Chuvash language is only a one element [word] is not really monoelemental. Besides, the Chuvash "p" in the word "pus" apparently developed from "b" (cf. Tartar "bash"—head), becoming unvoiced in the initial position under the influence of Finnic languages.

On page 116 of the same article, N. Ya. Marr considers the Chuvash word "jyvys"—tree a cognate of Latin "arbor"—tree, whereas Chuvash intervocalic "v" developed historically from a post-palatal "g" (cf. Tartar "agach"—tree), while Latin "b" developed out of "dkh."

In the same paper, N. Ya. Marr discovers a general element "tan" in the Georgian verb "i tan a" to carry over, and Latin "tan-gere"—to touch.* But he neglects the fact that that which looks monoelemental in Georgian, was not monoelemental in Latin, in as much as "n" in "tangere" is an infix, that is, a formant (a meaningful element), archaically a word with independent meaning (cf. perfect "tetigi"—I touched, supine "tactum" from "tagtum").

In his article "Language"† N. Ya. Marr establishes kinship between the German word "Himmel" (sky) and Russian "zemlya" [earth], breaking them down into two elements hi-mel and ze-mel. It is well known from Russian historical grammar that there could not have been any such element as "mel" in the word "zemlya" since "l" appeared later and did not belong originally to the root.

Such examples of inadmissible neglect of the history of individual concrete languages can be found in no small number in the linguistic works of N. Ya. Marr.

They bear clear witness to the fact that N. Ya. Marr actually substitutes for the study of the real history of words their forcible association with hypothetically established varieties of elements whose original forms were for him things in themselves. Element acrobatics outside of time and space actually led him to a shocking lack of historicity, to the denial of dialectics, the spirit of Marxism. In N. Ya. Marr's element analysis there is essentially no history at all. Therefore such an approach to the study of linguistic phenomena must be rejected by Soviet linguistics as obviously harmful and having nothing in common with Marxism.

---

*Ibid., p. 94.
†Ibid.

*Ibid., Vol. IV, p. 120.
†Ibid., Vol. II, p. 134.

This is where the defenders of four-element analysis will at once object that it is being contrasted with the comparative method which they had allegedly buried. Perhaps it sounds paradoxical, but the comparative method is much more useful as proof of the Marxist idea of development than Marr's notorious four-element analysis. If we compare the Latin word "angulus"—coal, Polish "węgiel" [coal] and Russian "ugol" [coal], we get, if not a complete, at least an actual picture of the real changes undergone by that word. The various steps of this change are traceable and documented in various languages.

The series "angulus—węgiel—ugol" is a reflection of an aspect of actual change and development comparable to a photograph of a speeding express train, which is the fixation of an aspect of its actual movement. At the same time, the Marr series of juxtapositions, such as for example [the Russian words] "ogon" [fire], "kon" [horse], "konura" [kennel], the Armenian word "kin" (woman) and the Russian "o-kun-at" [to dip],* supposedly proving consecutive development in the meaning of a single element "kon," is really a tortured abstract outline of an element's reincarnations, invented by the selfsame N. Ya. Marr.

Such an outline does not reflect real life. Consequently, it has nothing in common with Marxism, as Marxism is based on life, eternally changing and developing.

Some people say that the rational kernel of the four-element theory consists in [its recognition that] the original number of sound correspondences was incomparably lower than in modern languages.

It is quite likely that there were considerably fewer, but this gives no foundation for the affirmation that they were originally the same in all languages. Moreover, their original aspect and meaning could have changed so many times in the course of tens of thousands of years that all search for them would be like the search for a few drops in the sea.

Others try to phrase the matter in such a way that four-element analysis comes out a mere trifle, something like a completely inoffensive hypothesis which one should merely refine and correct. Simultaneously we are confronted with a long list of N. Ya. Marr's contributions, such as, for example, the establishment of the social significance of form, recognition of the development of language by stages, the dependence of changes in language on changes in the material base, and so on.

However, this is not the issue. Nobody is challenging or denying these contributions of Marr. The whole matter consists in asking: Are these theses of N. Ya. Marr confirmed by the data of actual languages, how correctly are they confirmed, and does this evidence help our professionals to carry through those tasks placed before them by the Party and the Soviet government?

If the main technique proving the protolanguage theory turns out in the hands of the Indo-Europeanists to be the comparative method, then four-element analysis is the corresponding technique for confirming Marr's Marxist theses. Take away the comparative method and the whole cumbersome Indo-Europeanist system will be left hanging in air. Take away four-element analysis from Marr and one gets unproved declarative statements.

This is why the question of four elements takes on special political significance. If it is absolutely correct, it then means that one or the other of N. Ya. Marr's theses is justified; if it [four-element analysis] is incorrect, everything remains proclaimed, but unproved.

Moreover, an incorrect method of verification is grist to the mill of the enemies of Marxism who consider Marxist theses generally unprovable. Hence, this is not a mere trifle as is thought by some comrades.

*N. Ya. Marr, "Contributions to a Semantic Paleontology in Non-Japhetic Language Systems," Selected Works, Vol. II, p. 285.

The four elements are the selfsame protolanguage. N. Ya. Marr himself stated this quite unambiguously in the paper "Japhetidology at the Leningrad State University":

"After all, if one must speak about protolanguage, the initial condition of voiced speech, this was a speech on a narrow scale of a particular profession, the speech of medicine men***"*

If voiced speech, once and originally the property of medicine men, developed from four initially identical elements, then the analogy between protolanguage and the four elements is complete.

As for N. Ya. Marr's second assertion, concerning the hybridized state of all the world's languages, it obviously exaggerates such a universal hybridization of languages. Languages did mix in reality, but mixed due to contact on definite geographical territories. Where there was no direct contact, the possibility of hybridization was virtually excluded.

In his excellent work "On Dialectical and Historical Materialism," Comrade Stalin says: "***the science of the history of society, regardless of all the complexity of the phenomena of social life, can become as exact a science as, let us say, biology, capable of utilizing the laws of social development for practical application."†

It is perfectly apparent that if Soviet linguistic science will affirm a priori, following Academician Marr, that all languages are hybridized, and if it will juxtapose Mordvinian "lish-me"—horse with Chinese "ma"—horse, it will find itself in the position of a fortuneteller, and can never become an exact science.

Only the utilization of the cumulative data of actual history, archeology, linguistics and anthropology can decide the question of the presence of real hybridization between languages.

It would be erroneous to think that all investigations by N. Ya. Marr are based on these theoretical assertions.

The third assertion is the sequence of stages in the development of human thought he erected.

In the report "The Linguistic Policy of the Japhetic Theory and the Udmurt Language" ‡ N. Ya. Marr outlines three stages in the development of human thought: (1) totemic, (2) cosmic and (3) technological.

The first stage, or totemism, is dated by Marr as coinciding with the period of primitive communism (See "Changes in the Techniques of Language and Thought."**)

This level is characterized by the image conception of totems or secret magic forces. The productive forces of collective work appeared in [these] images. This level corresponds to the period of pre-logical thought and kinetic [gesture] speech.

In another work, "Why It is so Difficult to Become a Theoretical Linguist," N. Ya. Marr characterizes pre-logical thinking in the following way:

"***men thought in mythical terms, in so-called 'pre-logical' thinking. Strictly speaking, they did not 'think' yet, they merely perceived mythically ***"**

Let us turn to the works of Vladimir Ilyich Lenin and see how he characterizes the process of human cognition. Lenin says:

"The approach of the (human) mind to a particular thing, the casting of its image (= understanding) is not a simple, direct, mirror-dead action, but a complicated ambiguous, zigzagging one, including even the possibility of the withdrawal of phantasy from life; more than that: the possibility of transformation (and unnoticeable, unconscious transformation at that) of the abstract notion, the idea into phantasy (in final analysis = god)."‡‡

*N. Ya. Marr, Selected Works, Vol. I, p. 259.

†History of the Communist Party of the Soviet Union (Short Course), p. 109.

‡N. Ya. Marr, Selected Works, Vol. V, p. 495.

**Ibid., Vol. II, p. 441.

††Ibid., p. 400.

‡‡V.I. Lenin, Philosophical Notebooks, 1947, p. 308.

If the great scientific giant, the Marxist V. I. Lenin, affirmed that in the process of cognition there is only the possibility of phantasy's flight from reality, then N. Ya. Marr in "correcting" Lenin, created a special totemic stage of thought which represents the absolute flight of phantasy from reality.

It is perfectly clear that the point of departure of this Marr scheme has nothing to do with Marxism.

The hypothesis of four initial elements emerged necessarily from the hypothesis of the existence of a totemic stage of thought, because the elements, according to Marr, were techniques of addressing the totem.

If, following Lenin, we deny the possibility of the existence of a totemic stage of thought, then all grounds for the four elements disappear.

The cosmic stage, which N. Ya. Marr equates with the origin of voiced speech, represents the culmination of totemism. The conception of three elemental forces—the upper, middle and nether sky—makes its appearance. At this stage the productive totems are replaced by cult [totems]. "*** The sun," says N. Ya. Marr in the article "The Science of Language Viewed on a World Scale, and the Abkhazian Language," "was a deity like the sky and, as a part of it, was known by the same name."*

At the technological stage, in connection with the growth of productive forces, the names of objects and tools appear in their true meaning.

The artificiality and abstractness of such an outline, utterly unrelated to any concrete history, is completely obvious.

The fourth fundamental assertion of N. Ya. Marr is the theory of development of word meanings, closely related to the outline mentioned above.

As has been mentioned, voiced speech, according to Marr, begins at the stage of cosmic thinking. The names of the upper, middle and nether skies were transferred to analogous phenomena, such as cloud, moon, bird, either according to the law of calling parts by the whole or according to association of images, for example, circle, line, soul, etc. The word meaning sky was transferred also to parts of the body, such as hand, eye, leg, etc., and to abstract concepts like conscience, faith and others. In passing over to usage in everyday economic life, the same terms become the names of corresponding persons or things.

Thus, the essence of N. Ya. Marr's semantic theory is reduced to transformations of the original name of the cult totem.

Such a theory, strengthened by the theory of the four elements, opened for N. Ya. Marr new and extensive possibilities for arbitrary and a priori elaborations.

It is not without interest to note that for Marr element analysis was most intimately related to this developmental outline of meanings and subservient to it. Let us look at some examples to see how he manipulated the four elements in connection with the scheme outlined above.

In his article "[Contributions] to a Semantic Paleontology in Non-Japhetic Language Systems"† N. Ya. Marr juxtaposes such words as Russian "kon" [horse], "oko" [eye] (o-kon), "ogon" [fire], Turkish "gyun"—day, German "Hund"—dog and Russian "konura" [kennel]. The kinship of these words, according to N. Ya. Marr, is determined first of all by the fact that they all contain the element "S", and secondly by the fact that the consecutive development of such meanings is quite easy to deduct from the outline he has sketched. The word "ogon" [fire] is an original attribute of the cosmic term "upper sky"; from here it is extremely easy to deduct the Turkish word "gyun"—day, because "day" is a natural derivative of "the upper sky." If parts of the body, according to Marr's outline, were closely connected with cosmic names—totems, then it is not difficult to add here the word "oko" [eye], and, since originally domestic animals were also totems, naturally there is nothing to prevent the inclusion here of the German word "Hund"—dog. But according to the law of functional semantics the word for dog was transformed to the word for horse (cf. kon-ura). What then stops us from concluding the series with "kon" [horse]? Such is N. Ya. Marr's uncomplicated dialectics of development.

*N. Ya. Marr, Selected Works, Vol. IV, p. 61.

†Ibid., Vol. II. pp. 272-3.

Here we also become convinced that the investigation of real historic ties between Russian, Turkish and German and the study of the development of word meanings in close relationship to the actual history of these peoples and of their material culture has actually been replaced by an artificial scheme. It is not concrete historical facts which are used as evidence, but the idea of potentially possible transformations in the meaning of the names of cosmic totems.

These four fundamental theoretical assertions are the quintessence of the entire system of arguments which N. Ya. Marr utilizes as soon as he tries to prove, with the actual data of language, any theoretical thesis, whether his own or a Marxist one, whether it concerns the development of language by stages, the connection of language with thought, or the social significance of language forms.

In this connection the question arises: can anything at all be demonstrated through the use of such obviously worthless means? Anybody who understands even a little about language and Marxism will say that no matter what artifices are used nothing can be proved here.

Prof. A. S. Chikobava is absolutely right when he says that the practical problems of Soviet linguistics are not solved by Marr.

Tens of thousands of workers in the field of language in the Soviet Union have already become convinced that four-element analysis and abstract developmental schemes of the meanings of words cannot help practical endeavor.

Under such circumstances it is quite appropriate to mention the remarkable words of our leader Comrade Stalin, spoken in November, 1935, at the first All-Soviet Stakhanovite Conference.

"The facts of science," says Comrade Stalin, "have always been checked by practice, by experience. What kind of science is the science which has lost contact with practice, with experience? If science were what it is made out to be by some of our conservative comrades, it would have disappeared long ago from among mankind. Science is called science precisely because it does not recognize fetishes, is not afraid to raise its hand against the obsolescent, the old: it listens sensitively to the voice of experience and practice."*

It would not harm some of our conservative comrades to keep these wise words of our leader Comrade Stalin in mind. They have succeeded in making a fetish of Academician N. Ya. Marr's crudest errors and have regarded criticism of these errors as a crime against Marxism.

If the research methods of Academician N. Ya. Marr do not correspond to the requirements of the Marxist dialectical method, where should one look for a solution? The solution consists in utilizing in linguistic research the Marxist dialectical method, the chief features of which have been excellently presented in Comrade Stalin's inspired work "On Dialectical and Historical Materialism."

Does the above mean that N. Ya. Marr should be completely rejected and Soviet linguistics built anew?

[We] think that such a conclusion would be erroneous. The problem would be correctly solved if Soviet linguists undertook a re-examination of N. Ya. Marr's theory in order to determine what is valuable and productive in it and to reject all the patently erroneous theses, particularly the four fundamental theoretical assertions discussed above. We must further develop the progressive side of N. Ya. Marr's theory, using the Marxist dialectical method in our investigations.

*J.V. Stalin, Problems of Leninism, 11th edition, p. 502.

Either Forward or Backward*

By G. SANZHEYEV

1. The Causes of Stagnation in the Development of Soviet Linguistics.

The editors of the newspaper Pravda initiated a most timely free discussion "in order through criticism and self-criticism to overcome the stagnation in the development of Soviet linguistics and to give a correct direction to further scientific work in this field."

Stagnation characterizes our linguistics and is actually a reality. This can be confirmed somewhat by a small but typical fact. In November, 1949, the N. Ya. Marr Institute of Language and Thought of the U.S.S.R. Academy of Sciences organized a conference of linguists with the participation of representatives from scientific institutions of a number of Union republics and provinces. And then suddenly and unexpectedly several theoretical reports were scratched from the conference's agenda (about development by stages in language, on content and form in language) because we, the linguists, turned out to be unable to prepare these reports at the necessary scientific level.

What is more, we speak of development by stages in language, but do not know what stages there are. We speak of class languages, but we do not know how they are related to ethnic and national languages, and to this day we have not a single work which shows the nature of any class language or proves the legitimacy of even speaking of such. We speak about the paleontologic method aided by Marr's four elements but nobody, besides N. Ya. Marr himself, has used these elements particularly seriously, nor are they used now (the illiterate exercises of certain "linguists" are, of course, not counted). And so on and so forth. All this has led to stagnation in the development of Soviet linguistics. This explains why the Indo-Europeanists feel so free here, while we, the students and followers of Academician Marr, are in a state of utter confusion.

The basic and main cause of this stagnation is that all criticism and self-criticism is utterly lacking among us linguists. Those "discussions" which have taken place in recent years in connection with the well-known decisions of the Party on ideological questions, and the discussions in our press have either been of too general a character or have been limited to the "analysis" of some mistakes of individual linguists. The linguist whose mistakes underwent "analysis" (we use the term in quotation marks because the participants in the "discussions" simply repeated in their own words what had already been said in the press, without contributing anything significantly new of their own) sometimes left the meetings unsatisfied.

This happened because the person criticized did not always receive comradely help and suggestions from the critics as to how one should do further research on the linguistic problems in question. In these "discussions" the fundamental problems of language study were not discussed on their merits and not even raised, while thorny issues were avoided.

In short, these "discussions" were more frequently carried through for form's sake and in order that everything might remain as before until the next just statement in the papers: if no articles were forthcoming, that meant there was nothing to discuss, and everything was "in order!"

It is characteristic that from 1940 to 1950 there was in the U.S.S.R. Academy of Sciences not a single meeting, not a single discussion at which the problems of comparative historical grammar were discussed. And this regardless of the fact that during those very years the workers at the Academy of Sciences were almost fully occupied with compiling comparative grammars of a number of languages, until finally, in April, 1950, without any broad or even limited discussion or specific analysis of the work done by a large staff, the Presidium of the U.S.S.R. Academy of Sciences "declared" that it was wrong even to raise the question of this work!

Thus it turns out that Soviet linguists should not undertake research on similarities and divergences between related languages, but should limit themselves to a general denial of the notorious proto-language. This means that in comparative linguistics, whose importance was related highly by F. Engels, we disarm ourselves in the face of bourgeois linguistics with its various reactionary racist "theories." The study of connections between related languages is turned over as a monopoly to this bourgeois linguistics. This is where timidity in the face of theory and un-Bolshevist fear of difficulties lead us.

Some perplexity among linguists was aroused through the absence of criticism of N. Ya. Marr's work from a Marxist-Leninist position (there was no lack of vicious criticism from the Indo-Europeanists). And this criticism was absent because we, the students and followers of Academician Marr, considered it "untimely" and alleged that it could support and encourage the hopes of the partisans of bourgeois linguistics. For example, several substantial divergences between Academician Marr's statements and the theses of the classics of Marxism-Leninism in a number of linguistic problems were glossed over ("class" languages in pre-class society, the origin of voiced speech, the autochthony of the Turks in Asia Minor, etc.).

The most astonishing thing about the behavior of our linguists is the almost complete neglect of the specific statements on language in the works of the originators of Marxism-Leninism and the total absence of concrete investigations starting from the correct linguistic suggestions of Marx, Engels, Lenin and Stalin. What is more, it was often tacitly assumed that in case of divergence between the classics of Marxism-Leninism and Marr, it was not the former which were right but the latter (particularly on the question of the origin of articulate voiced speech).

And all this in spite of all the repeated and widely known demands of N. Ya. Marr himself.

Of all the controversial questions of Soviet linguistics we will dwell below only on the question of development of language by stages.

2. Remarks on Stages.

What is the development of language by stages, what is a stage in the development of language and what should our attitude be toward Academician Marr's theory?

What is involved is the recognition or rejection in principle of the legitimacy of even raising the problem of stages in the development of language. Some Soviet linguists admit that this problem is stated correctly by Academician

*Pravda, May 23, 1950, p. 4.

Marr, although he did not give it a correct solution. Other Soviet linguists, including Prof. Arn. Chikobava, consider that this is not a legitimate problem for linguistics. The essence of these differences can be formulated briefly in the following manner. The partisans of Academician Marr consider, in complete agreement with the theses of materialist dialectics, that language develops not only by evolution, i.e., by quantitative changes in various aspects and facets of language, but also by revolution, by skips and mutations, i.e., by the transition of this language from one qualitative state into another, ending the evolutionary path of development, all of which in the long run is determined by the corresponding changes in the means of production of a given society.

Thus a stage is a definite, qualitative condition in the development of language, a period of its evolutionary development before the explosion of the old and the emergence of a new qualitative condition.

But the opponents of Academician Marr, including Prof. Chikobava, assume on the contrary that language in its development knows no stage jumps, i.e., transitions from one qualitative condition to another. Thus they break with the basic positions of materialist dialectics, with the basic theories of Marxism-Leninism regarding the laws of development in nature and society in general.

Academician Marr's inspired contribution was that in full agreement with the theses of materialist dialectics for the first time in the history of linguistics, he fully stated and attempted to solve the question of the development of language by stages or through skips. The statement of this problem and the attempt to solve it (we agree, completely unsuccessfully) is in full agreement with the following lines of K. Marx: "***although the more developed languages have laws and definitions in common with the least developed ones, it is precisely the divergence from this universal and general element which constitutes their development."*

3. The Theory of Stages in Mongolic Studies.

Without here undertaking an examination of the condition of the theory of stage development in Soviet linguistics generally (as this will, of course, be illuminated in the articles of other participants of our Pravda-sponsored discussion), we would like to describe how matters stand in this respect in the specific study of Mongolic languages. After the death of Academician Marr, we, the students of Mongolic, delved deep in the study of Mongolic phonetics, syntax and vocabulary, and as a result have reached the following conclusions.

(a) At an earlier stage of their development Mongolic languages were characterized by the fact that agglutination (the addition of endings and suffixes to the stem and root without changing the latter) occupied in them a subordinate role, since the chief means of expressing lexical and other categories was the internal change of the word, conventionally called by us "inflection." Such "inflection" in our opinion replaced in rather remote times a diffused (differentiated) condition of language, about which for the moment we can only guess (but it was a period when men could not yet differentiate "thou—you," "I—we" or "cattle-herder—cattle owner"). In a definite period of social development, in connection with changes in the social consciousness of men, diffused speech is replaced by "inflection," as a result of which appear the differences: bi—"I" and ba—"we;" ti (now chi)—"thou" and ta—"you;" dzüge (now dzöö)—"to carry, to drag;" dzuga (now dzoo)—"to store, to bury in a ditch;" dzegü (now dzüü)—"to carry on one's person" and dzagu (now dzuu)—"to carry in one's teeth;" from the once undifferentiated word tigna or tygna—"to listen, to eavesdrop, to scout" in the period of "inflection" there came tigna (now chagna)—"to listen" and tagna—"to scout, to eavesdrop."

*K. Marx and F. Engels, Works, Vol. XII, Part I, p. 175. Emphasis mine. -- G.S.

In all these examples the phonetic differentiation is accompanied by a differentiation in meaning of the several variants of one old word. Consequently we get Marrian semantic clusters (true enough, completely different in content from those which were established by N. Ya. Marr from Japhetic linguistic data), i.e., sometimes entire groups of words which can be traced to one common root or, according to N. Ya. Marr's terminology, an archetype. Archetypes of this kind, of which there is a considerable number in the Mongolic languages, undoubtedly bring us close to Marrian elements, presented by Prof. Chikobava in a very simplified and partly distorted way.

Moreover, perhaps we would not arbitrarily and without justification compare Mongolic words with Georgian, Celtic or American, taking into account some quite dubious semantic derivatives (deflections) and clusters of the kind "hand-woman-water" and particularly [avoid] all that N. Ya. Marr with excessive zeal traced back to "sky." We should remember K. Marx and F. Engels' indication that the "real Mongols busy themselves more with rams (Hämmeln) than with skies (Himmeln)."*

For the discovery of the phenomena reported above, we, the students of Mongolic languages, are indebted to Academician Marr's theory of elements and semantic clusters, the theory of functional semantics, which occupied a large place in the thinking of that scholar and to paleontologic analysis, which need not necessarily be reduced to the manipulation of the four elements.

(b) In that period in which the early Mongol tribes began to take over a nomadic cattle-raising culture, some extremely essential changes began to occur in their speech, which led the early Mongolic dialects to a transition from one qualitative condition (stage) to another. The new qualitative condition of early Mongol speech is characterized by the fact that in the latter "inflection" is dying out as a significant device of language; the synharmonia of vowels becomes only a formal-phonetic system lacking any substantive content in lieu of the [earlier] meaning category. At this time, agglutination, having driven out "inflection," becomes the chief means of expressing the language's new grammatical and lexical categories. The whole history of Mongolic languages for approximately the last two thousand years consists of an unflagging battle of two opposites: the old ("inflection" surviving until today as synharmonia of vowels) and the new (agglutination)—a battle in which the new is gaining more and more of a victory over the old. The gradual reduction in the importance of "inflection" is expressed in the gradual change in the vocalic system, in the breakdown of the vowels' synharmonia.

Consequently, Mongolic (and Turkic) languages were not agglutinative from the beginning and we tend to connect this transition of these languages from one qualitative condition (stage) to another with the transition of early Mongol tribes to nomadic cattle herding, as it is fact that these events generally coincide chronologically and this can hardly be accidental.

4. The Types of Changes by Stages in Language.

Not every change by stages in language must be accompanied by a change in typology according to the table by levels (amorphousness—agglutination—inflection, as it seemed to N. Ya. Marr in 1926-28), particularly after the primitive-commune stage was left far behind (a fundamental mistake of N. Ya. Marr is that his changes by stages occur beyond the threshold of civilization and somehow stop in the periods of the formation and existence of class societies). After

*K. Marx and F. Engels, German Ideology, 1935, p. 148.

all, the ancestors of Kant and Hegel with their inflected speech wandered about in the skins of wild animals at a time when in the "amorphous" Chinese language there was already a rich and very varied literature on all branches of knowledge of the times (we do not even speak of modern Chinese, as according to Marr's 1926-28 scheme this language would be considered less developed because of the absence in it of inflection, than the language of the ancient Germanic peoples).

Even simple observation, not research, will show that changes by stages occurred: (1) in Chinese—within the framework of the same typology, without inflection or agglutination; (But with what extraordinary power does "inflection" reveal itself in that language in the form of sound tonality, to a degree unknown in any other language in the world! This is why it is completely unpermissible to describe this mighty language of a mighty people with the terms "amorphous" or "lacking in form" and to pitch it into a heap with the least developed languages of the world.) (2) in Indo-European languages—within the framework of the same inflected typology (it is indubitable, for example, that that which occurred with Russian in the Pushkin period represented a stage change in the language, although inflection still remained); the same can be observed in other languages of the world.

On the other hand, not every typological change in language can be the representation of its transformation by stages, as can and does occur under conditions of hybridization of languages differing typologically but at the same stage of development (Mongolic languages at their meeting point with dialects of the Chinese and Tibetan languages in the Kukunor and Amdu regions or with Iranian [dialects] in Afghanistan). After all, the path of formation of languages is quite variable. After all, in a small territory K. Marx and F. Engels found three ways in which national languages were formed: "***in any developed contemporary language speech which arose spontaneously became a national tongue, sometimes due to historical growth of language from ready-made materials, as in Romance and Germanic languages, sometimes through the hybridization and mixing of nations, as in English, and sometimes through the concentration of dialects into a single national language, conditioned by economic and political concentration."* What then can be said of the many languages beyond the limits of Western Europe, particularly languages of earlier periods, about which N. Ya. Marr wrote: "***the more archaic the type of community, the easier the coming together and the separation***"

One cannot find the correct path by comparing, for example, Chinese with German without taking into account the concrete history of the languages under investigation; one can obtain results only when one compares the language of contemporary Germans with that of ancient Germanic peoples, or by juxtaposing modern Chinese with that spoken in the third century B.C. Languages of different systems and typology can be compared while seeking generalizations, only after they have undergone individual historical investigation which takes into account the concrete history of the social development of the peoples, carriers of the language. Academician I. I. Meshchaninov's attempt to find a solution for the problem of development by stages through a comparative study of certain syntactic indicators (subject-predicate) in some languages of our North, Far East and the Caucasus was unsuccessful because so far we know nothing of the past conditions of these languages.

Either forward from Marr—under the shining arch of a Marxist-Leninist science of language; or backward from Marr—into the past: to the Marr of 1922, to whom we are apparently called by Prof. Chikobava, or, what is even worse, into the fetid swamp of bourgeois linguistics. A third path ("Marrism," for example) does not and cannot exist.

*Ibid., p. 414.

Against Stagnation, For the Development of Soviet Linguistics*

By Professor F. FILIN

The great October socialist revolution provided linguists with great possibilities for freeing their creative work from the narrowness and one-sidedness of traditional linguistics and from many of its unscientific fallacies. It armed Soviet linguistics with a genuinely scientific method of research, that of Marxism-Leninism.

The outstanding scientist and linguist Academician N. Ya. Marr played a distinguished role in the struggle for progressive Soviet linguistics and left behind a rich linguistic heritage. During the Soviet years of his creative work Academician N. Ya. Marr formulated the new teaching on language, which he designated thus to distinguish it from old, bourgeois linguistics.

Academician N. Ya. Marr was able to note the general contours of materialist linguistics in its application to the analysis of a wealth of factual material of various languages of the world, first of all the languages of the Soviet Union.

And yet, as the newspaper Pravda correctly states in its editors' note to Prof. A. Chikobava's article, Soviet linguistics is in an unsatisfactory state, is at a standstill at the present time. This is expressed first of all in the sharp lag of language theory behind the needs for further development of the language culture of the Soviet people, in the lack of proper deductions from the historical development of languages and their present state, in a kind of disorder in our linguists' theoretical thinking, and in their impotence to solve major problems of the science of language.

The reasons for this unsatisfactory state are, generally speaking, correctly indicated in the articles by Prof. N. Chemodanov and Prof. G. Sanzheyev published in Pravda, May 23, and for this reason I shall not dwell in detail on this question. I shall only say that one of the major reasons for stagnation in linguistics is the lack of the needed critical evaluation of the obsolete and erroneous propositions of Academician N. Ya. Marr, the danger of a dogmatic approach to the heritage of our outstanding linguist. It is perfectly obvious that appropriate critical work must be done.

But on what foundations should this critical work be performed? The answer is perfectly clear: on the foundations of Marxism-Leninism. This incontestable proposition is formulated also in Prof. A. Chikobava's article, published in Pravda May 9. The works of Marx, Engels, Lenin and

*Pravda, May 30, 1950, p. 3.

Stalin, the basic statements of the classics of Marxism-Leninism on language and thought must lie at the basis of Soviet linguistics.

However, Prof. A. Chikobava interprets the tasks of Marxist-Leninist linguistics in an extremely peculiar way. The main line of his criticism of Academician N. Ya. Marr's teaching is aimed at denying the unity of the language-building process, stage development, the paleontology of speech, the class nature of language in a class society; it is aimed at upholding the "comparative-historical" (formal-comparative) method of bourgeois linguistics. The latter (defense of the formal-comparative method) is the principal aim of his article and, incidentally, also of Comrade Serebrennikov's article in Pravda of May 23. True, Prof. A. Chikobava writes that "comparative-historical analysis needs to be perfected," but the path this work of perfecting is to follow remains the author's undisclosed secret.

Just what is the formal-comparative method?

The "comparative-historical" linguistics advanced at the beginning of the 19th century was a step forward in the study of language. It paved the way for determining correlations among related languages of a given "family."

Such established correlations which made up the common stratum in the languages of a "family" placed linguistics on a firmer historical base and allowed the classification of languages according to the degree to which they were related to one another. For the 19th century (with the probable exclusion of the end of the past century) comparative linguisguistics was a considerable advance in the study of speech. F. Engels was entirely right in his brilliant criticism of Dühring when he noted the successes of this linguistics. It does not, however, follow from this positive evaluation of comparative-historical linguistics by F. Engels that one of the founders of Marxism shared the theoretical premises of the bourgeois science of language. In defending the "comparative-historical" method, the opponents of Academician N. Ya. Marr's theory (including Prof. A. Chikobava) always refer to the passage cited in F. Engels' polemic with Dühring, but "forget" F. Engels classic piece of research called the "Frankish Period," in which the theoretical premises of the "comparativists" are virtually shattered asunder.

The "comparative-historical" method (especially with the appearance of works by the German linguist A. Schleicher) concealed contradictions in itself from the very beginning, contradictions which later led bourgeois linguistics into a blind alley. On the one hand, correlations were established between languages within the confines of a "family" or "branch" which, in the majority of cases, actually existed; on the other hand a faulty, idealistic approach was established to the very essence of speech, to its historical development.

The fact of greater or less closeness of certain languages to one another cannot be denied and never was denied by Academician N. Ya. Marr. For example, the Slavic languages (Russian, Ukrainian, Belorussian, Polish, Czech, Bulgarian, etc.) are close to one another. The Slavic languages have traits in common with the Baltic (Lithuanian and Latvian), Germanic, Romance, Indian, Iranian and several other language groups comprising the Indo-European system ("family" in the obsolete terminology) of languages, even though the common nature of these traits is considerably less than among the Slavic languages themselves.

But how can the common nature of these traits be explained historically? The comparativist answers: if there are regular correlations among two or more languages, these languages are related. "Two languages are called related when both are the result of two different evolutions of one and the same language formerly in use," wrote A. Meillet, head of the French bourgeois school of linguists, who died in 1936.*

On the basis of assumed "relationship" all Indo-European languages can be traced to a single "ancestor," a "proto-Indo-European language." In precisely the same way, the Finno-Ugric, Turkic, Semitic and other language systems are alleged to have had their own "proto-languages." According to the "comparative-historical" method, the "proto-language" was spoken by a "proto-people" who lived in a comparatively small territory, the "proto-homeland."

But how did the numerous modern languages of different systems develop from a "protolanguage?" The comparativists answer: by a prolonged evolutionary process of fractioning which is allegedly a general law in the history of languages. Thus, for example, because of overpopulation of the area they occupied (or for various other reasons), the "proto-Indo-Europeans" at one time moved from their "proto-homeland" (searches for which are still being unsuccessfully conducted in various parts of Europe and Asia), and began to split up into groups. Correspondingly, their language was subjected to a splitting-up. From the "proto-Indo-Europeans" came the "proto-Germans," the "proto-Balto-Slavs," the "proto-Indo-Iranians," etc. The "proto-Balto-Slavs broke up in turn into the "proto-Slavs" and the "proto-Balts," and the "proto-Slavs" broke up into new groups among which were the "proto-Russes." The "proto-Russes" broke up into new branches, etc., on down to the modern speakers of the numerous Russian, Ukrainian and Belorussian dialects.

On these premises the entire ancient and middle period of the history of peoples is portrayed as a continuous stream of break-ups, of endless migrations, of conquests of alien territories, of complete annihilation or absorption of neighboring tribes and peoples.

We note that modern data of Soviet history, archeology, ethnography and anthropology reject this entire scheme as unscientific, though of course cases of break-ups, migrations and conquests which actually took place in the past are not denied.

But how does one determine the peculiarities of the "protolanguage," which is the main goal of the "comparative-historical" method? For this, words and forms compared within a system or group are traced to a "proto-form" by means of a peculiar arithmetical equation. The totality of "protoforms" is alleged to have constituted the basis of the "protolanguage." All the historicity of the bourgeois comparative method in linguistics is reduced to the reconstruction of "protoforms," while the very mechanism of "reconstruction" rests wholly on the idealist concept of changes in speech as being a purely immanent, evolutionary process entirely independent of social conditions, of the peculiarities of thought. It is all the same to the comparativist, for example, under what socio-historical conditions Russian "vorona," Bulgarian "vrana," Polish "wrona" and Kashubian "varna" were obtained from the hypothetical "proto-Slavic form": "vorna" [raven]. In essence, the real history of tribes and peoples does not exist for the bourgeois "comparative-historical" method: real or supposed speech changes are described as though they occur somewhere in space. This is understandable when one considers that the comparativists regard language as a self-sufficient "organism," independent of everything.

It is no accident that the "genealogic classification of languages" advanced by A. Schleicher and championed by Prof. A. Chikobava is based on a concept of language as a kind of biological organism with a certain admixture of the well-known biblical legend of the Tower of Babel and the "mixing

*"A. Meillet, Introduction to a Comparative Study of the Indo-European Languages, 1938, p. 50.

of languages " and certain other vestiges of "mythological thought."

As for the history of peoples itself, the historical premises or conclusions of the comparativists are not organically related to linguistic analysis itself or to its results. They are a kind of appendage, an "external" history of language which is usually altogether absent from the works of the comparativists. The desire to remain at all costs within the confines of "purely linguistic" analysis leads to attacks on an approach to language as a social phenomenon, reflecting the struggle of antagonistic classes in a class society. The error of Prof. A. Chikobava, according to whom a national language is allegedly of a supra-class nature, is related precisely to the essence of the "comparative-historical" method.

We add to what has been said above that the "comparative-historical" method deals almost exclusively with description of the evolution of sound changes and grammatical forms. It ignores the laws of vocabulary and semantics (allegedly accidental phenomena not subject to generalization), as well as qualitative changes in the very content of the language. Hence, this method should more accurately be called the formal-comparative rather than the comparative-historical method.

The formal-comparative method has still another side logically ensuing from it and having far-reaching scientific and political consequences.

Employing this method, the comparativists "explain" only what is common to a system or group of languages, ignoring what is unique, peculiar to one language only. Moreover, this uniqueness is what comprises the main part of the particular language. The "explanation" of the comparativists reduces totally to the reconstruction of "protoforms." That which can be traced back to a "protolanguage" comprises the "primordial" stratum of the language, while that which does not enter into the "protolanguage" scheme is either borrowed or vague, unknowable. But with respect to borrowings—real or more often supposed—the comparativist is given free rein for all sorts of conjectures and political speculations.

For example, the unscientific tradition has been established in bourgeois linguistics of regarding a large group of words in the Slavic languages as borrowed from the Germanic languages. Let us take for example the word "buk" (tree) [beech], and the derived "bukva" [letter, character]. Because of its absence in other Indo-European languages except the Germanic, this word cannot be "traced" to a "proto-Indo-European form" and, consequently, it is "not primordial " in the Slavic languages but is borrowed from the Germanic languages. But why not suppose that it was not the Slavs who borrowed from the Germanic peoples, but vice-versa, the Germanic peoples from the Slavs? It turns out that this cannot be supposed because allegedly the Germanic peoples were always more cultured than the Slavs and borrowings by "cultured" peoples from "uncultured" ones do not occur! Thus, such words as "khleb" [grain, or bread], "vazhny" [important], "bronya" [armor], "izba" [hut] and many others turn out to be "alien" for the Slavs.

Let us recall also that the notorious "Norman" hypothesis and others like it in the language sense rest precisely on the formal-comparative method.

What, then, is the comparativist's notion of a language which actually has existed and does exist now, including the Russian language? Any concrete language is alleged to be composed of two parts. One part of the language came to the people speaking it as a heritage from the "proto-people" —this is the primordial part. The "primordial" stock is the basis for all changes, all innovations in the language. The other part is constant borrowing. But what in such a case is left a people speaking their own language if even the basis of the "primordial" part of their speech was not created by them but by a "proto-people" millenia remote from them? They can only freshen up the heritage they have acquired and borrow from their neighbors.

Thus, the formal-comparative method reduces the language-building activity and originality of a [given] people to zero, and provides extensive opportunities for all sorts of cosmopolite disputations.

But let us imagine for a moment that a "protolanguage" did actually exist at one time. In such a case the question naturally arises as to what were its historical roots, what was the relationship of the "protolanguages" of various "families" to one another. Formal-comparative linguistics (with the exception of certain dissidents of bourgeois linguistics who sketch fantasies on the theme of a world "protolanguage") considers this question out of place, ruled out. Consequently, after the restoration of "protoforms" science has nothing more to do; the world of the unknowable lies beyond this!

For the comparativist the relationships between languages of different "families" are reduced merely to external influences, to clashes. Each "family" of languages has lived its own closed, inner life since time immemorial, endowed by nature (or by God) with its own special qualities. It is entirely understandable that such a "theory" was widely used and is used by those who love racist ranting. It is known, for example, that the "facts" of formal-comparative method played no small role in the formulation of the "race theory" of the Hitlerite "masters" who held that the "highly cultured" "proto-Indo-European" ("proto-Aryan" in their terminology) language was preserved in its purity and inviolability only in the German language. The formal-comparative method provides all grounds for use by the racists, whether its champions admit it or not.

Lastly, I shall point out that the complete blind alley into which "comparative-historical" linguistics has turned is even recognized as such by certain contemporary bourgeois linguists. The well-known French linguist J. Vandries published an article in 1946 in which, paying his due to the formal-comparative method, he at the same time writes that this method has completely exhausted itself and that nothing more can be expected of it.

In defending the formal-comparative method against Academician N. Ya. Marr's paleontology of speech, Prof. A. Chikobava and others are dragging Soviet linguistics backward to a path long ago traversed by the science of language.

The obsolete canons of bourgeois linguistics ceased to satisfy more discerning linguists even at the end of the past century. The Russian student of the Caucasus, N. Ya. Marr, occupied first place among them. At the beginning of his scientific work several native languages of the Caucasus which had not yet been subjected to research by the method of formal-comparative linguistics seemed, according to the notions of the priests of science at the time, to be languages "without clan and tribe," languages which did not relate to any language "family" whatsoever. The young N. Ya. Marr set himself the task of tracing the inner relationships of the Georgian language with other "homeless" languages of the Caucasus; he even attempted to compare the Georgian language with languages of the Semitic "family." After long years of research, the fundamentals were laid down for Japhetic linguistics, for the doctrine on the Japhetic system of languages. A study of basic phenomena of the Japhetic languages, backed by work on monuments of material culture, led N. Ya. Marr even before the revolution to conclusions which were incompatible with formal-comparative linguistics. Analysis of survival characteristics of Japhetic speech showed that in the distant past the Japhetic languages were closely connected to the languages of other "families" at the early stages of their development.

This led in turn to a broadening of the subject under investigation, to emergence from the confines of a single Japhetic "family"—something which was already contrary to traditional linguistics. Elements began to be found which were common to the Japhetic and non-Japhetic languages and which could not be explained in terms of the "theory" of borrowings. In particular, N. Ya. Marr was intrigued by the presence of words common to Russian and to the Japhetic languages (such as "pechat" [seal, stamp], "salo" [fat, grease, lard], "kniga" [book], and others in their early meanings, meanings which do not correspond to their modern meanings).

The very legitimacy of such juxtapositions was backed by the facts of ancient history, archeology and ethnography, as well as by special sound correlations which were regarded sceptically even then by the comparativists who did not allow (as even now) for even the possibility that there could be any type of mutual relationships between different language "families" other than purely external influences, borrowings.

The results of many years of research were summed up by Academician N. Ya. Marr in his work "The Japhetic Caucasus and the Third Ethnic Element in the Creation of the Mediterranean Culture" (1920). Here Academician N. Ya. Marr advances the following hypothesis: the Indo-European languages of the Mediterranean area were formed as the result of the hybridization of the Japhetic languages with the original Indo-European ones. However, this hypothesis was soon rejected by Academician N. Ya. Marr himself inasmuch as it did not explain how the aboriginal Japhetic and Indo-European languages were formed which together formed a hybrid. In this work Academician N. Ya. Marr still did not break with the "protolanguage hypothesis" or with bourgeois genealogical classification of languages (which is precisely why Prof. A. Chikobava commented favorably on the work).

After 1920, not ceasing his investigation of language material, Academician N. Ya. Marr began a serious study of the classics of Marxism-Leninism. N. Ya. Marr saw in the application of Marxist-Leninist methodology to practical research work the only reliable way out of the blind alley which formal-comparative linguistics had entered. This was the decisive turning point in Marr's creative scientific work, and at the same time it marked the beginning of the creation of progressive Soviet linguistics. Hypotheses were advanced which have already been elaborated on in the article by Academician I. I. Meshchaninov published in Pravda, May 10.* Hence, I need not deal with this matter.

I will only note that the new methodology required the creation of a new technique of linguistic research. This new technique of Academician N. Ya. Marr took the form of the paleontology of speech with analysis according to elements. However, it still proved to be far from perfect. Mocking Marr's paleontology of speech and juggling with the facts, the adherents of the formal-comparative method directed the brunt of their criticism at discrediting the entire factual side of Academician N. Ya. Marr's research work. However, their arguments were not at all convincing.

Naturally, there is much in the works of Academician N. Ya. Marr that is subject to dispute and is erroneous even with respect to facts, but these vital shortcomings in the essence of his work await more thorough investigation. Marr's errors must be disclosed and eliminated from current linguistic work, but this must not be done in the way it is done by Prof. A. Chikobava and Candidate of Philological Sciences B. Serebrennikov. What is the value, for example, of Prof. A. Chikobava's accusations that Marr fostered racism, accusations based on "skillfully" selected quotations? Because in Marr's stage classification of the languages of the world (which absolutely represents an unfinished scheme and which is erroneous to the extent that it is based solely on morphological features) the Chinese or Georgian languages appear at stages preceding the Indo-European languages, Prof. A. Chikobava hastens to draw the following conclusion: Academician N. Ya. Marr denies these languages (Georgian and Chinese) [the possibility of] further development.

This conclusion does not in the least correspond to reality: unlike certain comparativists, Academician N. Ya. Marr did not equate the content of a language and its form. He wrote the following regarding the Georgian languages in the world*** The Georgian language is capable of conveying concepts of abstract thought fully and without distortion. Works of both the Asiatic and European cultured society are easily translatable into Georgian. It also possesses sufficiently rich means for nationalizing achievements in the applied sciences and technology. In it is the leaven of internationalism achieved by dint of enormous labor."*

Academician N. Ya. Marr believed that there were great possibilities for a tempestuous growth and flowering of languages in a socialist society. His expression, "a native tongue is a powerful lever for a cultural upsurge" became an enchanted phrase which corresponded to the content of Marr's investigations. What we need is an appropriate critical appraisal of the real and not the imaginary errors of Marr.

It is not an easy matter, but it is possible to end the stagnation in which modern Soviet linguistics finds itself. A Marxist Leninist science of language must be built up not without Marr, but with his heritage and relying on what is most important, what is basic: the works of the great scientists, Marx, Engels, Lenin and Stalin.

*Current Digest of the Soviet Press, Vol. II, No. 19, pp. 3-11.

*N. Ya. Marr, The Georgian Language, Stalinir, 1949, pp. 11-12.

On Certain of N. Marr's General Linguistic Theses*

By Gr. KAPANTSYAN

I welcome the decision of the editors of Pravda to open a discussion on linguistic problems "in connection with the unsatisfactory state of Soviet linguistics."

I also feel it necessary to express great satisfaction with Arn. Chikobava's brilliant article "On Certain Problems of Soviet Linguistics." Arn. Chikobava raises a number of problems daringly, profoundly and from many points of view. In criticizing many linguistic problems as Academician N. Marr conceived them, he exposes their un-Marxist trend and nature. The author of the article indicates correctly that "the fundamental statements of Marx, Engels, Lenin and Stalin on language and linguistics have been replaced in the work of many linguists by Academician N. Ya. Marr's incorrect premises on linguistic theory. In case after case, lip service to Marxism-Leninism turns out in reality to be defense of N. Ya. Marr's fundamental errors."

It may be that nowhere here in the U.S.S.R. has every statement of N. Marr been so canonized as in Armenia, where his every remark has been made into infallible dogma. For example, it was here that A. Garibyan and E. Agayan considered Marrism and Marxism to be synonymous. Moreover, they frequently preferred the former to the latter and reference to various of Engels' propositions which contradicted those of Marr encountered mute hostility. Very detrimental was the effect of G. Serdyuchenko's articles in the press and his address to the presidium of the U.S.S.R. Academy of Sciences co-ordinating session of all the academies, as was also the article by N. Bernikov and I. Braginsky in the newspaper Kultura i zhizn, etc. The earlier approach by Literaturnaya gazeta was particularly tendentious. All this produced an incorrect orientation and really initiated "the stagnation in the development of Soviet linguistics" to use the expression of Pravda's editors. At the same time, a situation has arisen in which it is becoming impossible to do positive work on the immediate tasks of our motherland's linguistic development. (See A. Chikobava's article.)

I shall not refer here to N. Marr's role as a student of Armenian and Georgian [cultures], partly as archeologist and ethnographer, later as creator of Japhetidology, meaning the theory of the genealogic kinship of the so-called Japhetic languages, the number of which was gradually broadened to include not only Caucasus languages but subsequently others as well (Basque, Etruscan, Urartu, Elamite, etc.) until their imagined genealogic connection with the Semitic ones disappeared. By Japhetic languages, N. Marr understood a stage in the development of all languages all over the world. Here the comparative historical method of study, correct though not exhaustive, was replaced with the famous element analysis. The search went on in all languages for four unfortunate elements and for them alone, with an arbitrary analysis of words. In my book "Hayasa—the Cradle of the Armenians," I wrote the following, at the risk of its being slandered by the "critics" (which did happen), about these elements. "Beginning with 1923-24, in his discussion of linguistic and ethnogenetic questions, N. Marr refused to recognize kinship between languages, their genealogic classification, [language] families and such, as well as the factor of migration. But his universalism in proposing just one single glottogonic process, with its development by stages and 'paleontology,' which, if you please, are based on four morpho-phonetic elements initial for all languages—all this was erroneously elevated in contrast to the real tangible history of given languages with their peculiarities, regularities, relationships, etc."

With such a universal approach, unhistoric and cosmopolitan, N. Marr compares not only languages of any kind whatever, words in their contemporary phonetic condition (consequently, regardless of the fact that they might have changed beyond recognition), the structure of language, and so on, but also the most minute peculiarities of these individual languages. For example, modern Georgian is closer structurally to contemporary New Armenian than it is to Old Georgian, which is of course an accidental coincidence; in an article ("From Pyrenean Guria") "the dialectic peculiarities of the Guria patois of Georgian and the Suletian dialect of Basque (in Spain—G.K.) are shown in relation to each other."*

One might recall here Marr's insistence upon the eternal class nature of language, even in the period of savage hordes or in the primitive clan community, although later, during the Baku discussion, he was forced to retreat because of strong opposition, saying: "Whenever there is a collective organization founded not on blood, then I use the term 'class'*** I took this term 'class' and used it with a different meaning; why not use it?" †

On the question of practical linguistic development in the period of the proletarian revolution and later, N. Marr expresses opinions which are inconsistent with the interests of the proletariat and the revolution. Thus, for example, he says: "***unless the revolution through which we are living is a dream, there can be no talk of any palliative reform of language or grammar, nor consequently of writing or spelling. Not reform, but radical reconstruction, the shifting of this entire superstructural world onto new tracks, to a new level and stage of development of human speech, into revolutionary creativity and the creation of a new language." ‡

All this is expressed beautifully, of course, and, moreover, has application to revolution. But, again, it is not scientific or historic nor is it concrete in dealing with a given language.

For example, contemporary Russian spelling rather contributes to a single national, highly cultured and elaborated orthoepy, and does so without any sharp break with earlier writing. The introduction of such allegedly "folk" pronunciations as zhyz in lieu of zhizn [life]; shto [what], while chevo [of what], chemu [to what] continue to be used; petachok or pitachok [instead of legitimate pyatachok—a five-kopek coin]; etc., will hardly make for progress. A revolution in spelling must be undertaken where pronunciation greatly differs from spelling, as in English, or where because of its complexity writing has become the attribute only of scholars or of a few individuals, as in Chinese.

Where a revolution in language is concerned, its needs, its historic inevitability must be demonstrated. After all, grammar is not directly connected with changes in social structure and production. It is good to speak of a new stage, but for the speaker [of a language] is it not a matter of indifference whether he forms grammatical relations according to the pattern—pishu [I write], pishesh [you write],

*Pravda, May 30, 1950, pp. 3-4.

*N. Ya. Marr, Selected Works, Vol. II, p. 411.

†N. Ya. Marr, Contribution to the Baku Discussion on Japhetidology and Marxism, Baku, 1932, p. 39.

‡N. Ya. Marr, Selected Works, Vol. II, p. 370-1.

pishet [he writes], etc., or the pattern—ya [I] pish, ty [you] pish, on [he] pish, etc., the pattern—dom [the house], doma [of the house], domu [to the house], etc., or according to the pattern—kino [motion picture theater] (stands), kino (the building of the kino), kino (I went up to the kino), kino (I sit in the kino)? Finally, there are languages like Georgian where the verb must inevitably bear in itself a relationship to the object (direct or indirect) when a word for the object is also present. For example, s-tsem-s ("gives") where final "s" defines the third person of the subject, while the first "s" superfluously indicates again the existence of another word side by side, i.e., the object, which is indicated.

One may ask if one can force a Georgian not to use these objectival prefixes any longer. And will the actual grammatic consciousness of the Georgian tolerate such an abrupt change now? What for? It would be the same as if we were to try to abolish with a stroke of the pen the use of the animate gender in the Russian language and were to say "I see the ox" as we say "I see the table,"* or if we abolished the masculine, feminine and neuter genders. This did not take place in English in the Middle Ages, but the groundwork had been laid in the absence of gender endings. Caucasus mountaineers continue to distinguish masculine, feminine, animal and object genders, while Bantu languages group nouns according to outward appearance (round, flat). Modern Armenian in the Ararat [region], as distinguished from all other modern and archaic Armenian dialects, even uses the genitive case (ending in "va") for words of time. One may ask, can one reject all these ancient phenomena of formal grammar in order to create a new level in the development by stages (which one?) of language?

We do not even always change the vocabulary. Our revolutionary practice in the post-October period certainly did not follow the predicted path of transformation by "stages" of language, grammar, orthography, etc., as suggested by N. Marr.

Apropos, I should also like to say a few words about phonetics. Many enthusiastic admirers of N. Marr defend the position that every phonetic change is socially conditioned. This can refer to those cases where such a change is used for stem formation (word formation) or for the expression of grammatical function, but in other cases as where, for example, [sound shifts] occur as a consequence of palatalization, metathesis or assimilation, they do not have such significance. In a letter to Bloch, F. Engels once referred to this crude sociologizing in [dealing with] sound shifts. Actually, what sounds in the Russian language did we change and for what purposes?

In this connection one would also like to call attention to the phonetic aspect of N. Marr's elements—SAL, BER, ROШ, YON. The question is: were such sounds possible in the earliest times in the mouth of a savage? After all, animals make diffuse and inarticulate noises and such hominid sounds, complete with closed syllables, could hardly have been worked out and uttered distinctly. And we do not even mention that among African savages (Bushmen, Hottentots) there have survived up to six kinds of suction and clicking gutteral "sounds," similar to turkey cries. So that even according to historic phonetics, there could be no such elements as SAL, BER, etc., and if the contemporary names of certain tribes have such a phonetic appearance, it does not follow that hundreds of thousands of years ago their pronunciation was the same, even if one postulated the existence of these elements against [the evidence of] the entire history of human speech formation.

But N. Marr not only sets down what the elements were, he makes their changes depend directly on the ideology of the times. In the article "Language and Thought" he writes: "Ideological changes determine phonetic shifts. Because of this, the initial linguistic elements, four in number, have undergone numerous changes in the process of their development. Following the same law of opposites, they reach in their development the state of a single sound, be it vowel or consonant."* Until his death, N. Marr continued in a completely arbitrary manner in his investigations to subdivide words into these sound fragments and in all the languages of the world, to give them arbitrary meanings which he needed for his predetermined explanations.

He never showed the specific historic development, inevitable for every word. The late form in existence was considered phonetically fit for such element analysis at the sacrifice of a study of its history. Thus neglecting sound laws, N. Marr "establishes" the community of the words Japhet, Prometheus and Karapet. But the Armenians borrowed the last word from Iranian, where kara means "clan," "tribe" as well as "army" (similar to Georgian eri —"people," "army," also to Russian polk [army, regiment] and German Volk—"people"); and Persian pet (Georgian speti) means "commander," "chief." Consequently, [in Persian] karapet meant "clan chief," "tribal leader," and the origin of Armenian karapet—"precursor" has no relation whatever with Semitic Japhet and Greek Prometheus.

Thus arbitrarily, ignoring the specific characteristics of each language, one can relate any words and establish their kinship. Only if one does not know the history of the [Russian] word "ruka" [hand] can one divide it into the elements "ru" and "ka." For the syllable ru was once nasalized (ro) as it still is in Polish and was written with a large jus,† and thus cannot be regarded as similar to the verb root "rushit" [to destroy] (from the root ru, also found in Latin: ruō—to destroy). Through such arbitrary manipulations, words meaning "hand" in different languages are transformed into new phonetic combinations meaning "woman," "water," "strength," "cunning," and the like. On the basis of such element "analysis" all basic peculiarities of German as well as Gothic are explained as traits [held] in common with particular Caucasus languages of the same Japhetic system: German and Svanetian, also Gothic with Megrelian and Chau ("Language and Thought").

In the same work N. Marr connects the origin of dialectics with the Germanic language system, as if dialectics could not have existed in a different linquistic milieu of thinking. He says: "In the main section of our report on the development of thought, attention should be called to the fact that after the Greeks, philosophy and the theory of cognition receive their greatest dialectic development (be it idealistic or materialistic) in an environment in which German was spoken, German—a language of an older system than Greek. <u>This is no coincidence.</u>"‡(Emphasis mine—G.K.) This approach is undoubtedly wrong. Neither the age of the language system nor the German language itself is relevant here. The development of dialectics has no relation to the fact that Hegel and Marx spoke German. They would have created this dialectics if they had thought in Russian, English, French, etc. Consequently, this is pure coincidence.

Among "definitely confirmed theses" N. Marr includes: "The singular did not exist at first and the plural developed from the same form as the singular. But nevertheless plurality came first and then later singularity, as its part, as its opposite."**

From the study of the category of number in [many] languages we know very well that this numerical category, as well as others, was originally quite fully represented in ancient languages as a part of concrete original thinking. In the most backward languages of savages we notice the word designation not only of the concept of singleness (using any sign), but also of duality, when this one word indicates

* [In Russian an animate masculine noun bears the form of the genitive case when used in the accusative.]

*N. Ya. Marr, <u>Selected Works</u>, Vol. III, p. 100.

†[Ancient letter for nasalized "o"].

‡<u>Ibid</u>.

**<u>Ibid.</u>, p. 98.

the paired quality of the object, and also triplicity, and in some places even a fourfold quantity as among the Maori of New Zealand. Gradually triplicity and even duality die out in language and singleness and non-singleness (the plural, i. e., more than one) are kept. This happens because a word, endowed with particles to indicate number, gender, distance and definiteness actually become a burden for concrete thinking. Later on number was indicated simply through a separate word, a numeral, and this term contented itself with two numerical categories—singular and plural. This is undoubtedly progress in the development of language and thought, although a word designated as plural can refer to two objects (which logically is not plural [more than two]). As we can see, not everything was taken into account by N. Marr in dealing with the number category in language.

Later N. Marr notes that "there were no persons in conjugation: no first, or second***consequently there could be no conversation, i. e., no colloquial language. And if the two first persons were absent, obviously there could be no third person as a grammatical category***" * Only later do verbs acquire personal endings from pronominal particles, which had developed from independent pronouns, those former "totem substitutes."

It is not clear how it can be that there were no designations for persons in voiced, spoken language, which takes its inception from communication. These designations need not necessarily have appeared as particles as [they do], for example, in Russian (pisal-pisali) [he wrote-they wrote], or in French, where persons are not indicated (mange—we do not yet know the person or number). But the designations of person are indicated through the addition of personal pronouns, which now become formally functional little words. Further, N. Marr says that "generally there were no conjugations and declensions although there was voiced speech and people understood each other perfectly without need for such grammatical burdens as morphology, the study of forms." † However, we should not regard the concept of "form" narrowly as is done by many Indo-Europeanists and see in it only the form of the actual word. If men communicate through voiced speech and understand each other, the form can include also accent, word order and sound shifts within the word and finally a simultaneous gesture of the hand.

In the old science of language, according to N. Marr, "there were laws of phonetics—of sound phenomena, but there were no semantic laws—laws of the origin of a given meaning, laws for the intelligibility of speech and later of its parts, including words. The meanings of words received no ideological explanation." ‡

This proposition is generally correct but is left hanging in thin air because N. Marr offers no "semantic laws" and, when studying changes in word meanings, he does so, not on words of an original (related) root, but in words outwardly similar, accidentally selected from any language whatever and therefore non-historically ascribing an auxiliary function to the technique of speech, be it voiced or manual."

At the end of the book "Language and Thought," N. Marr declares: "Language exists only insofar as it is revealed in sounds; the action of thought takes place even without revelation (but in sound images, as internal speech—G.K.). Language, as sound, has a center of appearance; the center of the work of thought is cerebrally localized; but all this, particularly sound production, can always be formally (!?) correlated with thought or thought production. (Voiced) speech has already begun to yield its functions to the latest inventions, which incontrovertibly conquer distance, while thought goes on and upward from its unutilized past accumulation and its new acquisitions and will fully displace and replace language. The future language is thought growing in a technique free from natural matter. No language will withstand this, not even voiced speech which is still connected to nature's norms." *

These thoughts of N. Marr are either an enormous scientific prophecy or equally boundless phantasy. Actually, N. Marr seems not to reject the accompaniment of thought by various signal activities—hand movements and such—in "manual" speech, [or] sound images and their expression in voiced speech, etc. After all, we cannot deny deaf-mutes the act of thinking and similar association with the idea of motion.

According to N. Marr even voiced speech yields its (communication—G.K.) functions to new inventions, although it is thereby forgotten that this physical action also is conditioned and accompanied by us through the conception of language in sound. But N. Marr tears language from thought, which [actually] reveals to us two sides (form and content) of one process of man, historically elaborated, and man's highest process. He says: "The future language is thought growing in a technique free from natural matter." It turns out, according to N. Marr, that voiced speech still connected with the norms of human nature will give way to thought transmitted through a new technique. One might ask: and how will this thought of ours take place "outside of nature?" Dühring wrote in part about this when he said: "He who can only think with the aid of speech has never yet experienced what abstract and genuine thought really means." To this Engels answered: "If this be so, animals are the most abstract and genuine of thinkers, as their thoughts are never disturbed by the meddlesome intervention of language." †

I understand even scientific phantasy if it is based on certain preliminary, scientifically verified data. But the "scientific prophecy" of N. Marr presented above has rather a speculative lining and, it seems to me, is completely unmaterialist and unhistorical.

Finally, in connection with the above indicated ideas of N. Marr regarding the independence of thought from the specific elements of language and its control over its linguistic formulation, let us present his notions about the morphologic classification of langagues. They coincide with those first formulated by August Schlegel in 1827. A. Schlegel divided the world's languages into three categories according to their use of various kinds of affixes: the amorphous (like Chinese, where roots are unchangeable and there are no affixes); the agglutinative (with affixes of multiple utilization and single function) and the inflected (with developed changeable roots and affixes which can be inserted inside the root and have multiple functions). In his work "Actual Problems and Current Tasks of the Japhetic Theory," N. Marr wrote:

"Changes in thought are [seen in] three systems of voiced speech structure emerging in toto from various economic systems and their corresponding social structures: (1) primitive communism, with a synthetic speech structure, with polysemantism of words, without distinction of stem and functional meanings; (2) a social structure based on the appearance of various economies with social division of labor, i. e., the division of society by professions, the stratification of a single society into productive-technological groups representing primitive forms of guilds. To it corresponds a linguistic structure which separates the parts of speech, while inside the sentence—the different clauses, and in the clauses—its various parts, etc. Others [aspects of sentence structure] with different functional words which eventually change into morphological elements with stem meanings distinguished in words, and the growth of functional meanings side by side with the stem ones; (3) an estate or class society with technical division of labor and an inflected

*Ibid.

† Ibid., p. 99.

‡ Ibid., p. 103.

* Ibid., p. 121.

† F. Engels, Anti-Dühring, 1932, p. 58.

morphology."*

At first glance, this is a thoroughly materialist approach—a view of major shifts in the thinking of organizational systems of voiced speech dependent on the different systems of socio-economic formations and production. But in reality there is much schematization in N. Ya. Marr and a direct connection between formal linguistic constructs and socio-productive conditions. The immanent significance of the specificity of voiced language is completely ignored and its acclimatization over a very long period in the structure of the sentence, in speech, in other words in language. The first kind—the synthetic or amorphous (lacking affixes) is characteristic now of Chinese and Sudanic Negro languages although economically, culturally, and where production is concerned they stand on quite different levels. The language of the Eskimos is quite rich in the use of affixes, but their social condition is primitive, [devoted to] communal herding, and it is only now, thanks to Soviet organization and our national policy, that this language and others like it are being enriched because, as a linguist once said, "all languages have resources for the formation of new words. The need for them has only to arise." Finally, contemporary English, not to mention others, is losing its grammatical particles and thereby in part coming closer to the first type; does this mean that English as well as contemporary Chinese are backward languages, qualitatively equivalent to Sudanic Negro languages of the same type? One thing only strikes [us]: a developing typology of the amorphous-agglutinative-inflective kind extends from eastern Asia to western Europe to the shores of the Atlantic, although even in this area there is some lack of uniformity.

As is known, this trinomial typological view of languages was at the basis of N. Marr's analysis by stages with the initial constant elements SAL, BER, ROШ and YON, which developed differently in a given language as they subsequently evolved. A theoretical handling of this phenomenon's causes is given in Comrade A. Chikobava's article and I shall not deal with it here.

In the field of general linguistics N. Marr touched on many problems and questions, but the examples given above are quite sufficient to convey an objective idea of their indisputable materialism.

Linguistic problems are numerous and very broad in scope, and naturally this is not the place to linger on all of them. We have in mind specifically: the origin of language with the interrelation of gesture and voiced speech, the differentiation and hybridization of languages, the question of "protolanguages," the role of classes in class society, language and thought, language and writing, the structure of language and social development with its production and ideology, language as a superstructural category, immanency of changes, the different levels of changeability in vocabulary and, on the other hand, of construction-typology with sound and morphological content, artificial languages, linguistic policy, language of the future, etc., etc.

The contributions of Academician N. Marr consist mainly in that he posed linguistic problems materialistically in his approach to language as part of the cultural superstructure and particularly in his critique of the idealist position of the Indo-Europeanists, who pretended to spread their methods of investigation to other language systems. All these schools with their emphasis on the primacy of either form or the spirit or social psychologism, etc., with the limitations of the formal methods of comparativism, naturally could not become a genuine science of language for us. There could be no truly materialist theory there [among the Indo-Europeanists] and N. Marr criticized them severely. But was he himself successful in creating, at least in general terms, in a tangible treatment, a truly materialist Marxist linguistics based on dialectical and historical materialism, using all the accumulated material examined? As has been seen above, we cannot give an affirmative answer to this [question]. Too much is still declarative and speculative. Much is only touched on and a finished, truly Marxist treatment of even the main problems or aspects of linguistics is still lacking. Doubtless, the participation of many Marxist linguists is needed and it will probably take a long time.

On the other hand the role of Academician N. Marr as a student of Armenian and Georgian [cultures] and an investigator of the several contiguous areas of scientific interest [relating] to the peoples of the Near East, particularly the Japhetic peoples of the Caucasus, is enormous and incontrovertible. Here he is linguist, philologist, historian and archeologist, and with his enormous erudition and production (several hundred works, large and small) he was a true innovator and initiator of a new and scientific study of Georgian and Armenian [cultures]. His role is in no way minimized by the new, better-founded genetic determination of the Georgian language as related to the Caucasus ones, given by I. Dzhavakhishvili ("The Primordial Nature and Kinship of Kartvelian and Caucasian Languages"), nor by my work on the genesis of Armenian, [viewed] not as an "Aryo-Japhetic" [language] hybridized in equal proportions as claimed by N. Marr, but as primarily "Asianic." At the same time we do not deny the fact of migration for various tribes and peoples—it has been noted in the case of the English (from Germany), Bulgarians (from the Volga), Hungarians, Turks, etc., and in very ancient times of the Cimmerians, Scythians, Phrygians, Etruscans (from Asia Minor), etc. Marx said about the movements of nomads: "***the pressure of surplus population on productive forces forced the barbarians from Asia's plains to invade the ancient civilized states."* However we cannot explain through migrations many questions which are of an ethnogenetic, productive, cultural, etc. nature.

Now the problem is to end stagnation in our Soviet linguistics. For this we must critically review many of our premises, approaches and theories, including the general linguistic conceptions of Academician N. Marr. Soviet science must achieve in linguistics, in concrete language development in our multinational motherland as well as in formulating a general linguistic discipline, a genuine science of language in the light of Marxist-Leninist theory and methodology. Even in old Russia we had linguistic scholars outstanding for their time (Potebnya, Shakhmatov, etc.). Today bourgeois linguistics is at an impasse and only Soviet science enjoys all conditions favorable for its flourishing and dominance. We should always keep in mind Comrade Stalin's statement: "Science is called science precisely because it knows no fetishes, is not afraid to lift its hand against the obsolete, the old, and it listens carefully to the voice of experience and practice."

We must now be convinced of one thing, that our discussion on the pages of Pravda will reveal at this historic moment for Soviet linguists the possibility of "a correct direction of future scientific work in this area." (Pravda).

*N. Ya. Marr, Selected Works, Vol. III, p. 71.

*K. Marx and F. Engels, Works, Vol. IX, p. 278.

Pressing Problems of Soviet Linguistics*

By A. POPOV

How to Use the Scientific Heritage of N. Ya. Marr.

"Fifteen years of Soviet life have flown by at such speed that they measure a whole century in content, creating before our eyes an epoch of world importance, an historic epoch, not [merely] rare but unique."†

These expressive words of N. Ya. Marr from his report "Transformations in the Techniques of Language and Thought" (published in 1933) can be applied with particular effect to creative 15 years in Soviet science, which have elapsed since the death of the founder of the new linguistics. It seems perfectly natural therefore, to think now about the need for a broad discussion of N. Ya. Marr's basic theses—in order to divide the incontrovertible part of his work, confirmed by the facts, from the doubtful and erroneous, which is not in agreement with the actual reality contained in the concrete linguistic material collected and studied in recent times.

N. Ya. Marr himself frequently repudiated his own constructs, if he saw that they disagreed with the facts. This characteristic of his scientific work can probably be seen best in the works of 1926.

There in the introduction to "Stages in the Development of Japhetic Theory," a collection [of works] published that year, he states openly that it was "a collection***of articles, most of which reflect opinions given up long ago and some only recently, [opinions] which for us, in large measure *** are already dead and in the mortuary," "a kind of 'bouquet' [made] of fallen leaves already withered." ‡

In almost every Marr article of 1926 we find abrupt and categorical announcements of a complete change in methods of work, the very way in which questions were posed, etc. At this time N. Ya. Marr speaks of a number of major changes and turns, of a new view of facts which he himself had earlier given a different interpretation, of diametrically opposed explanations, etc.

Without dwelling on N. Ya. Marr's numerous other statements in the same spirit, let us note merely that shifts were observed in his creative work both before and after 1926, so that we have chosen that year only as the most vivid illustration of the famous linguist's penchant for change in his diversified activity.

From what has been said it is already perfectly obvious that the whole of N. Ya. Marr's scientific heritage cannot be used equally well, particularly since he was first active as a bourgeois scientist and only later spontaneously adhered to the Marxist-Leninist point of view. Major shortcomings in the work of Soviet linguists result largely from the fact that many of them do not separate in this heritage the extremely valuable accomplishments of the late academician from his erroneous theses, many of which he himself repudiated about 25 years ago.

This inability to distinguish within Marr's heritage can unfortunately be observed even among certain linguistic specialists, not to mention representatives from other sciences, and is to be explained by the continued presence among Soviet scientists of occasional formalist vulgarizers, incapable of rising to a genuine understanding of historical and dialectical materialism. This is a very serious fact and the reason the discussion opened on the pages of Pravda. It is quite timely and necessary.

Prof. Arn. Chikobava's article, a very sharp, harsh and needed one, in our opinion, poses some questions on the wrong plane. We do not intend to enter in direct polemics with the author and shall limit ourselves merely to a feasible elucidation of several urgent questions of the day.

*Pravda, May 30, 1950, p. 4.

†N. Ya. Marr, Selected Works, Vol. II, p. 427.

‡Ibid., Vol. I, p. 1.

Two Kinds of Questions Treated by Marr.

N. Ya. Marr's ideas were extremely versatile and diversified. Nevertheless, if one rises above the details, one can divide into two categories the fundamental questions which interested him and which are in a strict sense linguistic in nature.

To the first belongs all that is connected with initial appearance, the origin of language in general, with "the humanization of the ape" under the influence of primitive work processes, the very first steps of mankind in this direction.

Into the second should be placed all questions connected with the study of the gradual development and spread of voiced languages and language systems in a relatively later period (approximately from the so-called Aurignacian period—some 25,000 to 30,000 years ago).

Naturally, all the questions of the first kind are very controversial and present such enormous difficulties for their final solution that it is hardly possible to expect here convincing results in a short time. Probably many years will yet pass before mankind learns to understand even partially the question of origins of the first communicating gestures and of the simplest articulate sounds—the initial gesture and initial voiced speech on earth.

The first attempt to make sense of these extremely ancient phenomena more or less graphically was made by N. Ya. Marr and reduces itself basically to the theory of the original elements, which he tried to discover in the vocabulary of contemporary languages with the help of the so-called "paleontologic analysis" ("element analysis").

Regardless of the extraordinary ingeniousness of the basic idea, this attempt could not produce anything of practical value in view of the extremely "worn out," "effaced" nature of the ancient roots after their long life, and the complications in almost every word in the form of various suffixes and prefixes, etc., that is, the general obscurity surrounding ancient phenomena due to the accumulation of new, more powerful ones. In addition, N. Ya. Marr himself hesitated a long time in his choice of the number of elements, deciding first on 12, then three or five such initial units; finally he stopped at four—for purely empirical reasons, although he admitted that he could not explain why there were just four of them. It must be said that very many people—linguists, archeologists, ethnographers, historians—tried to include the "four elements" in their work, regardless of N. Ya. Marr's own warnings that the origin of elements goes back to times in which prevoiced speech prevailed, that formal paleontologic analysis "leads and has everywhere led to an endless number of errors,"* that "to utilize the Japhetic theory in history *** is very difficult." †

*Ibid., Vol. II, p. 17.

†Ibid., Vol. III, P. 174.

It is regrettable that all these warnings went unheeded and "element analysis" assumed some very ugly forms in the hands of various kinds of vulgarizers who had no idea how complex these problems were.

In this respect one must agree fully with Prof. A. Chikobava and admit that one of the major weaknesses of our linguistic work has been the distortion, the nonsensical use even to this day of "elements" by occasional vulgarizers, regardless of repeated critical statements in the press by such an authoritative person as Academician I. I. Meshchaninov, who has many times stated that such practices had to end.

Without touching on any of the other problems raised by N. Ya. Marr in the course of trying to explain the initial origin of speech, let us turn now to questions of the second type, connected with the study of later distribution and development of languages and their systems.

Here the contributions of N. Ya. Marr are enormous. However, for a correct understanding of this [contribution], familiarity with a wide range of factual material in many languages of different systems is absolutely essential. This is why many persons have completely underestimated or understood in a distorted way N. Ya. Marr's excellent ideas in this field. Obviously, even here some things have grown obsolete in these 15 years and should be reworked, but the main outline of the picture drawn by N. Ya. Marr is undoubtedly correct, as can be confirmed by the enormous volume of factual material drawn from different languages.

This is not the place to go into detail on this. We shall only say that this picture has no relation whatever to the "four elements" or to any other unproved or erroneous theses. As for the singleness of the glottogonic process and the development of languages by stages, one should indicate the rather serious uncertainty surrounding these concepts, which cannot be applied with any serious validity except to the earliest periods of human thoughts and human language. In later times, languages preserve only insignificant traces of such early conditions—traces which can be revealed with a great deal of labor as a result of meticulous scientific investigation; sometimes they cannot be discovered at all.

It should be recalled, by the way, that towards the end of his life N. Ya. Marr used the term "development by stages" much more warily. In his earlier works we find a different situation: he deliberately allowed himself peculiar "exaggerations," to use his own expression, considering this "an unavoidable methodological technique." *

Therefore, far from everything in these early works should be taken literally. It is particularly difficult to establish an exact concordance among various of N. Ya. Marr's definitions and terms, when to the exaggerations mentioned ("overbending of the stress") is added the fact already referred to, that his views evolved rapidly. We cannot see in his works a formally finished theory, supplying answers for all questions. He too spoke of this repeatedly.

Let us Take the Valuable, Reject the Obsolete.

No Soviet scholar can deny the enormous contributions [made by] N. Ya. Marr in various fields of linguistics. These contributions are in no way limited to Caucasus studies; they are incomparably broader and have basic importance. (Here we have not mentioned many of N. Ya. Marr's indisputable and important accomplishments of a fundamental character, as well as many of his basic errors. There is no way of stating all this within the limits of a newspaper article.)

Discussion should not consist in rejecting all or most of N. Ya. Marr's general ideas and his results but in figuring out how to select from the late scholar's enormous scientific heritage what is actually of value, rejecting the obsolete and erroneous, such as the notorious "classes" ("class-tribal formations" in N. Ya. Marr's words) in pre-class society (paleolithic!). This task is very difficult; but it is feasible; it will necessitate among other things a new edition of N. Ya. Marr's works. The existing one is totally unfit for use, because articles are printed in it in no recognizable order and without editorial explanations and notes. This leaves the young, inexperienced reader completely helpless and at the mercy of Marr's thought, powerful but stormy and not always consistent, eternally searching. Volume V of the Selected Works is compiled in a particularly unsatisfactory way and contains the largest number of obsolete articles. One should also add that the specific examples chosen by N. Ya. Marr to support his frequently profound ideas are, in the majority of cases, unsatisfactory and fail completely. This is understandable: he had no time to search for carefully refined examples—in the heat of struggle he used the first weapon at hand. All this shows that one cannot recommend the "indiscriminate" reading of N. Ya. Marr's work to a beginner: it can do more harm than good.

On the Historical Comparative Method.

The question of the historical comparative method in linquistics, already broached by Prof. A. Chikovava, needs to be mentioned. N. Ya. Marr never denied the legitimacy of such a method. On the contrary, he even planned to extend its [sphere of] application and produce a comparative grammar of various systems. Nevertheless, he objected frequently to the abuse of formal sound correspondences within the framework of any single system of languages. [This abuse] can be observed even now among foreign linguists (particularly Indo-Europeanists and partly also students of Finno-Ugric). N. Ya. Marr's statements on this method contained no few exaggerations, but there also was and is very much that is valuable and incontrovertible. Specifically, it is to him that we are obligated for rejection of the reconstruction of "protolanguages," of fantastic "protopeoples." Only his ideas permit one really to understand the error in such reconstructions, based on tracing back the several languages in a system to an ancestor-language, which was thought of as the main trunk from which branches eventually emerged [as] the individual languages of a given system. The actual process of language formation is incomparably more complicated than this gross and actually false picture—only N. Ya. Marr determined this. However, thanks to his harsh attacks on the comparative method of the Indo-Europeanists, many linguists received the impression that all "comparativism" should be most rigorously avoided. This is, of course incorrect, even from N. Ya. Marr's point of view, because without comparison of forms in various languages, and on a historical plane at that, there can be no scientific linguistics.

But one should not ascribe too much importance to formal phonetic correspondences without semantic analysis and a consideration of the actual historical conditions under which a given word or grammatical form, etc., appeared. Nor should one reject the examination of noticeable similarities (lexical and others) in the material composition and structure of languages of different systems. Only then will the requirements which N. Ya. Marr set for linguists be fulfilled. He only wanted them to reject the narrow, formal comparativism of excessively orthodox Indo-Europeanists with whom he had occasion to struggle; he did not want total rejection of the comparative method. This is why, in spite of Prof. A. Chikobava, we think that this method is applicable also to the new science of language—but in a basically new, completely different version, allowing one to speak of a certain approximation of linguistics to the actual history of language—in the sense of a precise method of investigation.

Unfortunately, because of his stormy and multiple activities, it was simply impossible for N. Ya. Marr to provide models of such comparative investigations of the new type,

*Ibid., Vol. II, p. 118.

and none of his students and followers were inclined in this direction. Besides, a scholar like Academician I. I. Meshchaninov, who took N. Ya. Marr's place, attracted his numerous students primarily in the direction of a profound study of syntax, which in itself is quite important and interesting but which is only one side of the question; it has not furnished an impetus toward full development of the comparative method in the sense discussed above. Here work still lies ahead but, of course, neither within the framework of "element analysis," nor with the prospect of a return to protolanguage notions.

From what has been said above it seems sufficiently clear that the large scientific heritage of N. Ya. Marr is very uneven. One cannot reject the wealth which lies in this heritage, but neither can one blindly, formally, consider everything the originator of the general science of language said and wrote unalterable and infallible.

If we adopt the only correct policy of serious, sober evaluation of the great accomplishments and significant errors of N. Ya. Marr, Soviet linguists will succeed in quickly eliminating the shortcomings mentioned. We know the way to it is led by the Leninist-Stalinist science of the historical process, of which the science of language must also be a part.

Let Us Develop Soviet Linguistics on the Basis of Marxist-Leninist Theory*

By ACADEMICIAN V. VINOGRADOV

The Role of Academician N. Ya. Marr in the History of Soviet Linguistics.

The Soviet science of linguistic culture, of language as the direct reality of thought (K. Marx and F. Engels), as the most important means of human communication (V. Lenin), as a tool of development and struggle (J. Stalin), must occupy an important and honorable place among those social sciences which, guided by a precise knowledge of the laws of social development, are called upon to make an active contribution to the building of a new, socialist culture for humanity.

In the light of the philosophy of dialectical and historical materialism, in the light of what Marx, Engels, Lenin and Stalin taught, Soviet linguistics sees more deeply and broadly the general prospects for investigating the historic laws of the development of human speech in general and the individual languages of the world in particular.

It was natural that on the new paths of Marxist investigation all basic theses and categories of bourgeois linguistics had to undergo critical revision, re-evaluation and change. The task of creating a general theory of materialist, Marxist linguistics was posed sharply and urgently.

One of the first linguists in our country to recognize this task soon after the great October socialist revolution was Academician N. Ya. Marr. He set boldly about making it a reality.

A scholar of unusually wide scientific horizons, historian, ethnographer, archeologist and linguist, with an excellent knowledge of many languages of various systems, N. Ya. Marr began energetically to clear a path for the elaboration of a general materialist science of language. He impetuously overcame old scientific traditions, courageously admitting his numerous previous and equally numerous new errors and freeing himself of them.

The role of Academician N. Ya. Marr in the development of Soviet linguistics is very great. He was the first of the linguists of prerevolutionary training to rid himself of many prejudices of the bourgeois-idealist science of language, and he waged a fierce, uncompromising battle with them in the name of materialist linguistics. He attempted to destroy the whole system of bourgeois formalist comparative-historical linguistics and to replace it with a new universal comparative-historical conception which described from a materialist point of view (utilizing data from the most different languages, representing the most diverse types) the general paths of the development by stages of language and of its dialectic connective, thought, beginning with the stage at which voiced speech originated.

One cannot but be astonished at the great daring of the Soviet scholar, the grandiose nature of his plans, the significance of the results he achieved. The name of N. Ya. Marr has entered the history of Soviet philological science as that of an audacious innovator, the creator of a new materialist conception of the development of human speech, the originator of a broadly ramified linguistic trend, divided into numerous currents.

Although we contemporary Soviet linguists can no longer regard much of linguistics with the eyes of N. Ya. Marr, nevertheless, to a greater or lesser degree, Academician Marr helped and is helping all of us to see and recognize in a new way the goals, tasks and paths of Soviet linguistics.

One way or another, Soviet linguists are continuing the work of Academician Marr when, in the struggle with bourgeois-idealist linguistics, they are elaborating a materialist linguistics, based on Marxism-Leninism.

In the history of the development of Soviet linguistics, N. Ya. Marr incontrovertibly occupies first place among our country's linguists.

On the strength of this, the followers of the great Soviet scholar began to transform his theories into dogma and to view Academician Marr as a compulsory and unavoidable bridge between all Soviet linguists and the classics of Marxism-Leninism, even in those questions which Academician N. Ya. Marr himself never touched on.

Complex, contradictory and, in many points of emphasis, very distant from the practical tasks of contemporary philological education, the doctrine of N. Ya. Marr, without any critical evaluation, has become in recent years the training ground of all young Soviet linguists, who have absorbed it as the full expression of Marxist-Leninist linguistics. In connection with this, a gulf developed between that theory of general linguistics learned by the young investigators and those current problems and questions as yet unsolved, which frequently come up anew from the living needs of Soviet culture. These were questions of technical linguistic specialization which they encountered at every step in their scientific practice and for which they could find no answers in the doctrine of Academician N. Ya. Marr.

"Stagnation in the development of Soviet linguistics" (Pravda, May 9, 1950) became evident to wide circles of Soviet public opinion.

Three Views of the Significance of Academician N. Ya. Marr's Doctrine.

If one should penetrate the thicket of words about the two orientations in Soviet linguistics to the living, historically

*Pravda, June 6, 1950, pp. 3-4.

specific multiplicity of scientific trends in the field of Soviet linguistics, then, leaving aside obsolete, archaic tendencies and moods among our linguists, one must admit that among Soviet students of language three fundamental attitudes toward the doctrine of Academician N. Ya. Marr and his significance for contemporary Soviet linguistics are sharply delineated.

I. According to the first point of view, the Marxist general theory of language has already been created by Academician N. Ya. Marr. It remains only to apply it to various languages, to the investigation of various concrete linguistic questions, "fill out its bases," as it were.

Here are some of the most typical formulations:

"The new science of language, based on Marxist-Leninist methodology, is the general and only scientific theory for all the particular linguistic disciplines."

"*** The only scientific linguistics is the new science of language. No other Marxist linguistics exists or can exist."

"In a political sense the doctrine of N. Ya. Marr, generated by Soviet society, is (in specific linguistic data) a component and organic part of the ideology of socialist society."* (Emphasis in all quotations, mine—V.V.). If one excludes the unintelligible reference to the "specific linguistic materials," then one is left with the affirmation that in all questions of linguistics every Soviet person, every member of Socialist society, must follow blindly and indisputably the doctrine of N. Ya. Marr.

"The enormous body of data accumulated by the old linquistics" can be critically utilized only on the basis of the methodology of N. Ya. Marr's doctrine, on the basis of Marxism-Leninism. And here, when the methodology of N. Ya. Marr's doctrine is not equated with Marxism-Leninism, then Marxism-Leninism comes out second best.

Such an attitude toward Academician N. Ya. Marr's doctrine contradicts those appeals which Academician Marr himself directed to his students. Academician Marr fought vigorously against "passive acceptance" of his work.

The representatives of this point of view are quite numerous all over the Union.

II. According to the second point of view, the foundations of Marxist linguistics have been laid down and established in the works of N. Ya. Marr; a Marxist-Leninist science of language in all its basic theoretical theses can be created only on the basis of Academician N. Ya. Marr's conception, only on the basis of the creative development of his heritage. In accordance with this, N. Ya. Marr's new science of language "continues to develop and to become more precise."†

As one of the main "refinements," there occurred at the end of the thirties the change or, more correctly, the replacement of N. Ya. Marr's paleontologic element analysis with an equally anti-historical, formal comparative analysis of so-called "sentence structure" in languages of different systems. Academician I.I. Meshchaninov wrote the following about it: "Paleontologic analysis according *** to the four elements dropped out some ten years ago, as not corresponding to the basic theses of this analysis. The paleontologic approach to language envisages qualitative shifts in it. This had to happen also to the original word roots. In the progressive march of the historic process they turned into stems of a growing number of words. Under such conditions the four mentioned elements could (?—V.V.) be considered applicable only in a definite period of the development of human speech. These initial periods were studied intensively by Marr himself. His followers during the last 10-15 years have concentrated their work primarily on the historically recorded languages of written and oral speech and particularly on their present condition. Paleontologic analysis was included in just such a framework, limited to the tracing of observable changes in linguistic forms in each separate language and to comparative juxtapositions of this continuing process in different groups of languages in varying systems."*

In this declaration, the hesitation and lack of precision in settling the question are remarkable: paleontologic analysis, so very fundamental in N. Ya. Marr's doctrine, "dropped out some ten years ago," while at the same time it did not drop off; it is being used but "has been restricted" to a narrow framework. What kind of a framework is it? On the one hand, it is "the tracing of changes in linguistic forms in each separate language." But since the beginning of the 19th century any history of language, regardless of its methodological base, has dealt with this, and never has this activity been known as "the paleontologic analysis of Academician N. Ya. Marr." Exactly in the same way, the "juxtaposing" study of the formal grammatical typology in languages of different systems has little to do with Marr's speech paleontology. Thus, the seal of Marr is left, but a new meaning is added to the whole set of corresponding questions. Only the general principle of juxtaposing and comparing the structures of languages of different systems is here inherited from Marr.

In this connection, Marr's term "paleontologic analysis" frequently acquires among this group of representatives of the new science of language a meaning completely contradictory to that given to it by Academician N. Ya. Marr. For example, in the article "The Problem of Stages in the Development of Language," Academician I. I. Meshchaninov writes that the analysis of a word's semantics, analysis of the meaning of a morphologic indicator (for example, the formation of such [Russian] adverbs as "taikom" [secretly], "iskoni" [since time immemorial], etc., from nouns), analysis of the transition of a word from one part of speech to another, etc., deals with "a specific manifestation in its historically recorded life. This will be what we usually call paleontologic analysis***"† In this case, "paleontologic analysis" in no way differs from that which traditional formal comparative-historical linguistics calls historical analysis of a word, a form, etc. Even the criterion of qualitative change in the meaning or function of a word, etc., is here expressed no more clearly than in many conceptions of bourgeois comparative-historical linguistics.

Frequently admissions are made in this connection: "The formal description of linguistic structure should not give grounds for a one-sided emphasis on narrowly formal analysis. Marr demanded that one reveal in the form under investigation its content, its social designation, which as yet are inadequately reflected in scientific investigations."‡

Thus, starting from several of Academician N. Ya. Marr's theses, the representatives of this branch of the new science of language "develop and refine" the basic ideas of Marr in such a peculiar way that nothing, or almost nothing, of Marr is left in them. The result is that Marxist

*F.I. Filin, "On Two Orientations in Linguistics," Journal of the Academy of Sciences, Division of Literature and Linguistics, Vol. VII, No. 6, 1948, pp. 448, 495-6.

†I. I. Meshchaninov, "On the Situation in Linguistic Science," Journal of the Academy of Sciences, Division of Literature and Linguistics, Vol. VII, No. 6, 1948, p. 484.

*I.I. Meshchaninov, "The Works of N. Ya. Marr on Language," Anniversary Symposium of the Academy of Sciences, Devoted to the Thirtieth Anniversary of the Great Socialist Revolution, 1947, pp. 784-5.

†I.I. Meshchaninov, "The Problem of Stages in the Development of Language," Journal of the Academy of Sciences, Division of Literature and Linguistics, Vol. VI, No. 3, 1947, p. 173.

‡I.I. Meshchaninov, "Marr - the Creator of Soviet Linguistics," Journal of the Academy of Sciences, Division of Literature and Linguistics, Vol. VIII, No. 4, 1949, p. 293.

linguistics has so far not been built by N. Ya. Marr and actually cannot be built on the basis of his doctrine alone.

Here is another illustration.

On the basis of the formal-typological comparison of languages of various systems, a chart of development "by stages" of sentence structure was elaborated by representatives of this branch of the new science of language. This formal syntactic development "by stages" of sentence structure is a completely different reckoning by stages than the one found in Academician N. Ya. Marr's doctrine. Of course, the delimitation of several types of sentence structures, characteristic of different languages in the world, is important for linguistics. But to make a given type of sentence structure the basis for characterizing the whole structure of the language, and to determine the stage of its development according to this criterion, is unhistorical. In this case the concrete historical-materialist study of the whole syntactic structure of the language is replaced by the analysis of subject-object relations within a type of sentence (i.e. the clarification of relations of subject and predicate or, more simply still, of the predicate [in relation] to subject and object). What is more, such analysis does not require from the investigator an intelligent, live knowledge—i.e., a social understanding—of the language under analysis.

One of the partisans of this formal linguistic exercise admits: "An obviously incomplete picture was obtained: the subject-object sentence structure was equated with the structure of the language as a whole." * And at the same time, as is generally known, different kinds of sentence structure (and therefore, allegedly also different stages in the development of sentence structure) can coexist in the same language, for example, in contemporary Georgian or Chukchee. In this connection, Prof. A.S. Chikobava correctly states: "Apparently, the elaboration of a chart of development by stages can lead to tangible results only if it is erected not deductively and a priori, but inductively, by languages, taking full account of the history of these languages. ***"†

Naturally, under the influence of incontrovertible linguistic facts, in 1947 Academician I.I. Meshchaninov had to give up his chart of the formal development by stages of sentence structures. He became convinced, on the one hand, that sentence structure can remain outwardly the same, but that "its meaning changes;" therefore, very little attention had been paid until then to the meaning aspect of sentences. On the other hand, various sentence structures coexist side by side in the same language. Therefore, "stages and transformations in them" are as yet undetermined. "To define the various stages and their transformations, given the complexity of their dialectic conditioning, must *** [be done] first of all by analyzing the historic path of the language's development using specific and carefully checked data from each separate language***" (with comparative digressions to languages of other systems). "Transitions by stages can be traced through the data of individual languages, even individual linguistic groups (families). Perhaps it will be possible to reveal also a general scheme of transitions by stages." ‡

A new path in the study of stages is indicated: the study of a given language in its historical context, then the comparison of languages of a single group (family) and, as a last step, comparison of languages of different systems in their typological and stage analogies. Then "the concept of stage will be refined."

It is apparent that these critical observations cannot replace the Marxist, historical-materialist treatment of the question of development by stages of language and thought, conditioned by the laws of social development. After all, the problem of stages in linguistic development was broached (true, from an idealist position) even by A.A. Potebnya in the '60s and '80s of the 19th century.

Thus "the problem of stages in the development of language" in its new formulation, radically different from N. Ya. Marr's doctrine of stages in the development of linguistic semantics, collapses. Here, too, special attention must be called to the complete substitution for Academician N. Ya. Marr's doctrine of the development of the vocabulary and semantics of language by stages connected with social development of a completely different, formal doctrine of the development of sentence structure by stages. The form was left the same, but it was given a completely different content.

Even the editorial of Izvestia akademii nauk, Otdeleniye literatury i yazyka (Vol. VIII (1949), No. 6, "The Present-day Position and Tasks of Soviet Linguistics") states that "the elaboration of problems of development by stages of the world's languages from the positions outlined by Academician N. Ya. Marr has stopped almost completely" (p. 506).

Thus on many fundamental questions the development and refinement of Academician N. Ya. Marr's doctrine has not yet given such reliable and tangible results as could be boldly presented in university lecture halls under the name of Marxist-Leninist general theory of language (compare the evolution of Academician I.I. Meshchaninov's views in the books "The New Science of Language," "General Linguistics" and "Parts of the Sentence and Parts of Speech").

Meanwhile some linguists mechanically unite very different points of view under the name of a single "conception of a 'new science of language' created by N. Ya. Marr and I.I. Meshchaninov and which is Soviet Marxist linguistics."*

All this is simply to illustrate the idea that many of the representatives of the new science of language in their own scientific activity do not try to solve the fundamental problems of general linguistics solely on the basis of N. Ya. Marr's doctrine, but actually depart from his main theses. Marr's problem-setting is important for them, but not his methodology. That which they dogmatically accept in Marr's specific linguistic doctrine most frequently is beyond their direct, real scientific-research interests (Marr's theory of the origin of language, of manual and voiced speech, the general principle of linguistic development by stages, sometimes comparative paleontologic analysis and such).

A number of very general and frequently very valuable ideas of N. Ya. Marr about language and thought and about language and society are an attempt to apply the teachings of Marxist-Leninist classics to linguistic theory, but they sometimes lead to obviously erroneous conclusions due to the antihistorical way in which the class nature of language is understood. Also, the rejection of the genealogic classification of languages ("theory of protolanguage"), the call for the juxtaposition of languages of various systems, the effort (almost completely forgotten among the majority of linguists of this kind) to "connect" linguistics with history, archeology and ethnography—all these do not, of course, exhaust the whole essence and the whole content of Marxist linguistics.

"The developers and refiners" of Academician N. Ya. Marr's doctrine leave him and go off in various directions. They go for ideas to A.A. Potebnya, to A.A. Shakhmatov, to foreign bourgeois linguists like I. Trier. In practice, that is, through their works, one can see that in their own

*"A Discussion of the Problem of Classification by Stages in Linguistics," Journal of the Academy of Sciences, Division of Literature and Linguistics, Vol. VI, No. 3, 1947, p. 259.

†Arn. Chikobava, "Historical Mutual Relations of Nominative and Ergative Constructions According to the Data of the Archaic Georgian Language," Journal of the Academy of Sciences, Division of Literature and Linguistics, Vol. VII, No. 3, 1948, p. 234.

‡I.I. Meshchaninov, "The Problem of Stages in the Development of Language," Op. Cit., pp. 187-8.

*N.S. Chemodanov, "Structuralism and Soviet Linguistics," Journal of the Academy of Sciences, Division of Literature and Linguistics, Vol. VI, No. 2, 1947, p. 115.

scientific research practice they do not admit the possibility of limiting themselves to the general linguistic theory created by N. Ya. Marr. Nevertheless, they call upon Marr's name even while they are rejecting his basic conclusions and principles. The name of N. Ya. Marr seems to them sufficient guarantee for the Marxist nature of all their theories.

III. According to the third point of view, Marxist-Leninist general linguistics cannot lock itself within the framework of the so-called new science of language and [cannot] be based on it alone. The new science of language did not solve all the problems of Marxist theoretical linguistics; it did not even solve many of the most urgent current problems of our contemporary Soviet life (for example, the language of a socialist nation, the basic regularities in the development of languages of socialist nations, the formation of languages in bourgeois nations, the general literary language of a people in the period before the formation of nations, and many others). The solution to many questions proposed by Academician N. Ya. Marr, and later by his followers of different tendencies, cannot be considered final and Marxist. In N. Ya. Marr's doctrine the fundamental premises and categories of Marxist-Leninist linguistics are either in no way illuminated or are presented in obviously erroneous, distorted interpretations contradicting the theories of Marx, Engels, Lenin and Stalin.

The creative elaboration of Marxism-Leninism in the works of J. V. Stalin during the fifteen years since Marr's [death], our ever-deepening study of Marxist-Leninist philosophy, the growing interest in the problems of dialectic logic, the accomplishments of Soviet historical science—all this cannot but be reflected in radical changes in the actual phrasing of many linguistic problems when compared with that period of the Soviet era when Academician Marr was alive and working. Why then must the Marxist investigation of all the problems of general linguistics and of all those erroneously solved by N. Ya. Marr (for example, the question of the origin of language, of the single language in mankind's future, of the historical regularities in the development of language in pre-class and class societies, etc.) and those which remain unsolved and even those never raised by Academician N. Ya. Marr— [why must they] be considered the creative development of the linguistic heritage of N. Ya. Marr and not simply the elaboration of Marxist linguistics on the basis of the theories of Marx, Engels, Lenin and Stalin?

It is particularly difficult to be locked within the framework of the new science of language for those linguists who are concerned with the study of contemporary languages, the concrete history of a given language in connection with the history of the given people, or with the investigation of a group (family) of closely related languages. Such are the majority of our linguists. In Academician N. Ya. Marr's theories one can find numerous sharp, interesting, valuable ideas referring to this whole set of questions; but one can find there neither a precise and complete dialeccal-materialist definition of those linguistic or historical concepts which a research linguist of this kind can use as a starting point nor a broad, consistent reconstruction of the history of any language or group (family) of languages which would satisfy the requirements of contemporary Marxist science. For example, our Slavic linguistics obviously needs vitalization and renovation. One can resolutely affirm that Academician N. Ya. Marr's doctrine has not answered concretely and cannot answer the question of how to study Slavic languages in their history, in their relationships, mutual influences, subdivisions and differentiations from oldest times, since the very times of origin of the family of Slavic peoples and languages.

The concepts of "social convergence" and "social divergence" of languages are very general and historically indefinite. Academician N. Ya. Marr did not clarify the main types and laws of such convergences and divergences in various epochs of development in human society, in various socio-economic formations, in various kinds of productive relations, in all the multiplicity of concrete historical conditions. One cannot accept as clear the "conclusion" drawn from Academician N. Ya. Marr's general propositions by Academician I. I. Meshchaninov (I am replacing the reference in the quotation to Romance languages with corresponding parallels from Slavic languages): "If Slavic languages, including Russian and Ukrainian, arose from the blending of several other languages and reveal numerous common features, then in these converging so-called Slavic languages similar components participated in the same way in which they participated in the formation of the respective peoples, later nations. Thus are created the historically formed similarities between languages which are classified by groups." (Pravda, May 16, 1950.)

It is hard to imagine what this conclusion contributes to a graduate student or a budding Slavist. But here is what it means to a learned linguist and here is how this principle of convergence and divergence of various languages is used in actual practice: In his "Grammar of the Literary Kabardinian-Cherkess Language" (1948), Prof. N. F. Yakovlev deals with the ancient connections of Cherkess tribes, speakers of a language of amorphous structure, with the Eastern Slavs (this amorphous structure of the Adighe language "was still alive and quite strong" even in the 13th-15th centuries A. D. but was connected, according to Yakovlev, with the stage of savagery of the people "before the appearance and development of pastoral tribes"). He writes: "Place names such as Cherkassy in the Ukraine and Novocherkassk in the Don region serve as proof of the participation of Cherkess (Adighe) ethnic elements in the formation of the Ukrainian people." *

This kind of opinion and conclusion frequently leads the student of the history of Slavic languages into an impasse, and one should not be greatly surprised at the stagnation in the area of Soviet Slavic linguistics.

Nor should one be astonished at the fact that many Soviet investigators of specific languages, not finding in Academician N. Ya. Marr's doctrine any firm answer to the question perturbing them and honestly thinking Academician N. Ya. Marr's attempted answers impracticable and outside their ken (as a consequence of ignorance or inadequate knowledge of many other languages of various systems and their history), sometimes follow the path of least resistance in their specific research work, turning themselves over to our own bourgeois linguistic traditions or unwisely callfor help from foreign Varangians, turning to the "theories" of West European idealist linguists.

Of course all such anti-Marxist errors, deviations from the highway of Soviet materialist linguistics (of which I too am guilty), must be criticized and rejected resolutely, severely, thoroughly and with full knowledge of the matter at hand.

One cannot think that Academician N. Ya. Marr's doctrine is the only panacea for all linguistic illnesses. For example, in research on the history of the Russian literary language a thorough study of the Marxist-Leninist classics, their independent creative application to the uninvestigated questions of the language's history, and the combination of linguistic interests with cultural, historical, philosophical and literary ones, will contribute more than N. Ya. Marr's doctrine, which almost never touches the question of historical regularities in the development of literary languages from the point of view of historical materialism.

Thus, one need not reject all that is theoretically valuable and practically useful in the works of Academician N. Ya. Marr. It is necessary to re-examine critically his linguistic heritage, to take into account the extremely valuable scientific research effort of Marr and simultaneously his vulgar materialist errors in general linguistic theoretical

*Works of the Tsulikidze Kutaisi State Pedagogical Institute, Vol. IX, 1949, p. 136.

formulations. [It is necessary] to elaborate a Marxist-Leninist linguistics, free of all fetters, on the basis of the Marxist-Leninist classics, the accomplishments of Soviet historical and philosophical science, through the comradely common efforts of Soviet linguists, who must master the method of materialist dialectics.

Into this broad program, as a part of it, will naturally enter also the task of creative development and critical re-examination of the linguistic heritage of Academician N. Ya. Marr.

On Attitudes Toward the Prerevolutionary Linguistic Heritage.

The accomplishments of the preceding history of native Russian linguistics will be appraised depending on the various points of view as to whether Marxist linguistics has already been created in our country or whether it is still in process of creation. A great many representatives of the new science of language reject almost all previous Russian phililogical science. "Indulgences" are issued only for Lomonosov and Potebnya, while N. G. Chernyshevsky is viewed as N. Ya. Marr's predecessor. The views and accomplishments of individual Russian linguists of the past are analyzed not in their complex contradictions— in relation to their general world view, as a reflection of the social and historical conditions of society's life and class struggle—not in connection with the concrete historical study of the struggle between materialist and idealist ideas in the history of Russian social thought and Russian philological science, but only "on the basis of the methodology of Academician N. Ya. Marr's doctrine." This is why even questions of the priority of Russian philological science of the past, which in many areas of linguistic research was far ahead of Western European bourgeois linguistics, do not arise for the followers of N. Ya. Marr. Their rejection extends formally to the whole area of Russian prerevolutionary theoretical linguistics. It is self-evident that such rejection in no way precludes following (sometimes very uncritically) the theories and theses of Russian bourgeois linguists, for example, the works of A. A. Potebnya, A. A. Shakhmatov and others on syntax.

Academician N. Ya. Marr is himself in no way guilty of such contempt for the history of native Russian philological science. Nevertheless, in no other area of Soviet humanities is such nihilism regarding the accomplishments of Russian prerevolutionary philology so widespread as in the field of linguistics. And yet, after the discussions of the last few years on ideological questions, we all remember the remark of Comrade A. A. Zhdanov on Marxist philosophy:

"Marxist philosophy***is an instrument of scientific research, a method penetrating all natural and social sciences and enriching itself with the data of these sciences as they develop. In this sense Marxist philosophy is the most complete and decisive negation of all previous philosophies. But to negate, as Engels emphasized, does not mean just to say 'no.' Negation includes succession, means the absorption, the critical reworking and unification in a new, higher synthesis of all that is advanced and progressive, that has already been achieved in the history of human thought."* This point of view might also have been used in undertaking an appropriate critical appraisal of Academician N. Ya. Marr's linguistic doctrine itself.

V. I. Lenin wrote: "Marxism is distinguished***by a wonderful combination of complete scientific sobriety in the analysis of the objective state of things and the objective course of evolution with a most definite recognition of the importance of revolutionary energy, revolutionary creativity, revolutionary initiative of the masses and, of course, of individual persons as well***"†

In concluding this subject of attitudes toward our leading

*A.A. Zhdanov, Problems of Philosophy, 1947, Vol. I, pp. 259-60.

†V.I. Lenin, Works, 4th edition, Vol. XIII, pp. 21-2.

native philologists of the past, I should like to remind some of our exposing linguists of the remarkable words of J. V. Stalin about anarchists: "They know that Hegel was conservative and so, taking advantage of this fact, they loudly condemn Hegel as an advocate of 'restoration'***why do they do this? Probably so as to discredit Hegel and get the reader to feel that the 'reactionary' Hegel's method likewise cannot but be 'disgusting' and unscientific.

"In this way the anarchists hope to refute the dialectical method.

"We say that this way they will prove nothing but their own ignorance. Pascal and Leibnitz were not revolutionaries, but the mathematical method they discovered is recognized today as a scientific method. Mayer and Helmholtz were not revolutionaries, but their discoveries in physics lie at the foundation of science. Nor were Lamarck and Darwin revolutionaries, but their evolutionary method put biological science on its feet***why can it not be recognized that, regardless of Hegel's conservatism, he was able to work out a scientific method, called dialectical?

"No, the anarchists will prove nothing this way but their own ignorance."*

The Chief Obstacle in the Study of Contemporary Languages.

In the leading article of Izvestia akademii nauk, Otdeleniye literatury i yazyka [Journal of the U. S. S. R. Academy of Sciences, Division of Literature and Linguistics] (Vol. VIII, 1949, No. 6), the following statement appears: "***N. Ya. Marr created a general theory of linguistics, clarifying the basic phenomena of speech, beginning with the epoch of its origin to the flowering of national languages in a socialist society" (p. 502).

This is, of course, an extreme exaggeration. N. Ya. Marr did not raise or settle the question of developmental patterns in the languages of socialist nations. Nor can it be said that the solid, materialist, Marxist bases for the elaboration of a national language's history were laid with Academician N. Ya. Marr's doctrine. On the contrary, one can definitely say that antihistoricity in the reconstruction of the history of a specific language is a characteristic trait of the overwhelming majority of the works which subscribe to the new science of language.

The question naturally arises: is it possible, from within the vicious circle of Academician N. Ya. Marr's new science of language, to study, describe and explain the structure of such a developed language as, for example, modern Russian, thoroughly, from a dialectical materialist point of view? After all, if the general Marxist theory of language has already been created by Academician N. Ya. Marr, and if the new doctrine is the only basis for the elaboration of the separate linguistic disclipines, it is precisely to it that one ought to refer for Marxist-Leninist explanations of all basic linguistic categories: the sentence, word order, the word, phraseological unity, a complex sentence, a complex syntactic whole, the various grammatical, lexical, and stylistic categories, —in brief, all the main concepts which determine the general approach and methods in the study of modern Russian. Does the general linguistic theory of Academician N. Ya. Marr offer us much for such a study? Very little. And in this sense Prof. A. S. Chikobava is correct, albeit uncompromisingly harsh: "All the positive things that are being done in this connection (preparation of grammars and dictionaries, be they for school use or historical in nature, the elaboration of rules for the literary language, etc.) are being done despite the linguistic theory of Academician N. Ya. Marr, for the simple reason that in solving the many problems indicated we cannot expect any help from element analysis" (Pravda, May 9, 1950).

Actually the problem of the sentence in its relation to thought, the problem of historical regularities in the origin and development of various kinds of sentences in languages

*J.V. Stalin, Works, Vol. I, pp. 302-3.

belonging to different systems and in the history of a particular language, from the point of view of dialectical and historical materialism, are completely unsolved in N. Ya. Marr's doctrine. In his "General Course on Language" Marr offers the following definition of the sentence (apparently for structures of all inflected languages): "The sentence is an expression, by means of words which signalize notions and ideas, of a definite thought reflecting the mutual relations of the words in the sentence; the relationships of objects find formal expression through word alternation especially for that purpose -- what in grammar is called declension. This is achieved not only through expression of the mutual relationships of the objects but also through agreement of the words designating these objects, just as in life the members of any productive organization are coordinated."*

The general materialist orientation of this definition of the sentence is unmistakable. But equally unmistakable is the mechanical, vulgar, straight and direct transfer of general sociological categories and ideas into the sphere of grammatical relations, which is typical of Marr's materialism (the analogy between word concordance and the concordance in life of the members of any productive organization). In addition, Marr's definition of a sentence stands outside history and therefore is static and metaphysical. This is why Soviet linguists do not use this Marrian definition of a sentence.

In his work "General Linguistics," Academician I. I. Meshchaninov defined the sentence as follows: "The sentence*** represents an integral grammatically shaped unit, expressing the direct reality of thought."† It is known that Marx and Engels characterized language as the direct reality of thought.‡ Therefore Academician I. I. Meshchaninov's definition of the sentence is unclear and imprecise. After all, the same can also be said about the word, and, if "unit" is used in a different sense, about language as a whole. This is why in another of his works, "Parts of the Sentence and the Parts of Speech," Academician I. I. Meshchaninov preferred to use the definition of the sentence which was given by Academician A. A. Shakhmatov.

Naturally, in the theoretical study of the problem of the sentence in its relation to thought, from the position of dialectical materialist logic, it is necessary to start from the Leninist theory of reflection and from the leads given by V. I. Lenin in his article "On the Question of Dialectics."

From this point of view one should describe the main kinds of sentences in every language in their relation to reality and the forms of thought, taking into account the over-all peculiarities of a given language's structure and the possible conflicts and lack of connections between form and content. According to the nature of the [various] reflections of reality, one can distinguish the modal varieties of sentences, for example, in Russian: the imperative, diverse meaning variants of the interrogative, etc. The category of modality, expressing the relation of speech to reality, remains completely unexplored in the context of a general Marxist theory of language. And yet, the importance of its dialectical materialist clarification is obvious. It is well known that elaboration of sentence theory in idealist, West European bourgeois linguistics is in an impasse. According to one of the latest calculations (that of the German Romance language scholar, Lerch), the number of different definitions of the sentence is already above 200.

The words of F. Engels on dialectical logic are well known: "Dialectical logic, in contradistinction to the old, purely formal logic, is not content to enumerate and juxtapose without connection the forms of movement of thought, i. e., the various forms of thought and inference. On the contrary, it deduces these forms one from another, it established between them a relationship of subordination and not of coordination; it develops higher forms from lower ones.*

Naturally, this same problem is faced also by the general theory of language in view of the dialectical connection between language and thought. In this context the study of simple and complex sentences, as well as that of more complex syntactic units, has hardly begun in Soviet linguistics, either in relation to living modern languages or in relation to the history of forms and types of sentences in the history of individual languages. In any case, Academician N. Ya. Marr's doctrine cannot be of any assistance in this area.

One can derive much more valuable leads from the words of Academician N. Ya. Marr on the question of the Marxist theory of the word and its meaning, on other questions of semantics. Words, says N. Ya. Marr, have no other meanings "beyond those generated by a given order, created by a given economic life and the world view emerging from this structure."† One must admit that the materialist doctrine of Academician N. Ya. Marr concerning the word and its meaning, "the laws of semantics," is a qualitatively new stage in the history of the treatment of problems in historical lexicology. And this represents an even greater accomplishment of Marr when one considers that our native science even in the prerevolutionary period, transcending its contemporary bourgeois West European linguistics in this field, proposed and defended the principle of regularity (and not accident) in the semantic changes of words (the works of A. A. Potebnya and Academician M. M. Pokrovsky).

N. Ya. Marr proposed the theses about the historical changeability of the category "word" itself, about qualitative transformations in its social perception, conditioned by the history of material culture, the history of the means of production, and connected with various stages in the development of thought. Nevertheless, N. Ya. Marr was not able to determine the historical regularities of semantic changes in words at the various stages in the development of a language and [was unable] to connect these regularities with the laws of the history of the life of society discovered by Marxism. He used a very dubious and unreliable, almost a fantastic instrument—paleontologic element analysis. However, there is reason to believe that N. Ya. Marr (as distinguished from the majority of his followers), in theory, did not consider the paleontologic element analysis he used to be universal, equally applicable to all stages and in all periods of a language's development; i. e., [it was not] completely metaphysical.

"***The technique of word construction was not only formally but also ideologically different, as thought itself was at various stages of human development," wrote Academician N. Ya. Marr. "The point is not only that before the telegraph, the telephone and the airplane there were no corresponding words, but also that words were not put together as they are [now]. Nor were the words put together as are the more common words, for example, in the Russian word 'sozdatel' [creator], 'sovest' [conscience] ***These words [belong] to periods of logical thinking, words built according to a plan, thought through logically, and not through association of images and the functions connected with them."‡ Essentially this means that [in dealing] with the concrete history of the lexical systems of any developed language, for example, Russian, paleontologic element analysis is generally inapplicable (even from N. Ya. Marr's point of view).

In the area of the history of a language, Academician N. Ya. Marr's doctrine gives some very general indications

*N. Ya. Marr, "General Course on Language," Selected Works, Vol. II, p. 49.

†I.I. Meshchaninov, General Linguistics, Leningrad, 1940, p. 27.

‡K. Marx and F. Engels, Works, Vol. IV, p. 434.

*F. Engels, Dialectics of Nature, 1934, p. 100.

†N. Ya. Marr, Selected Works, Vol. II, p. 198.

‡Ibid., p. 418.

of the need to proceed in the historical study of the vocabulary from the real filiation of meanings "established by their evolution, which keeps step with the evolution of the history of material culture and social relations." * But for use in the study of the contemporary lexical system (vocabulary) of any language, one can extract from Academician N. Ya. Marr's doctrine only some abstract suggestions to study words in a language system in connection with the social world view, as "a product of social life," to take into account the mutual influence of lexical and grammatical meanings as well as the dialectical connection between word and sentence. Such statements do not [exactly] contradict the main theses of Marxist-Leninist classics, but they do not give a worked out Marxist definition or description of the word and of meaning on either a philosophical or historical linguistic level.

We do not even have as yet a completely satisfactory and full definition of the word for even modern Russian and languages of the same system; we still lack a description of the meaning content or the semantic structure of the word at various stages of the development of language and for languages of different systems; we still do not have a thorough and many-sided historical materialist explanation of patterns in the connection between the meanings of words and the history of social ideologies and material culture. Consequently, in the area of word semantics also, the modern investigator of the living [spoken] language is forced (while taking into account the general principles of the semantic doctrine of Academician N. Y. Marr) to turn directly to the guiding instructions of Marxist-Leninist classics for a correct dialectical materialist and historical statement of the word as a linguistic unit designating and generalizing objects and phenomena of reality [which are] reflected in social consciousness.

It is natural to proceed from here to the question of grammatical categories as direct or indirect reflections of social experience. What does Academician N. Ya. Marr's doctrine offer the Soviet linguist in this direction? Not much. In Marr's words, a language's grammatical structure also touches very closely upon the laws of semantics. "Semantics possesses its own grammar with its own morphology." † The socially conditioned, qualitative transformations in the semantics of words are connected with radical qualitative changes in the grammatical structure of language. In this area too one can discern the materialist direction of Academician N. Ya. Marr's theory. Grammatical categories and meanings, according to Marr, are generated by social life and reflect objective reality. But how? This remains unclear. N. Ya. Marr pointed to the fact that in inflected languages (such as Russian) grammatical meanings acquired a very abstract character. "Inflected morphology, whether it be declension or conjugation," writes Academician Marr, "appears to us as an expression in the superstructure, of course, merely as a reflection of external relations between objects in space or time, expressed with the aid of signs, which mean nothing more than these merely abstract relations, without reference to objects and their peculiarities in a social or individual context." ‡

N. Ya. Marr distinguishes a later "grammar divorced from life" and ancient grammar, apparently immersed, as it were, in life. In the most ancient stages of linguistic development, grammatical forms and categories apparently reflect directly social relations, the real content of life. The threshold of the stage separating these types of grammatical "thought" is unclear in N. Ya. Marr's [works], which is perniciously reflected in the ideas about historical grammar held by the followers of the new science of language. Thus, Prof. N. F. Yakovlev, in his "Grammar of the

*Ibid., Vol. III, p. 242.

†Ibid., Vol. I, p. 190.

‡Ibid., Vol. II, p. 310.

Khabardin-Cherkess Literary Language," writes: "Originally, at the initial level of development of the primitive community, due to the direct connection of language and thought with man's material activity, logical and grammatical forms coincided with their real content. In a class society, due to the transformation of language into a superstructure, grammatical forms and the forms of thought find themselves in many cases in contradiction both with each other and with their real content" (p. 26).

The most remarkable part of this reasoning is the statement that language became a superstructural category only in class society. What is the root of this mistake? In such "laws" of the direct expression of class relations in grammatical categories according to Academician N. Ya. Marr's doctrine: "***Degrees of comparison are of social origin. They are a superstructure of a class, estate, order. At that, the word utilized now to indicate a higher grade, be it comparative or superlative, once expressed not one or the other of the higher grades of that idea, which is [now] expressed through an adjective with which it has coalesced (sic-V. V.), but [it expressed] membership in that higher stratum, be it an estate or a class, which was ruling, without any additional indicator (suffix or prefix) [and] its name, [its] totem—was socially evaluated as a high degree. The suffix, a word with the same function of forming a degree of comparison, actually indicated membership in the corresponding ruling stratum*** Degrees of comparison, like adjectives generally, receive [definite] form only after clan society***" *

Can one apply this theory about the grammatical category [viewed] as a simple, direct activity of passive reflection (Lenin, "Philosophical Notebooks" [in Russian] (1938), p. 336), even if it be of social origin, to the study of contemporary languages? Obviously not.

One could point also to a series of linguistic categories which did not receive any dialectical materialist explanation in Academician N. Ya. Marr's and his followers' doctrine (for example, the so-called "meaning categories") but even as it is it is clear that Academician N. Ya. Marr's theory does not give the student of living modern languages a Marxist method for the study of their grammar and vocabulary.

The History of Language and the Doctrine of "Stage Transitions."

According to Academician N. Ya. Marr's doctrine each language makes up one of the links of the single glottogonic (language forming) process: "It is the result of complicated historical blendings," "of convergences and divergences" of various languages. So too, for example, is the Russian language. According to the words of Prof. F. P. Filin, who collected Academician N. Ya. Marr's comments on the Russian language, many tribes and peoples, later nations, united one way or another through a community of socio-economic conditions, took part in both the process of creation of the Russian language as well as in its further development up to the present.

Given such views one cannot really speak of the originality [independent existence] of the Russian language, the Russian people and Russian culture. In the struggle with bourgeois nationalism it was important to N. Ya. Marr to emphasize strongly the international foundations of the Russian language, its primordial connection with other languages in the U.S.S.R. "From this the new science of language draws the conclusion that there is historical community [oneness] between Russian and the languages of many other Union nationalities; genetically they are interwoven among themselves in the preceding stage of development." † One thing

* Ibid., p. 278.

† F. Filin, "Genetic Mutual Relations of Russian with the Languages of Other U.S.S.R. Peoples in the Works of N. Ya. Marr," Symposium of the All-Soviet Central Committee on the New Alphabet [Dedicated to] N. Ya. Marr, Moscow, 1936, p. 130.

only is not explained: why the grammatical structure and the material composition of Russian and, for example, of Georgian or Esthonian, are completely different. Given such methodological purpose in Academician N. Ya. Marr's doctrine in proving the "community" of all languages in the world, the complex "hybrid nature" of every language, one can understand his statements that "languages of one and the same class in different countries, given an identical social structure, display more similarity of type to each other than do languages of different classes of one and the same country or one and the same nation."*

This thesis is, of course, antihistorical. Thus, in a feudal era, it is possible that different languages co-exist among different social groups of one and the same people (usually, true enough—for different social functions), but, in the period of capitalist development, within the nation's borders there reigns a language common to the nation. In addition, N. Ya. Marr thought that a language's grammar was created by a class and not by the people. All this tells us that Academician N. Ya. Marr's doctrine cannot serve as a reliable and incontrovertible base for the reconstruction of the history of a language.

In this case one must start directly from the theories of Marxist-Leninist classics about kinds of productive relations, about socio-economic formations, about regularities in social development in the feudal era, during feudalism's decay and the emergence of bourgeois relations, about basic class contradictions and divisions in every era and types of social world views historically conditioned by social relations (after all "whatever a people's pattern of life—so the pattern of their thoughts," according to J. V. Stalin's aphoristic formula).† It is on this foundation that the concrete history of each language must be erected—while taking into account the individual historical pecularities of its development. And yet, in this area of investigation, for example, in relation to literary Russian of the feudal era, conditions in our country are obviously in a bad way. There is much talk of the all-Russian basis of the literary language of Kievan Russia. However, the class basis and class differences in ancient literary Russian, in its lexical and semantic system, as well as the survivals in its structure and vocabulary of preceding stages of development, are left unclarified, uninvestigated.

Academician N. Ya. Marr's doctrine can offer us even less positive [help] in solving the question of the formation of national languages and their paths of development in capitalist and socialist society. The new formulation of the question of the nation, the formation of national languages, the growth of national languages in capitalist and socialist societies, given in the works of V. I. Lenin and J. V. Stalin, was not sufficiently utilized by Academician N. Ya. Marr. The teaching of Lenin and Stalin on national languages defines the fundamental historical varieties or types of national language formation and the fundamental historical regularities in the functioning of these processes.

Essentially, a national literary language is a qualitatively new system of literary language, whose roots go deep into popular foundations. J. V. Stalin's thoughts on bourgeois and socialist nations introduce essential new corrections in the Marxist theory of the formation and development of national languages. The study of class stratifications in the language of a bourgeois nation and of the class orientation of the various styles in the national literary language under conditions of bourgeois development are intimately connected with the elaboration of a historical study of style in literary language, the study of styles as systems of expression for class ideology. This task was completely alien to N. Ya. Marr.

Meanwhile, under the influence of the same struggle against bourgeois nationalism, one can observe in Academician N. Ya. Marr's doctrine some overt distortions of the Marxist understanding of national speech.

For N. Ya. Marr the national language is a class [phenomenon], be it a feudal, bourgeois or petty-bourgeois, "so-called national language which claims to be of the whole people."* "There is no common national language, but there is a class language***"†

In his article "Writing and Language" N. Ya. Marr introduces some refinements in his previous understanding of national language not only as a class, bourgeois [fact] but as a "dead and***stabilized" language. He writes: "In 'Language and Writing' emphasis was placed on the fact that when education turned into a weapon for ideologically lulling to sleep vital working class movements, writing (previously the property of only the ruling classes) was given to the masses, democratized just in order to quiet the class conscious stirring of the working people and to enslave ideologically the oppressed, to forestall or liquidate incipient revolutionary movements of exploited social strata*** In reality, though the national written language was bourgeois or feudal-bourgeois, nevertheless, in the period of its growth and flowering, it was in no way dead and stabilized; it was a live standardized language of the ruling social stratum. It could not be otherwise: it was created by social strata once young, drawing their creative organizing forces from the tools of a new high technology that they had conquered. These strata carried language to a wider and more creative community, struggling with the limited ideological views and sluggishness of social strata historically doomed to destruction." ‡

Lenin's teaching of two cultures and two nations within the borders of each nation in the period of capitalist development remained unknown to N. Ya. Marr. This is why he held on to his peculiarly phrased theory of "a single stream" in the evolution and understanding of the several paths of development of the literary, national linguistic culture in the capitalist era. It is self-evident that N. Ya. Marr could not have used Stalin's teaching about the socialist nation and, as the basis of it, have posed the question of regularities in the development of languages in socialist nations.

All this indicates that Academician N. Ya. Marr's doctrine has lagged far behind Marxist-Leninist theory of social development, just the one which must underlie the building of a Marxist history of language. Such a truly scientific, Marxist, materialist history of language can be contrasted without fear by Soviet linguists with any other history of language elaborated from idealist bases (that is, all kinds of bourgeois idealist histories of language).

The Study of Groups (Families) of Related Languages.

After over 100 years of almost unchallanged dominance, bourgeois formal comparative-historical linguistics has now reached an impasse. The antihistorical theories of "protolanguages," which lead deep into Biblical tales and idealist romantic illusions about a single initial human language, were dealt some shattering blows by N. Ya. Marr. To the majority of N. Ya. Marr's followers it seemed that under these blows the concept of "kinship" between languages and the concept of a group or "family" of related languages should have also collapsed. The concept of "protolanguage" in bourgeois West European linguistics is a metaphysical one. It does not rest on any historical material foundation and is utilized in the formal and simplified reconstruction of the common or initial language of very distinct families and groups of languages, which came into being in very distant prehistoric and historic eras. Naturally, the term "pro-

*N. Ya. Marr, Selected Works, Vol. II, p. 415.

†History of the Communist Party of the Soviet Union (Short Course), p. 116.

*N. Ya. Marr, Selected Works, Vol. II, p. 355.

†Ibid., p. 415.

‡Ibid., pp. 380-1.

tolanguage" and the concept which goes with it must be rejected by Soviet linguistics. But does this mean that, along with the concept of "protolanguage" and "proto-homeland," one should throw out those incontrovertible facts of material unity and closeness, of material kinship of such languages as, for example, the Slavic: Russian, Polish, Czech, etc., or even more closely: Russian, Belorussian and Ukrainian (where we presuppose a common Slavic base)? Obviously not. These facts demand explanation. There is no concrete historical explanation of all these phenomena of kinship and connection between languages and groups (families) of languages which led to their geneologic classification in N. Ya. Marr's doctrine of the development of language by stages. N. Ya. Marr was looking for new avenues for the solution of all these problems, on the principle of thesis and antithesis, very frequently falling into "contradictory general statements."

By radically denying the geneologic classification of language, he wanted to discover the historical stages of the hybridization of languages and peoples on the wide expanses of world history and [hoped to] find here the explanation for the emergence of systems of related languages.

The significance of N. Ya. Marr's work in this field consists in his utilization, for the solution of ethnolinguistic problems, of the immense bodies of data from archeology, ethnography and the history of material culture. However, the principle of "convergence" and "divergence" of languages and peoples, suggested by Academician N. Ya. Marr, based on paleontologic element analysis of the most diverse tongues, did not lead and cannot lead to a concrete historical interpretation of the facts of "oneness," structural similarities, the material kinship of such groups of languages as the Slavic, Romance, Iranian and such, that is, those facts which are not so much the product of formal comparative-historical Indo-European linguistics and its methods as they are the very [facts] which gave rise to this field of bourgeois comparativism.

N. Ya. Marr assigned too little significance to the internal processes of uniform change in languages, united for social and historical reasons through a common lexical body and structural features. This is why N. Ya. Marr was unable to give either a satisfactory historico-methodological explanation for the origin of linguistic "kinship" or to reveal the concrete-historical conditions for the emergence of individual linguistic systems or of diminutive linguistic groups, united through the presence of more or less close material bonds. Academician Marr's views on the process of development by stages of a common human language, on systems of languages "according to the periods of their emergence," on the genesis of individual languages, such as Russian, etc., changed constantly in connection with the instability of the results of paleontologic element analysis. The linguistically tangible community of the more closely "related" languages and groups of languages remained without specific explanation and, with the rejection of paleontologic analysis, even quite unexplainable for the new science of language.

And yet nobody can deny the tremendous importance of the historical study of the material ties between related languages of the same type. While rejecting with N. Ya. Marr the antihistorical and reactionary theory of "protolanguage," Soviet linguistics cannot be content to repeat the largely erroneous history-by-stages and ethnogenetic inventions of Academician N. Ya. Marr. In recent times it [Soviet linguistics] has even completely ceased research in this area and has begun to await timidly new discoveries from the archeological and ethnogenetic investigations of Soviet historians. This situation undoubtedly demands a radical change.

It is self-evident that the material kinship of languages consists not only in the community of a certain part of the vocabulary (including here also the word-forming morphemes) but also in a greater or lesser similarity of grammatical structure. In revealing the historico-social foundations for the emergence of such familes or systems of languages (as the Slavic ones), Soviet linguistics must also take into account the fact of the subsequent general trend of linguistic changes in the corresponding groups of related peoples (as well as with the actual, historical bonds between these peoples). Nor is there any need, while figurout out the socio-historical reasons for the emergence of the differences, for example, between Slavic languages and dialects, to refer constantly and without fail to the blending of these peoples and languages with other peoples and languages (for example, south Russian pronunciation of unaccented "o" as "a"—under Chuvash influence, Russian full vocalism—survival from languages of the pre-Indo European stage, etc.).

Thus, comparative-historical grammars of Slavic, Germanic and other Indo-European languages were buried alive by N. Ya. Marr and his followers. To replace the old in this field, Academician Marr and his school did not offer anything new, [anything] more or less historically reliable and based on fact, beyond certain hypotheses.

Among contemporary followers of N. Ya. Marr, the constant references to social convergence and divergence, while explaining linguistic kinship, while explaining [the presence] of common and distinct linguistic processes and phenomena among such peoples as the Slavic, Germanic, etc., have become an irresponsible game because of the absence of new concrete investigations in the field of mutual influences and hybridization of languages of different systems at the most ancient stages in their development.

The partisans of Academician N. Ya. Marr's doctrine themselves, if they wanted to become historians of the most ancient period of any language, for example, Russian, were forced to adopt an eclectic halfway point of view, hesitating between Academician N. Ya. Marr's doctrine and traditional bourgeois comparative-historical linguistics. In this connection, the following comments by Prof. F. P. Filin in his "Outline of the History of the Russian Language Before the 14th Century" is quite characteristic:

"The Slavs, as any Indo-European group of peoples, took shape over thousands of years in the process of convergence and divergence of many and multi-ethnic human communities. In this connection, the new science of language was confronted with a whole series of extremely complex problems of Slavo-Cimerian, Slavo-Sarmasian, Slavo-Celtic and other connections*** Apparently, even before the full emergence of clan structure, the Slavic tribes gradually took shape from numerous and unstable communities*** With the definitive establishment of clan structure, ethnolinguistic relations become somewhat stabilized. To this same period one must ascribe the final organization of Slavic groups of tribes as a definite linguistic unit***" Thus the presence of a common base for all Slavic languages is admitted. But at once stipulations are added: "There is nothing 'primordial' in Slavic languages that could be traced back to any ideal protolinguistic unity." And yet "it is indisputable that in many cases the several variants of one and the same phenomenon represent changes in a common initial form which once belonged to all Slavic languages and dialects."

Here, for all to see, is admitted the presence of a common linguistic base or of a common linguistic fund of "all Slavic languages and dialects." Thereby is admitted the historical "kinship" of Slavic languages, revealed in similar or identical processes of development in their systems.

There is even less reason to deny, for example, the close kinship of languages in the Eastern Slavic group: Russian, Belorussian, Ukrainian, and their development from a common source. The editors of the "Russian-Ukrainian Dictionary" were completely correct when they wrote recently of the Ukrainian language: "Emerging from a single, Eastern Slavic root, reflecting and confirming the eternal friendship and brotherly bonds of the Russian and Ukranian peoples, their languages during centuries developed in mutual connections and unity."

Thus, Soviet linguistics cannot undertake to deny a kinship of languages which is material and not metaphysical, [which is] historically shaped in specific historical conditions; [nor can it deny] a certain uniformity in their development which is connected with this. It is therefore obliged to concern itself in addition to the stage study of language also with the comparative study of historically emerging systems of related languages [and this] on new methodological foundations—the Marxist history of material and spiritual culture. The comparative-historical study of systems of related languages (Slavic, Germanic, Iranian, etc.) must be revived for a new life, illuminated by the bright light of Marxist methodology.

Conclusion.

A general Marxist linguistics must be created through the comradely efforts of Soviet specialists in various languages on the basis of creative utilization of the thinking of Marx, Engels, Lenin and Stalin in the concrete investigation of all languages of the world in their genesis, social history, their historical connections and mutual influences. The scientific heritage of Academician Marr must be utilized, but Marxist linguistics is much deeper, wider and fuller than Academician N. Ya. Marr's "new science of language." It is impossible to transform Academician Marr's theory simultaneously into a dogma and a guide to action. N. Ya. Marr himself was against it. He wanted his doctrine to meet "not only acceptance and passive assimilation but also a creative revolutionary attitude and, if necessary, reworking*** otherwise there is only one direction—backward." All basic theses and conclusions of Academician N. Ya. Marr's linguistic theory must be critically re-examined in the light of Marxist-Leninist linguistics.

On the Road to a Materialistic Linguistics*

By Professor L. BULAKHOVSKY

I.—Since "language is the most important means of human communication" (V. I. Lenin) and language as a "weapon of development and struggle" (J. V. Stalin) is one of the important elements of human relations in general, Marx, Engels, Lenin and Stalin did not neglect questions of linguistics in their diversified activity.

We have the materialist theory of the origin of language presented in Engels' work "The Role of Labor in the Process of the Ape's Transformation into Man." The statements of K. Marx and F. Engels on the relation between language and consciousness ("German Ideology") are widely known as are J. V. Stalin's observations ("Anarchism or Socialism?").

V. I. Lenin's theory of reflection offers a key to an understanding of language as one of the forms of nature's reflection in man's cognition and, moreover, in the process and development of cognition. V. I. Lenin's observation about the generalizing nature of words is very important: "Any word (speech) already generalizes*** Emotions indicate reality; thought and words are the same."†

What materialist semantics is, or, more correctly, what the direction is in which it should be elaborated on comparative historical foundations, is taught by the numerous observations of the Marxist classics dealing with particular sociologically important words. The Marxist classics have many observations of prime importance dealing with style as well: about translations, on the style of agitational literature, on ridding language of unnecessary foreign words and expressions, etc.

V. I. Lenin determined the leading social factor of the formation and dissemination of literary languages in bourgeois society: "All over the world the epoch of the final victory of capitalism over feudalism was associated with national movements. The economic basis of these movements consists in the fact that the conquest of the internal market by the bourgeoisie and state unification of territories with a population speaking the same language, accompanied by the elimination of all obstacles to the development of this language and to its literary utilization, are needed for the complete victory of commodity production. Language is an extremely important means of human communication; the unity of language and its unimpeded development are important conditions for trade which would be free and broad, corresponding to contemporary capitalism, and for a free and broad grouping of the population by all the individual classes [as well as], finally, conditions for the close link of the market with each and every boss, salesman, or purchaser."*

Comrade Stalin has given the classic definition of a nation, which is extremely important for linguistics: "A nation is a historically formed stable community of people which arose on the basis of common language, territory, economic life and psychological make-up which is manifested in a common culture."†

The whole enormous national construction of the U. S. S. R., the colossal, historically unprecedented fraternal unity of people speaking different languages and the most benevolent and persistent attention to their languages—all this is fully illuminated by the theory of Lenin and Stalin.

Comrade Stalin has formulated a view of mankind's future world language accurately and most convincingly.

A model of a thoughtful investigation of historical dialectology can be found, unfortunately unfinished, in F. Engels' "The Frankish Dialect" (in the article "The Frankish Period").

Firmly and decisively Engels recommended the comparative-historical method as the method of linguistic work: "The matter and form of the native language" become intelligible only when one traces its emergence and gradual development and this is impossible if one neglects, first, its own obsolete forms and, second, related languages living and dead. Obviously we are dealing here with a philologist who never heard anything about scientific linguistics, which has undergone such great and fruitful development in the last 60 years—and this is why Mr. Dühring is looking for "the highly instructive elements" of linguistics not in Bopp, Grimm and Dietz but in the late Heyse and Becker."‡ Let us compare with this Engel's letter to Lassalle (1859):

"Since I have been here I have been busy primarily with military matters and from time to time turned to my old hobby—comparative philology. But if one is busy all day with noble commerce, then in such an enormously vast science as philology one cannot transcend the bounds of purest amateurism. If once I harbored the daring idea of working out the comparative grammar of Slavic languages, I have long since given it up, particularly after the task was accomplished with such brilliant success by Miklošić."**

*Pravda, June 13, 1950, p. 3.

†V.I. Lenin, Philosophical Notebooks, 1938, p. 281.

*V. I. Lenin, Works, Vol. XX, p. 368.

†J. V. Stalin, Works, Vol. II, p. 296.

‡F. Engels, Anti-Dühring, 1950, pp. 303-4.

** K. Marx and F. Engels, Works, Vol. XXV, "Letters," p. 245. By the time Engel's letter was written the first two

If to all this one adds the significant material contained in the works of such serious Marxists with philological interests and training as P. Lafargue and F. Mehring, and of such major writers as M. Gorky who stood firmly on materialist positions, then one can say with sufficient justification that we have at our disposal everything needed for the development of materialist linguistics.

II. — We must answer the question: is a lot of scientific material accumulated earlier already obsolete? Does it no longer have any significance in linguists' actual investigative work?

Strictly speaking, the discussion concerns primarily the comparative-historical method. Academician I. Meshchaninov in his list of negative aspects of our linguistics says: "The formal comparative method and the reactionary hypothesis of a protolanguage have not yet been shaken off***"

I consider that this position is unfounded and harmful primarily for those possibilities which we have of elaborating a materialist linguistics, the principles of which go back to Engels.

The most frequently [heard] and the weightiest objection to the comparative method, an objection which has become a cliche, is that this method presupposes the existence of a "protolanguage" and is directly connected with "racialism" from which comes "racism," that is, the preaching of hatred of one race's representatives for another.

The concept of "protolanguage" has long since been criticized in Indo-European linguistics itself. But no matter what is said on this subject, the "protolanguage" or "protolanguages" under discussion have of course nothing to do with the meanings ascribed by "Indo-Europeanists" to this "protolanguage" as some kind of a single language of mankind or something similar. Use of the concept of "protolanguage" to apply to a concrete group of related languages is in no way related to whether languages can be traced from an initial multiplicity to singleness or vice versa, and can be so related only through misunderstanding.

Moreover, the last question must be settled dialectically and not with that superficial directness with which it is regretably not infrequently stated and resolved.

In the history of languages, i.e., of tribes and peoples who carry them, it has very often happened that a process took place either from multiplicity to uniformity or, the reverse, from uniformity to fragmentation. When all is said and done, we are convinced that this process will be resolved by the main historical factors in favor of uniformity in the distant future. Where the facts of language (and not abstract considerations) force us to deal more with factors of differentiation and where with the opposite is determined by the concrete material.

Furthermore, language and race are not directly connected. By language the Negroes of North America are unmistakably Indo-European; the Jews who use so-called "Yiddish" as a native tongue and those of the Romance branch who use a variety of Spanish are also Indo-European of the Germanic branch; inversely, Hungarians, Esthonians and other peoples who speak languages of another system are hard to distinguish anthropologically from other Europeans, but in a linguistic sense they are definitely not Europeans.

Whichever way and by whatever methods one studies the history of the languages of a given system, races are here irrelevant, although the simple fact needs no proof that the languages of a given system are distributed mostly among some ethnic groups and not others. If fascists and fascist-like rogues in science found it necessary to use the existence of linguistic families for conclusions of a racial or even racist kind, what has science to do with this?

What is more, the comparative-historical method does not necessarily imply the use of the concept of a "protolanguage" as the most ancient language of a given linguistic system: there are various points of view on this. Even among "Indo-Europeanists" there are few who believe now that the comparative-historical method is adequate even in phonetics and morphology to reconstruct this entire "protolanguage" (for the Indo-European group, this would mean an antiquity of about 5000-6000 years). But, if the facts of contemporary languages are compared with the documentary data, it is actually impossible, if one is thorough, to avoid re-creating the most ancient state of the languages of the given group in one trait or another. But all these are purely concrete questions and the debate does not concern them now. And when discussion centers on the closeness of such an incontrovertible type as the Slavic, Romance and similar languages, the reconstruction of their group's most archaic condition reaches very high probability.

Another objection [states] that the comparative-historical method is formalistic: it is alleged that they work with it while separating sounds from meaning. This objection is the result of taking technically simplified means of presentation for the essence of the matter. It ignores the simplest thing, that even phonetics cannot, absolutely cannot be studied in its comparative-historical context without etymologizing, that is, without comparing the meanings of words (whether this is done well or badly is another question, see below) and without allowing certain changes in meaning, that is, in the meaning component of the word.

The comparative-historical method has a quite dissimilar appearance in the works of various authors. Moreover, any convinced supporter of this method can point to a number of its deficiencies, unresolved difficulties and, in certain authors, ideological components unacceptable from a Marxist point of view.

We cannot therefore keep from asking ourselves, what do we accomplish objectively by defending the particular significance of the comparative-historical method, if only as one of the linguistic methods in the field of the history of language? What is it that speaks in us? Our training? Habit? Inertia? Inability to evaluate the perspectives opened from other positions? Inability to overcome survivals of bourgeois thinking? Hardly. He who has dealt long and frequently with the facts of his science, who has seen how these facts yield to certain methods of investigation and stubbornly refuse to yield to others since they cannot, (and after all this something happens to all others who have a sufficiently serious preparation in the corresponding field of science), he naturally is convinced that the approaches with which he handles the facts (as long as there are none better) are just those which cannot be rejected without harm to the work at hand.

The comparative-historical method has rendered the greatest services in the field of linguistic science. Its practical usefulness has not been exhausted. There are still very many questions concerning Indo-European languages and those of other systems which can and should be solved by employing it. The limits of its usefulness, its degree of perfection and the possibilities of improving it—all that is another matter. We think that the comparative-historical method should not be transformed into a bugbear by labelling it "bourgeois," because this will have no useful effect except to harm science, which demands thoroughness and adaptability in handling facts.

The value of this method consists in just this: when piles of motley linguistic facts taken at a given moment are approached with intention to compare the present condition in one way or another with preceding ones, one can proceed with confidence from a scientific premise which has proven itself in most cases, [namely] that phonetic correspondences between the preceding and subsequent conditions must have occurred consistently. Speaking in general terms, that is,

volumes had appeared (in German) of a comparative grammar of Slavic languages by Fr. Mikološić, Phonetics, 1852, and Theory of Stems, 1859.

excluding several essential refinements—if comparison shows a definite correspondence in three words, then one should expect and can get confirmation for it in dozens and hundreds of other words.

So far as we know, there are no differences in principle about this method between "Indo-Europeanists" and the majority of specialists in other linguistic systems—students of Finno-Ugric, Semitic, Turkic and other languages who, with complete success, that is, with direct results, have utilized this basic approach of the comparative-historical method. The discussion rather concerns one or another detail than it does principle. The importance of this principle for the linguist working on the history of language was not denied even by N. Ya. Marr. As to how he used the concept of phonetic law and whether the concrete regularities he discovered are accurate, that is, do they correspond to the facts, that is a separate matter. On this point the floor can be held competently only by students of Kartvelian and specialists in other Caucasian languages.

But even the notion of phonetic regularities operative in language, as it was worked out around the eighties of the 19th century, has been refined many times in investigative practice: its biological explanations have long since been rejected by the neogrammarians even in bourgeois science; among the attempts made to find a more satisfactory explanation there are many which are completely unacceptable from the standpoint of materialist linguistics and some about which the last word has not yet been said.

Much was done in Europe and in Russia even before the revolution to determine the methods of comparative-historical analysis. For example, a definite role was played by the efforts, continued in Soviet times, directed toward the rational elaboration of a series of techniques dealing with "analogies" which cut across phonetic regularities and with related phenomena, particularly in the area of morphology. The method has undergone a most careful verification through linguistic geography which emerged from dialectology as a scientific discipline, which thoroughly studies life in the social context of individual words, etc.

III.—Can the comparative-historical method be replaced at this time by another? I will not speak of a purely historical one: it does not raise any objections on principle and has been and will be successfully used, for example, in the Russian language field. But this method (the documentary history of language) does not lead far beyond mere empiricism and has in no way offered anything to deserve any special endorsement as theoretically or practically new.

N. Ya. Marr contrasted the comparative-historical techniques with his method of paleontologic analysis according to the four elements (earlier a larger number). Let us not argue about this method, what has concretely been achieved with the aid of this method and what can still be achieved. The languages which I know are basically not in the category of relics which the late academician wanted to reveal. But, working in the Ukraine, I could not and still cannot bypass N. Ya. Marr's work—it appears to be the only one dealing directly with the Ukrainian language. I will not dissimulate; almost all this is quite strange for me and for many others familiar with it. It has a strange title: "Japhetic Dawn on the Ukrainian Farmstead. (Grandmother's Tales about the Hog Little Red Sun). Dedicated to the Second All-Ukrainian Convention of Orientalists." ("Farmstead" in the period of collective farms!) The very first page is strange: "For some—Venus of Milo and Vladimir the Little Red Sun, for others—the goddess Motyga or, what is the same thing, the goddess Ruka with the Hog Little Red Sun. Something is not right: there is no little sun of the feminine gender. But it is not our fault that in some places mother-truth has been covered with a fig leaf and the sun turned into a thing of very doubtful gender: neuter; notwithstanding a perfect awareness that the sun is feminine and that it is impossible to hoodwink our contemporaries by turning her, while she is still a woman in the consciousness of primitive matriarchal society, at once into a bearded representative of humanity."*

The etymologies are very strange. For example, the Ukrainian onomatopoetic verb "khryu+k-ati" [to grunt] is taken, and at the same time "khryo-k-ati" is mentioned, and—I can only quote, it is difficult to retell: "Later, the connection of 'hog' as a cult creature in relation to the totemic subjects of the same 'tribe,' more precisely of a definite socio-economic group, no longer Scythian-Celtic but of a ROШ union, emerges in the Ukrainian 'rokha' (hog) (from here 'rokh'—the grunting of a hog, 'rokhkati' to grunt, 'rokhkaniya'—grunting), while roq (<ro-k) > rok, for this meant 'sun' and eventually 'little sky.'"† Thus it is affirmed that "khryukat" [to grunt] and "solntse" [sun] are somehow related through meaning.

The whole article consists of such etymologies "by elements;" the reader, if he cares to, will find them by opening any of the first 75 pages of the "Learned Notes" of the Institute of Ethnic and National Cultures of the Peoples of the East for 1930, Vol. I.

Academician I. I. Meshchaninov, in his article written for the discussion, is actually ready to repudiate element analysis completely. This is good and it would appear that this question might be bypassed as obsolete. But the matter is not by any means as simple as it seems. Take any page in any work of N. Ya. Marr after about 1925; cross out anything referring to "elements" and decide whether ten or even five per cent of other material and statements would be left that are free of the theory on which the whole element method is based.

What I am talking about now is extremely serious: one cannot shake it off, cannot dismiss it with abstract phrases. The question is not completely settled by rejecting elements; many other [questions], sharp and important, are connected with it and one must settle it, looking the facts in the face, as they are.

Efforts to create semantics as a real science have been made for many years but have not given great results. Of course, it is not now what it was at the beginning of the century; but the state of linguistic science in this area is very far from the legitimate demands made upon it and this is hardly disputable.

Did Academician N. Ya. Marr give us another, more perfected semantics? His efforts were not directed toward the present day. Marr's interests lay in discovering the oldest stages of human thought as reflected in language, and the enthusiasm of his creative efforts as a linguist [lay in] re-creating, making clear the forms of man's "prelogical" thought.

Did he solve this problem? Are the "meaning clusters" he discovered convincing, as he claims? Are these notions and their connections characteristic of "prelogical" thought? We cannot and should not ascribe to the fabulously distant antiquity with which Marr dealt, those correspondences in meaning with which we deal today, and we are perfectly willing to tolerate [for antiquity] at least some of "the miracles" which are impossible for the cultured person of today to recognize. But if we take one or another of these archaic "meaning clusters" in a scientific context, and not in one of, let us say, artistic phantasy, while following the intuition of even a major scholar, we have no right not to ask for proof, that is, a body of scientifically elaborated data which allow of many-sided and repeated verification. Not everyone is competent to make such a check in the field under discussion; the floor belongs to the experts in Kartvelian and other Japhetic languages of the Caucasus, and to them alone.

But if they too, like the outstanding student of Kartvelian, A. S. Chikobava, could not see these "miracles" and, after many years of work in this field (although they undoubtedly studied the works of Marr long and carefully), were

*N. Ya. Marr, Selected Works, Vol. V, p. 224.
†Ibid., p. 234.

unable to see that which to him seemed already proved, then serious doubts are quite legitimate for us, who are not students of the Caucasus. Does the semantics of extreme antiquity he defends correspond to what really existed in that antiquity?

Among Marr's semantic "clusters" there are some the novelty of which arouses no astonishment. They have been and are observed (while taking into account the differentiating morphological criteria) in languages easily accessible to us all.

It is not hard to agree, for example, that the term "zemlya" [earth] lies at the basis of words for "niz" [base], that the terms for "vremeni" [time] and "god" [year] are connected with each other, that words meaning "space" acquire the meaning of "place." Any etymological dictionary of any of the Indo-European and non-Indo-European languages will fully confirm this kind of statement of N. Ya. Marr. But many of his other juxtapositions cannot but astonish us, and we naturally ask how and by what is it proved?

It occurs to one that the existence of a new semantics, created precisely among us, carefully documented and firmly based on the method of dialectical materialism, is not yet something we can be proud of as a fact of our scientific reality. The program of this important branch of linguistics and its method (not in declarations testifying to good intentions but in concrete application) is something which even today must still be created, which awaits its workers and requires considerable effort and of whole scientific teams at that.

Can one say that the materialist theory of the origin of language as given by Engels should be revised because we now have another one which is also materialist? One need only compare what Engels has to say on this subject with such statements by N. Ya. Marr:

"Comrades, a most profound misunderstanding arises when the origin of language is regarded as coinciding with the appearance of voiced speech, but it is no less fundamental an error when language is supposed from the first to have had a conversational function which today is primary. Language is a magic instrument, an instrument of production in the first stages of man's development of group production; language is an instrument of production. The need and the possibility of using language as a means of communication is a very late matter***"*

These and similar statements by Marr (there are many), widely publicized in many pamphlets, articles and books under the label of the latest word in materialist linguistics, force us (no matter how their author corrected them in the process of his work or how they were corrected by his followers) to reject them openly, completely, once and for all. Let us stick to the "uncorrected" Engels, or, if he be "corrected," then with something incomparably more convincing.

IV.—However, it would be a serious error to think that the efforts of linguistic thought made in connection with Marr's heritage turned out fruitless and that Soviet science has nothing to call its own true contribution. That which is summed up today as "the new science of language" and which includes quite disparate elements of different degrees of persuasiveness and diverse value was created partly by N. Ya. Marr himself, partly by his students who critically worked over his heritage (the most important of them is undoubtedly Academician I. I. Meshchaninov) and least of all by his direct followers, i.e., those who unquestioningly accepted all that he taught, even in the last period of his activity before his death.

I. I. Meshchaninov, freeing himself of many of his errors, took over from his teacher, among other things, three interests of first-class scientific significance. He raises the problem of constructing a comparative grammar of many mutually unrelated languages and solves this problem by using vast materials from languages of the Soviet Union until recently unwritten. He tries to illuminate the morphology and syntax of the unrelated languages he compares by dealing with grammatical categories as a suspension of the corresponding facts of thought (in the broad meaning of the word). Ideas (or concepts or groups of concepts) suspended in specific forms or syntactic combinations he considers as stage ideas, that is, corresponding to stages in the development of human thought in its dependence on the stages of economic development (labor activity).

All these currents in our science are fresh and new, and what we find on these topics in his books, particularly the one which came out in 1945, "Sentence Parts and Parts of Speech," deserves the most careful attention.

However, there is every reason to believe that I. I. Meshchaninov himself does not pretend that his works be considered, figuratively speaking, as walls of the future edifice of materialist linguistics already faultlessly and firmly erected. Nor can we consider them so. And when Pravda, opening the discussion, invites us to state our opinion freely and directly, then we must say: of the three mentioned basic tendencies, the first is closest to success. A grammar of languages which are of genealogically unrelated systems is possible and will undoubtedly become an interesting parallel field in our science, as is clearly shown by the works of Academician I. Meshchaninov. Has the author been able to give a convincing explanation of the forms and word combinations of paleo-Asiatic, American and other languages which he so carefully examines in his books and which until now have been poorly studied and little known? It is possible that Academician I. Meshchaninov is close to the truth in a number of cases but the danger exists that with the techniques of direct, or as one would say, surface analysis (that is, without taking into account the history of the respective language) which he is employing, one cannot obtain reliable data: many explanations of this kind are illusory just as were similar explanations of forms in Indo-European languages at an earlier period in science, when it still lacked the comparative-historical method. As for development by stages, that is, attempts to find a more or less direct reflection of economic eras in the facts of juxtaposed (compared) forms and word combinations of languages of different systems, in this respect it seems to us that we are offered very little that is convincing. So far the situation in these fields is pretty much the same as in phonetics, about which F. Engels wrote: "It will hardly be possible for anybody, without being ridiculous***to explain the economic origin of High German vocalic changes which divide Germany (in dialect matters) into two halves."*

One should not think, however, that appropriate researches are erroneous in principle, since the reflection of socio-economic structures in vocabulary is a scarcely disputable fact. (Academician Marr was correct methodologically in concentrating his search primarily in this field) and morphology, no matter how complicated it becomes as a result of historical accretions, nevertheless is actually dependent on lexical elements in language (particularly, for example, in agglutinative languages of the "pasting together" type).

Valuable results can be found to have been achieved along the road of the "new science of language." The role it played, together with N. Ya. Marr and after, deserves full sympathy as consonant with the grandiose linguistic development of the U.S.S.R. But in its scientific essence this doctrine is directed to the far distant past, and its connection with the present emerges not from it itself, but is created only as a result of the powerful demands of life. If one turns to the valuable things that have been created in Soviet times in the province of Russian, Ukrainian and Belorussian, one is forced to observe that the new science of language, although it had no few adherents, cannot flatter itself with the results which can be directly traced to its influence. Not in the flowering of dialectology as mass sci-

*N. Ya. Marr, Contribution to the Baku Discussion on Japhetidology and Marxism, Baku, 1932, p. 7.

*K. Marx and F. Engels, Letters, 4th edition, pp. 375-6.

entific enterprises of Union linguistic institutes, nor in the history of literary languages, created and energetically improved in Soviet times (the underestimation in this connection of the role primarily of Academician V. V. Vinogradov seems unjust to us), nor with the work on language of writers, particularly contemporary ones, which is connected with this discipline, nor in the diversified lexicological work connected with life, which, true enough, is still in great need of broad generalizations which are ripening, nor in good descriptive grammars (here it seems one can speak of even more extensive accomplishments—applicable to many languages in the Union), nor in the improvement of texts for middle schools, do we seem to find any direct accomplishments of the "new science of language."

V.—I should like to talk of at least some prospects of scientific development in linguistics.

In a multilingual country, where bilingualism, that is, the free use along with the native tongue of literary Russian as well, is by no means an exceptional fact, the problem of bilingualism in a linguistic context and particularly in the living context of the present would appear to arise of its own accord. One cannot fail to consider it a great deficiency, therefore, that although in following Academician N. Ya. Marr they talk a lot about the hybrid nature of languages, Soviet linguists unfortunately are almost uninterested in that area of specific questions which is directly related to this problem.

How is bilingualism formed and reflected in a child's speech? Precisely what kind of bilingualism is it, i.e., does it refer primarily to language types? What are the forms of bilingualism in the family? How does it look in live communication and under the influence of the school, etc., etc.? The hybrid character of all the world's languages is beyond any doubt, and Marr's passionate defense of this thesis is fully justified. But with all his enormous experience in this connection and given such an excellent object of observation as the Caucasus he so excellently knew (if only with its "mountain of languages"—Dagestan), Marr was unable to place his general theses of an historical nature on the firm foundation of a rigorously organized, scientifically systematized description of fact. Perhaps Marr did not do this because, while hastening to draw generalizations from prospects which attracted him of penetrating the remote antiquity of languages, he, as an exceptional polyglot and a man of enormous personal experience, did not find that he needed this work. However, we must contrast the scientific intuition of even a very great expert with something more durable, tangible, proven and verified. This must and can be done. We have at our disposal data—and, strictly speaking, extremely sparse data—dealing almost exclusively with the languages of the Indo-European system. This is clearly inadequate. We need incomparably more material.

One can and should also place on the firm ground of observation that which refers to the tendencies of living languages to draw closer to each other. In passing, I will observe that I do not see any basis for the critical observations which A. S. Chikobava makes about Marr's thesis that "mankind, proceeding toward economic unity and a classless community, cannot help applying artificial means, scientifically worked out, in order to accelerate this broad process." "Artificial means" are not necessarily "coercion" as the critic thinks.

A. S. Chikobava undoubtedly knows no less than others that there are no literary languages that are not artificial, that their organization and realization in the life of peoples presupposes factors of very strong conscious intervention and that the school (can it be considered a means of coercion?) is the primary factor in their penetration to the masses. One can also suppose with great probability that in a highly cultured, classless environment, which the communist society will be, the conscious aspect of socio-cultural processes will be much higher than what we are observing now.

Of exceptional importance from a materialist point of view (and in this respect there seem to be no differences of opinion) is the fate of lexicology and of lexicography, which is most intimately connected with it. It would be unjust to underestimate in the latter field those great successes of our science which are wholly ascribable to the Soviet period.

But all these successes are still inadequate for the scale of socialist construction of our time in an enormous country with its constantly growing scientific forces.

"The Dictionary of Contemporary Literary Russian" of the U.S.S.R. Academy of Sciences has great merit, but only the first two letters have appeared. There is as yet no Ukrainian-Russian dictionary of the Ukraine Academy of Sciences; there is no Belorussian-Russian or Russian-Belorussian Academy dictionary and so on. Neither the Russian historical nor the Ukrainian historical dictionaries have been made (put into shape for printing), etc., etc.

In the theoretical aspect, the struggle with errors and ill-intentioned distortions should not be carried on by statements alone. Soviet linguists must categorically show in the area of their specialty the strength of the dialectical materialist method which was placed in their hands (its strength in other areas has long since been proven through powerful results), and this demands, of course, great knowledge, creative thinking and attention to a multiplicity of facts, among them also "trifles."

One of the first conditions for the flourishing of linguistic science consists first and most of all in turning not to the paleontology of speech, a scientific discipline having its rights to consideration (but to incomparably less consideration than it has enjoyed until now), but to questions of living languages. In the Soviet Union, a country of numerous peoples enjoying equal rights, there is, of course, enough with which to occupy oneself; there is [enough data] to perfect the method. Scientific theory must be verified and justified through practice.

"The data of science have always been verified through practice and experience" (J. Stalin).

Materialist linguistics must start from reality, and only reality will determine its growth and true strength.

The History of the Russian Language and N. Ya. Marr's Theory*

By S. NIKIFOROV

The discussion taking place on the pages of Pravda on the condition and paths of further development of Soviet linguistics has confronted all Soviet linguists, including students of the history of the Russian language, with extremely significant problems of general linguistics as well as the concrete historical study of particular languages.

It is clear to Soviet linguists that their work must rest on the principles of dialectical and historical materialism. But there are major shortcomings in the creative application of these principles to the solution of specific problems, particularly the historical study of a given national language. A bold development of criticism and self-criticism is the chief means of rectifying these shortcomings.

It is necessary to determine to what extent the doctrine elaborated by Academician N. Ya. Marr offers the methodological premises for an exhaustively profound study of each language. This verification will be carried out on the results of the study of Russian, not only because of its special role in the cultural development of peoples in the Soviet Union, but also because the Russian language has been studied in its historical development by representatives of various schools, including N. Ya. Marr himself and the adherents of his linguistic theory.

The Russian national language is rich in dialects. The Russian literary language, documented since the 19th century, has a complicated and peculiar historical development. Therefore, the juxtaposition of initial theoretical positions and of concrete results of the work on the history of the Russian language by representatives of various schools makes it possible to determine the importance of N. Ya. Marr's theory in its study.

Quite a few of Academician N. Ya. Marr's theses are really incontrovertible; they proceed from the principles of historical materialism. The decisive one is the recognition of language as a superstructural phenomenon on a socioeconomic base, specifically, a means of formalizing and expressing the ideology of a given social collective. I shall not enumerate these theses, since it is not they which are now an object of controversy. The controversy hinges on whether there are in Academician N. Ya. Marr's linguistic theory any major theses which contradict Marxist-Leninist methodology.

It should be stated clearly and definitely that there are a number of such theses, that they must be pointed out, subjected to principled criticism. The way will thereby be cleared for a fruitful development of general linguistics as well as of the historical study of particular languages. The first such thesis is the treatment of the class nature of language.

Prof. A. S. Chikobava correctly indicated that Academician N. Ya. Marr used the concept of "class" in an un-Marxist fashion, that he saw evidence of classes in the primitive-communal structure.

Despite N. Ya. Marr, the question of a language common to a given nationality must be settled not abstractly for all times and all peoples, but specifically and historically. The following thesis of N. Ya. Marr is fully correct only for a feudal society: "In studying the documents of language, both ancient and most ancient as well as modern and most modern, one takes into full account that the given document was written in the language of a given social class and is not the language of the whole people in its totality."* In the capitalist era, when nations are formed, each nation is characterized by a common language, which is one of the characteristic traits of a nation. For purposes of class warfare the struggling classes utilize the ideological aspects of the common language (the semantics of a definite category of words and of a definite phraseology), but by no means its grammatical structure.

In the period of early feudalism, when the relationship between lords and peasants bore, in large measure, the character of external coercion and the relation between the lords themselves was closer, the literary (written) language played the role of a language common to the lords. This literary language could even be alien to a given people (as, for example, was Latin for the Germans—the language not only of the church but also of literature, which was most intimately connected with the church, and of education in general). Consequently, in the period of early feudalism there could be a significant difference between the speech of the ruling class and the speech of the socially lower classes, not only in the vocabulary, particularly in the semantics of socially saturated words, but also in the grammatical aspect of language.

This difference between the literary language of the lords and the speech of the lower classes, which was characteristic of feudal society, is also wholly applicable to the Russian language. This is confirmed, for example, by the investigations of F. P. Filin. He says: "***The old Russian written language basically reflects the speech of the city population or, even more narrowly, the speech of its socially highest classes—princes, their bodyguards, boyars and the strata of the monasteries and churches. The language of the rural population, of the basic masses of Eastern Slavs, is represented in writing indirectly, only in so far as one can speak of a certain community in the speech of the upper and lower classes of the population."† But the question of what does the difference between the speech of the lords and the speech of the socially subordinate consist in is not raised methodologically. In the above-mentioned work, in characterizing the language of tenth and 11th century writings of a businesslike nature ("Russkaya Pravda" [Russian Law], charters, treaties), F. P. Filin, states very hesitantly: "***The language of 'business documents' reflected the speech norms of the ruling strata in the population of old Russia which developed from an all-Russian linguistic base" (emphasis mine, S. N.).‡

Two questions remain unclear for the reader:

First. As F. P. Filin, an adherent of Academician N. Ya. Marr's linguistic theory, sees it, what is an "all-Russian linguistic base?" Does this concept differ in factual linguistic content (and not according to the interpretation of this content's genesis) from the content of the term "all-Russian language" as the Indo-Europeanists (A. I. Sobolevsky, A. A. Shakhmatov) understand it? Did Academician N. Ya. Marr's general linguistic theory help to make the understanding and the actual analysis of this con-

*Pravda, June 13, 1950, p. 4.

*N. Ya. Marr, Selected Works, Vol. 1, p. 262.

†F.P. Filin, The Vocabulary of Literary Russian of the Ancient Kiev Period, Leningrad, 1949, p. 227.

‡Ibid., p. 6.

tent more thorough, more closely corresponding to actual reality?

Second. How did the "speech norms" (according to this formulation we are dealing not with particular lexical or phonetic distinctions but with a deeper distinction) of the dominant strata differ from the "speech norms" of the "basic masses of Eastern Slavs?"

Unfortunately, the existing monographs and general treatises give no answers to these important questions either theoretically or in the investigation of specific material. The linguistic theory of Academician N. Ya. Marr was of no factual help in handling this matter and actually could not offer help in view of the erroneousness of the basic premise.

Academician N. Ya. Marr correctly thought it necessary to relate stages in the development of language with stages in the development of society and thought. However, his primary interests in the period of the emergence of language and the first stages in its development lead to his outlining stages of thought (and language) only for pre-class society: totemic and cosmic. The absence of sound evidence for the outlining of these stages has been convincingly shown by B. Serebrennikov.*

Neither N. Ya. Marr nor his closest followers actually dealt with the stages of development in thought and language in the history of class society. Students of the Russian language, however, deal primarily with the development of thought and language in a society possessing writing (from the tenth century to our days), that is, in different periods in the development of class society.

Investigation has shown that the dynamics of dialects and the character of literary Russian, the laws of the development of the Russian literary language and its mutual relations with dialects are different in different periods. We can distinguish four periods:

(1) The period of early feudalism.

(2) The period of the liquidation of feudalism and of rising capitalism when the Russian nation is emerging with a common language—an extremely important criterion of a nation.

(3) The period of capitalism. The struggle of the revolutionary-democratic trend in the development of Russian culture against the bourgeois trend develops at this time. In the process of this struggle certain words and turns of phrases (and also syntactic constructions) were selected from the nation's common language and acquired a revolutionary-democratic meaning. Also, a certain number of philosophical and political terms were created, expressing the philosophical and political views of democrats and socialists and used by them in the class struggle against the bourgeoisie. Despite Prof. N. S. Chemodanov, this process in no way leads to the disintegration of the common national language into two class languages.

(4) The period of construction of socialist society. In this period a single literary language expressing socialist ideology gradually displaces the local dialect traits which had been preserved until then in phonetics and, to a small degree, in morphology and vocabulary. In rare cases [this literary language] absorbs occasional words from the dialects and makes them part of the national language.

Historians of the Russian language, in collaboration with philosophers and with the historians of Russian culture, must ascertain these regularities in the development of language and thought dialectically connected with it. Without ascertaining these regularities the study of particular periods in the history of literary Russian, as well as the elaboration of general courses, lacks a sound methodological base, which in practice leads to subjectivity and erroneous conceptions as happened in V. V. Vinogradov's "Outlines of the History of Literary Russian, 17th to 19th Centuries" (1938 edition), or to general statements lacking in specific content such as the assertion of Prof. G. Sanzheyev: "***that which occured with Russian in the Pushkin period represented a stage change in that language, although inflection still remained."*

Closely related to the problem of stages in the development of languages stands the question of the origin and development of existing national languages.

How is the problem of the origin and development of the Russian language stated and solved by the representatives of various linguistic trends? What does Academician Marr's linguistic theory offer toward the solution of this problem?

In solving this problem, the major task consists in ascertaining the initial material from which the Old Russian language (Eastern Slavic tribal languages) was formed and its earliest paths of development.

Academician N. Ya. Marr and his followers state that all the world's languages developed from the four root-words SAL, BER, YON, ROШ, which were the most ancient totemic tribal names. According to N. Ya. Marr's theory, these initial elements subsequently change phonetically in various ways as a result of different elaboration (in respect to differentiation and clarity in the pronunciation of their component diffuse sounds) as well as in consequence of their different hybridizations resulting from the mixing of the earliest human communities. Therefore, four-element analysis is applicable to the words of all the languages in the world; it reveals the original composition and meaning of words. As an example, one can take N. Ya. Marr's analysis of the word rusalka [mermaid] which convinces us of its utter arbitrariness, as the make-up (origin) of this word is explained, without any linguistic reason, without taking into account the means of Old Russian word formation, in two ways: rosh > rus, therefore rus-al-ka, or: rosh > ru plus the first element (sal): ru-sal-ka.

It is obvious that this theory does not offer a key to the solution of the problem of the origin of Russian, because, according to this theory, the initial material is the same for all languages. No wonder Academician I. I. Meshchaninov, referring to himself in the third person, writes that they "consider such analysis unsuitable for periods of developed speech which have worked out more complicated stem structures. These students pass over in silence the question of the existence of these elements, in their Marrist sense, in the structure of language during the most archaic periods of its development,"† that is, he actually joins in the criticism of this most important thesis of Academician N. Ya. Marr, offered in Prof. A. S. Chikobava's article.

As is shown by history and the factual material of language, human language was formed in various places on the globe where the necessary conditions were present and therefore the initial material of aboriginal human groups was different.

The overwhelming majority of Soviet linguists, regardless of their attitude toward N. Ya. Marr's linguistic theory, do not deny either the historical facts of blending of primitive communities with their dialects into one community with a relatively common language (with prolonged retention of traces of the speech of groups making up the new community) or the "fragmentation" under certain conditions of a relatively uniform language into several languages. (On the divergent dialects is expressed the mutual interaction of each of them with the languages of the groups which were their neighbors.)

Prof. A. M. Selishchev, whose attitude to N. Ya. Marr's theory is negative, and Prof. F. P. Filin, a student of N. Ya. Marr, have the same explanation for the emergence of a certain unity of the Slavic languages as a result of the

*B. Serebrennikov, "On N. Ya. Marr's Research Methods," Pravda, May 23, 1950.

*G. Sanzheyev, "Either Forward or Backward," Pravda, May 23, 1950.

†I.I. Meshchaninov, "For a Creative Development of Academician N. Ya. Marr's Heritage," Pravda, May 16, 1950.

convergence of human groups.

But one cannot agree with the thesis that the only means of obtaining common linguistic elements is the process of hybridization, as Academician N. Ya. Marr affirms: "Language is a social phenomenon socially acquired***without the formation of social groups and their need for organized communication, without concerting sound symbols and meanings and without their blending with one another, no language could have arisen, much less any language have developed further. In this sense, the more common words there are in many of the languages which now exist, the more evident and easily ascertainable the formal connection between languages strewn over large distances, the more reason to affirm that these common features are a very late contribution, that their growth in particular languages is the result of very late, frequently repeated hybridizations" (emphasis mine, S. N.).

Some students of the history of Russian, following Academician N. Ya. Marr, exaggerate the role of hybridization in the development of Russian. They explain, through the hybridization of the Eastern groups of Russian tribes with the speakers of tribal languages of a different type, those phonetic phenomena of South Russian dialects which could have appeared (and, according to all the data, did appear) as a result of internal development. For example, N. P. Grinkova explains through such hybridization the reduction of unaccented vowels (akanye) and the palatalization of gutteral consonants (k, g) in South Russian dialects. See her conclusion on the origin of "akanye:" "In the light of the aforementioned considerations, South Russian akanye can be viewed as an ancient and characteristic feature of Eastern Russian tribal languages. It evidently reflects very ancient strata and the hybridization of these Eastern Russian tribal languages with languages of the most archaic typologies" (emphasis mine, S. N.).

A Marxist historian must, first of all, take into account the internal movements, the internal changes in language, conditioned by movements of social life of "converging" human communities. Certain lexical and grammatical forms can be created independently by the speakers of close ("related") languages from an identical initial material through internal movement stemming from similar conditions of social life.

It follows from what has been said that the comparative study of languages of different systems, as well as of languages of a single group, the Slavic in particular, is not only expedient on the basis of a Marxist-Leninist methodology but also necessary. Comparison of languages must be undertaken at similar stages of their development. Only such a comparison will guarantee the uniformity of the compared linguistic facts with their ideological and grammatical aspects.

Such comparison, of course, has nothing to do with that comparative-historical method, the representatives of which proceed only from phonetic or formal grammatical analogies, ignoring the specific history of languages.

All the above leads to the conclusion that in the future development of Soviet linguistics, resting on the method of dialectical and historical materialism, on the works of Marx, Engels, Lenin and Stalin, the many valuable theses of Academician N. Ya. Marr's theory, which is undoubtedly materialist in its foundation, must be widely used.

But this use must be creative and critical, not concealing and whitewashing (under the guise of incompleteness or the need for further verification) but resolutely rejecting the erroneous theses of his theory.

It is just through such an attitude to Academician N. Ya. Marr's heritage that the positive aspects of his doctrine will give us unmistakable help in raising Soviet linguistics to a methodological level worthy of our great Stalinist era.

On the Class Nature of Language*

By V. KUDRYAVTSEV

In his article "On Certain Problems of Soviet Linguistics," Prof. A. S. Chikobava says that the very "concept of a 'class language' is, if one takes into account the basic function of a language, self-contradictory and scientifically inconsistent," that "there are no class languages."†

Is this so? Is it true that the languages of all times and peoples are not of a class nature? To clarify this question, one must first define what a class is and then view language concretely, under definite historical conditions.

An exhaustive scientific definition of class is given by V. I. Lenin. "Classes," he says, "are called those large groups of people differing according to their place in a historically defined system of social production, according to their relation (for the most part fixed and formalized in laws) to the means of production, according to their role in the social organization of labor and, consequently, according to their means of receiving and the dimensions of their share of social wealth at their disposal. Classes are groups of people, one of which can appropriate the labor of the other, due to the difference in their place in a specific organization of social economy."‡

This is the scientific definition of class.

What is the Error of Academician N. Ya. Marr?

There were no classes in the primitive commune. This has been convincingly proven in J. V. Stalin's work "Anarchism or Socialism?" "There was a time," writes Comrade Stalin, "when men struggled with nature as a group, on principles of primitive communism. Then their property too was communist and therefore they almost did not distinguish between 'mine' and 'thine:' their thinking was communist."** In his work "On Dialectical and Historical Materialism," Comrade Stalin, characterizing the primitive commune as classless, says:

"In the primitive commune the foundation of production relations is the public ownership of the means of production. Fundamentally, this corresponds to the nature of productive forces in this period. Stone weapons and the bows and arrows, which appeared later, excluded the possibility of a struggle with the forces of nature and predatory animals on an individual basis. In order to gather the fruits in the forest, to câtch fish in the water, to build any kind of shelter, men were forced to work together if they didn't want to die of starvation or become the prey of rapacious beasts or neighboring societies. Labor in common leads to common ownership of the means of production as well as of the goods produced. There is as yet no notion of private ownership of the means of production, unless one considers private ownership of certain productive tools which are also weapons of defense against wild beasts. Here there is no exploitation; there are no classes."††

It is clear from the above that people in this social formation had no class consciousness either, and, consequently, there was no class differentiation in language. Therefore, Academician N. Ya. Marr is wrong when he says that language was of a class nature from its very beginning. N. Ya. Marr reached this erroneous conclusion because his very understanding of class was incorrect, unscientific and un-Marxist.

Classes arise in slaveholding society. Two antagonistic classes are discernable: slave owners and slaves. Their class consciousness is different.

Language is "practical***true cognition," "the direct realization of thought."* In so far as language and thought form a dialectical unity, class consciousness is unavoidably reflected in language also, forcing the class differentiation of the latter. In some cases, class differentiation can be so obvious that it is striking. Such a fact can be observed in Latin at the time of the second Punic war. According to P. Lafargue, at that time Latin "split up into aristocratic speech—sermo nobilis—and plebeian—sermo plebeius."†

Under feudalism class differentiation in language is quite noticeable and results from class stratification in society. In the feudal period many peasant dialects emergé, usually different from the language of the lords. Thus, for example, the French of 17th century feudal nobility is radically different from the language of the French bourgeoisie and peasantry. This aristocratic language, says Lafargue, separated the nobles from the other classes like a wall. The nobility, deliberately and ostentatiously, would not understand the language of the bourgeoisie and of the artisans and was contemptuous of it. Undoubtedly this language had a clearly expressed class character.

It is just such class languages in feudal Armenia and Georgia that N. Ya. Marr wrote about in his works. He discovered that in ancient Armenia there were two types of languages: keyan (Old Armenian spoken by the secular and ecclesiastic feudal lords) and reyan (peasants' and artisans' dialects). N. Ya. Marr justly saw a class character in this differentiation of language. Prof. A. S. Chikobava failed to upset this conclusion of N. Ya. Marr and concentrated all his criticism on Marr's erroneous view that, from its very beginning, language had a class character.

Further on, while mentioning the capitalist era and the formation of bourgeois nations, A. S. Chikobava affirms that "there are no class languages."

Prof. Arn. Chikobava's Statement Contradicts the Truth.

The history of language shows that, in the formation of nations and national languages, the earlier linguistic differences existing under feudalism gradually disappear. A linguistic community appears, stemming from community of territory, community of economic, political and cultural life. A common psychological make-up ("national character") is formed.

The nation's community of language is a completely indisputable fact, which can be illustrated by the history of the Russian language. The formation of the Russian nation and of the national Russian language took place over several centuries (from the 14th to the 18th century). In the 18th century the Russian language, as the national language of the Russian people, had become relatively unified. This fact is also cônfirmed by M. V. Lomonosov. In his work "On the Utility of Church Books in the Russian Language," he wrote: "The Russian people, inhabiting a large territory, speak everywhere a mutually intelligible language in towns and villages, irrespective of the large dis-

*Pravda, June 13, 1950, p. 4.

†Arn. Chikobava, "On Certain Problems of Soviet Linguistics," Pravda, May 9, 1950.

‡V.I. Lenin, Works, 3rd edition, Vol. XXIV, p. 337.

**J.V. Stalin, Works, Vol. I, p. 314.

††J.V. Stalin, Problems of Leninism, 11th edition, p. 555.

*K. Marx and F. Engels, Works, Vol. IV, p. 20, 434.

†Paul Lafargue, Language and Revolution, Academia series, 1930, p. 31.

tances."* While emphasizing the unity of the Russian national language, he adds: "As opposed to this, in some other countries, for example in Germany, the Bavarian peasant understands but little the one from Mecklenburg or the Brandenburgian the Swabian, although they all belong to the German people."

The testimony of Lomonosov indicates that Russian had taken shape as a national language by the middle of the 18th century while German had not yet jelled, since the German nation had not yet taken shape.

But the community of language does not mean that the national language is not of a class nature. Inasmuch as there are classes and a sharp class struggle under capitalism, there is class consciousness as well which is reflected in language. In a class society the national language, expressing social ideology and practice, acquires a class differentiation also. Class consciousness is reflected in the most varied ways inside the common national language.

In solving the problem of the class nature of language, Prof. A. S. Chikobava takes into account only one of its functions—a means of communication—and starts from the formal aspect of language. If a bourgeois, a landlord, a worker, a peasant, understand one another, if the phonetic, morphologic and syntactic structures are generally the same, then, according to him, the language must consequently be one and not of a class nature.

N. Ya. Marr never ignored the formal side of speech, but he always gave prime emphasis to the most essential thing in language—its semantics, its content, its close connection with thought. Expressing class consciousness, language itself becomes class in nature.

The class nature of language appears not in its phonetic or morphologic structure, but in content. Into the same words (for example, freedom, equality, brotherhood and such) the bourgeoisie and the proletariat read different meanings. V. I. Lenin exposed the class nature of the bourgeois use of words most mercilessly.

The class nature of a national language can be seen most clearly in dictionary work. For example, the interpretive dictionaries of literary Russian of the prerevolutionary period distorted, hid and confused in all kinds of ways the class essence of international political and philosophical terminology: revolution, class, party, agitation, propaganda, idealism, materialism, etc.

The class nature of prerevolutionary literary Russian was expressed, by the way, also in the fact that after October the people discarded all that was ideologically alien and unacceptable. The Russian language was cleansed of lexical rubbish, was enriched with many new words which reflect the new socialist life, the new world view. Our language has become ideologically different, distinct from prerevolutionary speech.

The National Language in Socialist Society.

Prof. A. S. Chikobava does not see or does not want to see the reflection of class consciousness in language. By denying the class nature of language, he makes the mistake of absorbing uncritically the old linguistic heritage. For if language be a non-class phenomenon, then all which was written in this language before the great October socialist revolution can be taken at its face value. But this is not so.

The national language in socialist society finds itself in a completely different position. As a result of the victory of socialism in our country, the survivals of capitalism are disappearing from the people's thinking, and, as a result, the national language becomes really one single language, common to the whole people and not of a class nature. This can be observed in the development of any language of a socialist nation in the U.S.S.R. As applied to socialist nations, A. S. Chikobava's thesis is correct.

*The Works of M. V. Lomonosov, With Explanatory Notes by Academician M. I. Sukhomlinov, Vol. IV, 1898, p. 229.

And precisely this circumstance—the existence of a single national language in every socialist nation—raises with all sharpness the question of its further perfection as a most important tool of culture and of the struggle for communism.

One of the guiding principles in the development of literary languages of the socialist nations of the U.S.S.R. must be the principle that language is of the people and accessible to them.

The literary language must be enriched through the use of the inexhaustible sources of the people's speech. The people are the creators of language. They refine the language, retaining in it what is valuable, bright, colorful, precise and accurate. And our literary language must be enriched with these pearls of popular speech, particularly the style of artistic literature.

A. M. Gorky, a magnificent connoisseur of the Russian language, insistently advised writers not to forget "the basic, spoken Russian language. One should sometimes read the bylinas [epic poetry], folk tales and generally be thoroughly familiar with the language spoken by the masses. There is much there that is musical and expansive.

"In all parts of our enormous country, this process of reorganization of language is now taking place, the process of rejection of certain words, their complete annihilation and the appearance of new words in their stead.

"Alongside of this an enormous process is underway of creating completely new word forms, new proverbs, doggerel and fables*** We should collect all this."*

A. N. Tolstoy tells how he acquired the real Russian language only when he turned to the sources of the Russian speech of the people, to the basic Russian language.

The Contemporary Language of Russian Literature

The language of contemporary Russian artistic literature is qualitatively distinct from the prerevolutionary one. Our literature was enriched with linguistically and stylistically brilliant works of A. M. Gorky, M. Sholokhov, A. Fadeyev, A. Tolstoy, K. Fedin and others. The contemporary Russian language is reflected in them in all its brilliance and beauty.

But, along with this, there are also no few works which need considerable improvement in language and style, as they are written carelessly, with numerous grammatical and syntactic errors. One should not forget that artistic productions are now read by millions of working people and that they learn literary Russian and master its riches from these models. This is why the responsibility of the writer has grown immeasurably at present: he has become the teacher of millions of working people. In educating Soviet people in a Communist spirit, he also teaches them the literary language.

In connection with this, one of the urgent tasks is the study of the language of Soviet artistic literature. A. M. Gorky used to indicate that literary criticism paid little attention to language and underestimated the significance of the word as the basic material of literature. Almost never does criticism take up analysis and appraisal of the language of artistic works. The linguists also have departed from the present day. This is why the study of the language of Soviet artistic literature is badly off. This is also confirmed by the fact that during the last ten to 15 years we have not had a single substantial scholarly work in this field. This discussion must make a break in this respect; it must turn the attention of critics and linguists to the study of the language and style of contemporary artistic literature.

The journalistic style of contemporary literary Russian is an original phenomenon. Never in all its history has this style flowered so as it has in the Soviet period.

Precision, clarity, truthfulness, a principled orientation—these are the basic qualities of the language of Bolshevist

*A.M. Gorky, Uncollected Literary and Critical Articles, pp. 176-7.

journalism.

A wonderful characterization of the language and style of Vladimir Ilyich's works has been given by Comrade Stalin. "Only Lenin could write about the most complicated things so simply and clearly, concisely and daringly—where each sentence does not speak, but shoots."* And further, Comrade Stalin says that in Lenin's speeches "there is unusual strength of conviction, simplicity and clarity of argument, short sentences understandable to all, the absence of ornamentation, the absence of bewitching gestures and effect-seeking phrases striving for an impression***"†

A model of precise, clear, compact, scientific-journalistic style can be found in J. V. Stalin's articles, reports and speeches. M. I. Kalinin, who knew Russian speech well and was a superb orator, said: "Now, if they asked me who knows Russian best of all, I would answer—Stalin. One should learn from him economy, clarity and crystal purity of language."‡

The rich prerevolutionary traditions (Herzen, Belinsky, Dobrolyubov, Chernyshevsky), the powerful influence of the language of Lenin and Stalin, the existence of magnificent conditions for social participation—all this has led to an unprecedented flowering of language and style in Bolshevist journalism. And yet, its language remains unstudied. We don't have a single scientific work on this topic. This is a serious deficiency in the work of Soviet linguists.

*J.V. Stalin, Works, Vol. VI, p. 53.
†Ibid., p. 55.
‡M. I. Kalinin, On Questions of Soviet Culture, p. 105.

During the Soviet period the collective farm village has undergone a radical change economically and culturally. Almost all Soviet peasants are literate. The books, movies, radio and newspapers have entered the daily life of our collective farm peasants. The Communist Party and Soviet government are steadily raising the cultural level of the masses of collective farmers. The thinking of the collective farm peasantry has also changed. Now the peasant is no longer an ignorant and browbeaten muzhik stuffed with superstitions, as he was under Tsarism, but a conscious citizen of his country, understanding political events.

In connection with this, enormous changes took place in the language of the collectivized village. The distinguishing peculiarities of dialects and jargon inherited from feudalism are disappearing: dialects are changing, coming closer to the literary language. But these new processes in the language of the collectivized village have not yet been investigated by Soviet linguists. Following an old tradition, our linguists are still looking for the archaic in dialects and show little concern for the new. This is why we do not have a single serious piece of research in the new elements in the language of the collectivized village, which were generated by socialist conditions of life and socialist way of thinking. This is also a major shortcoming in the work of Soviet linguists.

The discussion about fundamental questions of Soviet linguistics must improve not only the study of general problems, but also the working out of theoretical and practical questions of contemporary Russian and of the other national languages of the Soviet Union.

A Critique of Some of The Theses of the 'New Teaching on Language'*

By Professor P. CHORNYKH

The inadequate development of thorough, principled criticism and self-criticism among Soviet linguists and the incorrect tactics of representatives of the so-called "new science of language" toward the "heterodox" have led to the creation of an extremely tense situation in linguistics. The last few years have probably been the most difficult period in the history of Soviet linguistics, particularly of such branches as the comparative grammar of Slavic languages and the historical grammar of Russian. Moreover, the presence of stagnation, of "freezing," in some branches of linguistics is quite unfavorably reflected in the elaboration of others and also, in some measure, in the teaching of the native language in schools, as well as in the area of "linguistic practice" — the practical development of national languages.

There can be no disputing the fact that the characteristic features of Russian and the peculiarities of its development can best be revealed by comparing it with other Slavic languages, although it would be incorrect to deny completely the importance of a comparative grammar of languages of different systems. However that may be, F. Engels, who says in his "Anti-Dühring" that "the matter and form of the native language become intelligible only when one traces its origin and gradual development," for good reason goes on to say: "this is impossible if one neglects, first, its own obsolete forms and, second, the related languages living and dead."†

However, a materialist elaboration of a comparative grammar of related Slavic languages, with which the historical grammar of Russian is intimately connected, is hardly feasible without presupposing the common origin of Slavic languages, without an all Slavic (even if very relative) linguistic unity in prehistoric times. The comparative-historical study of Slavic languages leads inevitably to the conclusion that such unity did exist in the distant past. That which distinguishes the various Slavic languages from each other at the present time, [namely] differences in the pronunciation of many words and divergences in grammar and vocabulary, can, at least in the majority of cases, be explained and convincingly as a consequence of the fragmentation and splintering of a certain unity.

Without presupposing the original unity of Slavic languages, we would hardly be able to explain satisfactorily the observably startling closeness of contemporary Slavic languages. How could this have come about unless in the distant past the Slavic peoples had passed through a period in which they spoke a common language? Never in historic times were the Slavic peoples united within the boundaries of a single state.

But this simple presupposition is decisively rejected by "the new teaching on language," which proposes a universal thesis that language always and everywhere develops only from "multiplicity to uniformity" and demands in the final analysis that the similarities between languages of a given family (Slavic, Romance, Germanic, etc.) be explained only as a consequence of the "convergence" of languages (during an undefined period), and that the differences between these languages be explained chiefly as reflections of the "divergence" of these languages since prehistoric times. Thus Russian "veli" [they led], according to this view, is not the result of changes from Old Slavic "wiedli," which survives in Polish, but is actually a "divergence" preserved in Russian and Polish since prehistoric times when Slavic languages had not yet had time to jell as Slavic.

It is also usually emphasized that "convergences" and

*Pravda, June 20, 1950, p. 4.
†F. Engels, Anti-Dühring, 1950, p. 303.

"divergences" in languages of a given family result from corresponding transformations in the economic and social life of the peoples of a given group, but the matter is usually limited to unproven general statements. Not a single linguist of N. Ya. Marr's school has so far been able to show through specific examples from the history of a given language how the phenomena of "convergence" and "divergence" can be even ultimately due to the development of the material base. It remains the solemn duty of Soviet linguists to work out such a reconstruction of the history of Russian, or of any other Slavic or non-Slavic language, such an elaboration of historical grammar: a reconstruction based on the development of the social structure and social thought of the people speaking the language, and on the development of class struggle—in short, on the dependable basis of the Marxist-Leninist theory, historical and dialectical materialism, Stalin's brilliant definition of language as "a weapon of development and struggle."

The idea of "differentiation," the fragmentation of original linguistic unity, with which the fate of the comparative-historical method in linguistics is inseparably linked, does not contradict such a reconstruction of the history of a given language. Of course, in this field one must always take into account the actual historical conditions in which any linguistic group develops. Under different conditions the development of languages can assume a different character.

However, there are hardly any serious reasons to consider "reactionary" the very concept of an initial linguistic community, a linguistic unity whose disappearance under certain circumstances could actually lead to the emergence of groups of originally related languages.

In any case, the concept of the fragmentation of initial unity by itself, the notion of development from singleness to multiplicity (naturally up to certain historical limits, within a rigorously defined historical framework) did not seem "reactionary" to F. Engels, who approached this problem from the vantage point of a materialist understanding of history. Through his famous work "The Origin of the Family, Private Property and the State," he even helped to popularize this idea. It may be sufficient to recall the following from Engel's aforementioned book: "The example of North American Indians shows us how an originally single tribe gradually spreads over an enormous land mass; how tribes ramifying become peoples, whole groups of tribes, how languages change, not only becoming mutually unintelligible but losing almost all trace of the original unity***."*

In their critique of the "protolanguage theory," Academician N. Ya. Marr and his students always emphasized that the concept of the development of a group of languages from a protolanguage, the notion of kinship of languages within a group, is a tenet of racist ideology because from the admission of the isolated existence of language families developing as a result of the subdivision of an ancestral language it is only a short step to the recognition of the initial inequality of languages and the superiority of some languages (and peoples) over others. If, for example, one were to admit that Indo-European languages (of whatever origin) had from their very beginning been inflected and that inflection testifies to the "advanced" nature of these languages when compared with amorphous and agglutinative ones, one comes to the conclusion that Indo-European languages were initially higher than others.

However, the question is whether all bourgeois linguists who accept the theory of fragmentation of the initial linguistic unity really do hold that Indo-European languages must necessarily have been inflected from the very first and that inflection is a higher or even ideal form of grammatical structure. One can say without exaggeration that there are very few such linguists left nowadays.

* F. Engels, The Origin of the Family, Private Property and the State, 1949, p. 98.

On the contrary, no matter how startling [this may seem], the doctrine that inflective structure existed "from the start" in Indo-European languages, that Indo-European languages became Indo-European only from the time they became inflected and (what is particularly significant) that inflected languages were superior to others, is now connected mostly with such names as N. Ya. Marr and I. I. Meshchaninov, despite their repeated but unproven assertions that the new theory of how human speech developed starts from the idea of equality and "kinship" of all the globe's languages.

As is well known, according to N. Ya. Marr's doctrine of the development of languages "by stages" (a doctrine which, by the way, was recast several times and finally, in the words of Academician Meshchaninov, remained unfinished), there was at first neither agglutination nor inflection. "In the period of primitive communism" human speech was grammatically amorphous, which, simply stated, means that words were neither declined nor conjugated and had no inflection, affixes or prefixes. In time, at a new stage of social development, agglutinative structure emerges in connection with "social division by trades," and there appear besides amorphous also agglutinative (or "pasting together") languages possessing declension and conjugation but with weak inflection. Still later—in the period of "estate or class society," to use the same Marr terminology—along with amorphous and agglutinative languages there appear some with internal inflection (for example, Semitic) and some with external inflection (Indo-European). Thus, according to Marr, Indo-European languages are a crowning achievement in the development of human speech.

In his article "On the Question of Linguistic Stages," I. I. Meschaninov once would have liked to go even farther than N. Ya. Marr and assert that nowadays (grammatically) the most progressive of the Indo-European languages were French and English, which according to him were the latest, seventh, highest stage in the grammatical development of human speech.*

The adherents of the "new teaching on language," when criticizing the theory of fragmentation of languages, usually rely on a famous statement N. Ya. Marr made in 1924 in a short note which included no factual material whatever, called "The Indo-European Languages of the Mediterranean." [There he states] that Indo-European languages emerged not as a consequence of the fragmentation of the Indo-European protolanguage, but as a result of the transformation, the regeneration of the Japhetic languages of the Mediterranean in connection with the discovery of metals and their wide economic utilization. This is an interesting and scientifically fruitful idea, but one demanding substantial proof. To speak specifically of Eastern Slavic languages, one can state plainly that hardly anybody will be able to prove as an uncontrovertible fact that they come, for example, from Scythian languages, for the simple reason that at first, in antiquity, several distinct peoples speaking different languages were apparently called Scythians. Among these peoples there may possibly have been Slavs too. Second, and most important, we know too little of these [Scythian] languages. It is true that for quite a while we have had some (if very sketchy) data which permit raising the question of some possible connections of Slavic and particularly Eastern Slavic with Scythian, non-Slavic languages. Therefore, one could admit that Slavic languages emerged from non-Slavic, non-Indo-European ones in the process of their hybridization or "convergence" at a certain stage of the social and economic development of the prehistoric population of Middle and Eastern Europe. But this does not settle the question of common Slavic linguistic unity in the past.

Thus Marr's theory, pointed against the allegedly "reac-

*Journal of the U.S.S.R. Academy of Sciences, Division of Social Sciences, 1931, pp. 881 ff.

tionary" idea of protolanguage, against the theory of linguistic fragmentation, can itself be utilized in no lesser degree than the latter as an ideological platform of imperialism's colonial policy, granted the desire somewhere in the imperialist West on the part of some "eager seeker" after ideological justification of aggressive plans. In the given case, the counter agent must be the doctrine, emerging from the fundamental theses of Marxism-Leninism, of the equality of languages (in the sense of equal developmental capabilities given equal social and economic premises), of the equal value of all the world's languages as means of communication, as weapons of development and struggle.

The article which Academician Meshchaninov contributed to the discussion (Pravda, May 16, 1950) includes no new arguments, nor any new thoughts on the question of protolanguage, this matter apparently being considered long since finally settled. On the contrary, in this article too the author operates as formerly with such excessively general concepts as "convergence" and "divergence" in language, strengthening his reasoning with such expressions as "reactionary hypothesis." How cloudy such reasoning can be is to be seen from the following quote about Romance languages: "if Romance languages, including French and Spanish, arose from the blending of several other languages and reveal numerous(?) common features, then in these converging so-called Romance languages similar ingredients (?!) participate in the same way in which they participated in the formation of the respective peoples, later nations." (Emphasis mine — P. Ch.)*

For this reason, in the absence of sufficient clarity in the very raising of this question, I. I. Meshchaninov's statement that "the rejection of protolanguage is the beginning of materialist linguistics" remains unclarified.

In the aforementioned article of Academician Meshchaninov there is nothing significantly new about another extremely important question which in his article is classified among "problems requiring refinement and additional work," the question of the four elements and their phonetic variants.

As is well known, the linguistic aspects of N. Ya. Marr's theory are built wholly on an unproven premise that all words in all the world's languages always consisted and still do consist of these four elements (although mostly in a greatly modified form) as a consequence of the functioning of some universal phonetic laws not limited by either time or space. With the aid of these laws one can prove whatever one wishes.

It is not surprising that lately there have been more and more persistent rumors alleging that Marr's followers have given up or are ready to give up the doctrine of the four elements. We have quite a few more or less decisive statements by I. I. Meschaninov, beginning about 1946, rejecting (sometimes fully, sometimes partially) this doctrine. In his latest contribution to the discussion, Academician Meshchaninov confirms again that "paleontologic analysis, which traces qualitative changes in language, makes it possible even without element analysis to approach the developmental history of different languages through the use of their own data." Again it remains unclear what this permission granted linguists to engage in "paleontological" study of particular languages "through the use of their own data," means: [is it] recognition of the phonetic laws ascertained before Marr and Meshchaninov, that is, in other words, admission of the comparative-historical method into linguistics, or is it something else?

But is not the rejection of paleontological analysis with the utilization of the four elements also the rejection of the singleness of the glottogonic (language-forming) process and consequently, in some measure, of criticism of the "protolanguage" theory? After all, the critique of the theory of linguistic fragmentation was most intimately connected with the doctrine of a single "glottogonic process." And this whole doctrine was elaborated on the basis of element analysis.

* * *

We see that many of the fundamental theses offered by the "new teaching on language" did not survive the test of time, that they turned out to be either obviously erroneous or more or less controversial. The doctrine of four-element analysis takes first place in these ranks.

Unfortunately, the "enthusiasts" of the "new teaching on language" will probably never make up their minds to give up four-element analysis fully, because this analysis is correctly evaluated as the keystone of Marr's theory. Four-element analysis is the chief argument in the arsenal of the "new teaching on language." In case of a definitive rejection of this weapon, "the new teaching on language" must become a kind of repository of particular, diverse, though sometimes very interesting observations, aphorisms and general statements, which will await proof as before.

Even the very expression "the new teaching on language," the name of N. Ya. Marr's theory, cannot but be considered obsolete in our day. Its use is in no way justified. Actually, in what respect is this linguistic doctrine "new?" If it is new in relation to formal, idealistic, bourgeois linguistics, then why not call such a doctrine simply "Soviet linguistics, the Marxist-Leninist science of language?" Is it "new" in relation to Soviet linguistics? There is only one Soviet linguistics because there is a single theoretical base for it—the general methodological statements and the specifically linguistic statements of Marx, Engels, Lenin and Stalin. There can be no "new science of language" alongside it.

*I.I. Meshchaninov, "For a Creative Development of Academician N. Ya. Marr's Heritage," Pravda, May 16, 1950.

On Marxism in Linguistics*

By J. STALIN

A group of youthful comrades has suggested to me that I express my opinion in the press on linguistic problems, particularly where Marxism in linguistics is concerned. I am not a linguist and, of course, I cannot fully satisfy the comrades. As for Marxism in linguistics as well as other social sciences, I am directly concerned with this. I have therefore consented to reply to a number of questions asked by the comrades.

QUESTION: Is it true that language is a superstructure over a base?

Answer: No, it is not true.

The base is the economic structure of society at a given stage of its development. The superstructure comprises the political, legal, religious, artistic and philosophical views of society and their corresponding political, legal and other institutions.

Every base has its corresponding superstructure. The base of the feudal order has its own superstructure, its political, legal and other views and the institutions corresponding to them; the capitalist base has its superstructure; the socialist has its superstructure. If the base changes and is eliminated, then its superstructure changes and is eliminated after it; if a new base is born, then a superstructure corresponding to it is born after it.

In this respect language differs radically from the superstructure. Take, for example, Russian society and the Russian language. During the past 30 years the old capitalist base has been liquidated in Russia and a new, socialist base constructed. Correspondingly, the superstructure over the capitalist base has been eliminated and a new superstructure created corresponding to the socialist base. Consequently, the old political, legal, etc., institutions have been replaced by new, socialist ones. Despite this, however, the Russian language has remained basically the same as it was before the October revolution.

What changes occurred during this period in the Russian language? To a certain extent the vocabulary of the Russian language changed, in the sense that a large number of new words and expressions were added which had appeared as a result of the development of a new, socialist mode of production, the appearance of a new state, a new socialist culture, a new public opinion and morality and, finally, as a result of the development of science and technology. A number of words and expressions underwent a change in meaning and acquired new significance. A certain number of obsolete words disappeared from the vocabulary. As for the basic lexical fund and the grammatical structure of the Russian language, which comprise the basis of the language, after the elimination of the capitalist base they were not only not eliminated and replaced by a new basic lexical fund and a new grammatical structure, but, on the contrary, were retained in their entirety and remained without any serious alterations. They were retained precisely as the basis of the contemporary Russian language.

To continue. The superstructure is generated by the base, but this by no means signifies that it merely reflects the base, that it is passive, neutral and indifferent to the fate of its base, to the fate of classes, to the character of the system. On the contrary, having put in an appearance, it then becomes a most active force which contributes vigorously to the formation and consolidation of its base, takes all steps to assist the new order to drive the old base and the former classes into the dust and liquidate them.

It could not be otherwise. The superstructure is created by the base to serve it, to help it actively in taking shape and growing strong, to struggle vigorously to get rid of the old base and its old superstructure which have outlived their time. The superstructure has merely to renounce its role as servitor, to switch from the active defense of its base to an attitude of indifference to it, to an attitude of an equal approach to the classes for it to lose its quality and cease to be a superstructure.

In this respect language differs radically from superstructure. Language is generated not by one base or another, by the old base or the new within a given society, but by the entire historic development of society and the history of the bases over the centuries. It is created not by any one class but by the whole society, by all classes of society, by the efforts of hundreds of generations. It is created not to meet the needs of any one class but of the whole society, of all classes in society. This is precisely why it is created as the language of the whole people, as a society's single language, common to all members of the society. In view of this, the role of language as a servant, as a means of communication for people consists not in serving one class to the detriment of other classes but in equal service to the entire society, to all classes in society. Strictly speaking, this is the reason why language can serve equally both the old, dying order and the new, emerging one, both the old base and the new, both exploiters and the exploited.

It is no secret that the Russian language served Russian capitalism and Russian bourgeois culture before the October revolution just as well as it now serves the socialist system and the socialist culture of Russian society.

The same holds true of Ukrainian, Belorussian, Uzbek, Kazakh, Georgian, Armenian, Estonian, Latvian, Lithuanian, Moldavian, Tatar, Azerbaidzhanian, Bashkir, Turkmenian and the other languages of the Soviet nations which served the old bourgeois systems in those nations as well as they are now serving the new, socialist system.

It cannot be otherwise. Language exists, it is created, to serve society as a whole in the capacity of a means of communication for people, to be common to the members of a society and one and the same for the society, serving the members of the society equally, regardless of their class position. Language has only to depart from this position with respect to the entire people, language has only to show preference for and render support to a particular social group, to the detriment of other social groups of the society for it to lose its quality, for it to cease to be a means of communication of people in a society, for it to become the jargon of a particular social group, for it to degenerate and doom itself to extinction.

In this respect language, while differing fundamentally from the superstructure, is not, however, different from the tools of production, machinery, say, which can serve both capitalism and socialism equally.

To continue. Superstructure is the product of a single epoch in which a given economic base lives and operates. Hence the superstructure lives a short time, is eliminated and disappears with the liquidation and disappearance of a given base.

But language, on the other hand, is the product of a great many epochs, during which it assumes shape, grows rich and develops, is polished. Hence, a language lives incomparably longer than any base and any superstructure. Strictly speaking, this is why the birth and elimination not only of

*Pravda, June 20, 1950, pp. 3-4.

one base and its superstructure but of several bases and their corresponding superstructures does not lead historically to the liquidation of a given language and its structure and to the birth of a new language with new vocabulary and new grammar.

More than 100 years have elapsed since Pushkin's death. Within this period feudalism and capitalism were eliminated in Russia and a third, socialist order arose. Consequently, two bases were eliminated together with their superstructures and a new, socialist base came into being together with its new superstructure. However, if one were to take the Russian language, it did not experience any clear break and present day Russian differs little in structure from Pushkin's language.

What did change in Russian in this period? The Russian vocabulary was considerably augmented; many obsolete words disappeared from the language; many words changed their meaning and the grammatical structure of the language improved. As for the structure and grammar of Pushkin's language as well as its basic lexical fund, in all fundamentals it remained the basis of the Russian language of today.

This is fully understandable. Really, what sense would there be if language's existing structure, its grammar and basic vocabulary were to be destroyed and replaced with new ones after every upheaval, as is ordinarily true of the superstructure? What would be the point if "water," "land," "mountain," "forest," "fish," "man," "to walk," "to do," "to produce," "to trade," etc., were to be called not water, land, mountain, etc., but something else? What purpose would there be if words were to change in the language and word combinations in the sentence were to change not according to the existing grammar but according to a totally different one? Of what benefit to the revolution would such an upheaval be in language? History generally does nothing significant without a special need for it. One may ask, what is the need for such a radical change in language if it can be proved that the existing language with its structure is in the main wholly suitable to the needs of the new order? The old superstructure can and must be destroyed and replaced with a new one in a few years' time so as to give scope to the development of society's productive forces. But how can an existing language be destroyed and a new one erected in its stead in a few years' time without introducing chaos into the life of society and creating a threat of social disintegration? Who but Don Quixotes can undertake such a task?

Finally, there is one more radical distinction between superstructure and language. The superstructure is not linked directly to production, to man's productive activity. It is linked only indirectly with production, through the medium of the economy, the base. Hence, the superstructure does not reflect changes in the developmental level of productive forces immediately and directly, but after changes in the base, through the refraction of changes in production, in changes in the base. This means that the sphere of action of the superstructure is narrow and limited.

Language, on the other hand, is directly linked to man's productive activity, and not only to his productive activity but to every other activity in all aspects of man's work, from production to the base, from the base to the superstructure. Hence, language immediately and directly reflects changes in production without waiting for changes in the base. Hence, language's sphere of action, embracing all provinces of man's activity, is far broader and more diverse than the sphere of action of the superstructure. More than that, it is practically limitless.

This is the main reason why language, particularly its vocabulary, is in a state of almost constant change. The uninterrupted development of industry and agriculture, trade and transport, science and technology, requires that the vocabulary of language be broadened to include new words and expressions needed for their work. And language, reflecting these needs directly, supplements its vocabulary with new words, improves its grammar.

Thus: (a) a Marxist cannot regard language as a superstructure over a base; (b) to confuse language with superstructure is to commit a grave error.

QUESTION: Is it true that language has always been and remains of a class nature; that a single, non-class language common to a whole society and a whole people does not exist?

Answer: No, it is not true.

It is easy to see that there can be no question of a class language in a society without classes. The primitive clan society did not have classes and hence there could not have been a class language in it. There language was general. There was a single language for the whole collective. The objection that a class should be understood as any human collective, including the primitive commune, is not an objection but a play on words not meriting refutation.

As for subsequent development, from clan languages to tribal, from tribal languages to the languages of peoples and from the languages of peoples to national languages—everywhere, at every stage of development, language, as a means of communication for people in society, was common and single for the society, serving the members of society equally, regardless of social position.

Here I have in mind not the empires of the slave-owning and medieval periods, say the empire of Cyrus and Alexander the Great, or the empires of Caesar and Charlemagne, which did not have their own economic base and were temporary and unstable military and administrative combinations. These empires not only did not possess but could not have possessed a single language understandable to all members of society. They were a conglomeration of tribes and peoples who lived their own lives and had their own languages. Consequently, I am not referring to these empires and their like but to the tribes and peoples which comprised the empires and possessed their own economic bases and their own languages, which had developed in very ancient times. History shows that the languages of these tribes and peoples were not class languages but languages of the whole people, common for the tribes and peoples and understandable to them.

Of course, along with them there were dialects and local tongues, but the single common language of the tribe or people predominated over them and made them subordinate.

Later on when capitalism appeared and feudal disunity was overcome, when the national market was formed, peoples developed into nations and the languages of peoples into the languages of nations. History shows that national languages are not class languages but are common to the whole people, common to the members of nations and one and the same for the nation.

I stated above that as a means of communication among people in society a language serves equally all classes in society and in this respect is, in a manner of speaking, indifferent to classes. But people, particular social groups and classes, are anything but indifferent to language. They try to use language for their own interest, to impose their own special vocabulary, terminology, their own special expressions, upon it. The uppermost layer of the propertied classes, divorced from the people and hating them, stand out particularly in this respect. Such are the aristocracy of the nobility and the upper strata of the bourgeoisie. "Class" dialects, jargons and salon "languages" developed. The literature [on the subject] not infrequently wrongly qualifies these dialects and jargons as languages and refers to "the language of the nobility," "the language of the bourgeoisie," in contrast to "the language of the proletariat." or the "language of the peasantry." Strange as it may seem, it was for this reason that some of our comrades reached the conclusion that a national language was a fiction and that only class languages actually existed.

I maintain that nothing could be more erroneous. Can these dialects and jargons be considered languages? Absolutely not. This is, first of all, because these dialects and jargons do not have their own grammar and basic lexical fund. They borrow them from the national language. Secondly, because the dialects and jargons circulate within a narrow sphere among the upper strata of a particular class and are totally worthless as a means of communication for people, for society as a whole. What do they actually have? They have a selection of certain specific words which reflect the specific tastes of the aristocracy or the upper strata of the bourgeoisie; a certain number of expressions and turns of speech distinguished for their refinement, gallantry, and free of the "coarse" expressions and figures of speech of the national language, and, finally, a certain number of foreign words. Everything basic, however, that is, the great majority of words and the grammar, are taken from the national language, common to the whole people. Consequently dialects and jargons are ramifications of the common national language of the people, are lacking in any independence as languages and are doomed to stagnation. To believe that dialects and jargons can develop into independent languages which are able to drive out and replace the national language is to lose sight of historical perspective and depart from the Marxist position.

Marx has been referred to and one place has been cited from his article "Holy Max" where he wrote that the bourgeois had his "own language," that this language "is the product of the bourgeoisie," that it is permeated with the spirit of mercantilism and of buying and selling. With this quotation some comrades would like to prove that Marx allegedly believed in the class nature of language and denied that a single national language existed. If these comrades had approached the question objectively they should also have quoted another place in the same article "Holy Max" where Marx, referring to the ways in which a single national language is formed, speaks of the "concentration of dialects into a single national language resulting from economic and political concentration."

Marx, consequently, admitted the need for a single national language as the superior form to which dialects, as lower forms, were subordinate.

In this event, what can the language of the bourgeois be, which in Marx's words "is the product of the bourgeoisie." Did Marx consider it a language just the same as a national language with its own special language structure? Could he have considered it to be such a language? Of course not! Marx simply wanted to say that the bourgeois had profaned the single national language with its vocabulary of cheap commercialism, that the bourgeois, consequently, had his own cheap commercial jargon.

The result is that these comrades have distorted Marx's point. They distorted it by quoting Marx not as Marxists but as pedants without looking into the essence of the matter.

References are made to Engels and to the quotation from his pamphlet "The condition of the working class in England" where Engels says that "***in the course of time the British working class has become an entirely different people from the British bourgeoisie," that "the workers speak a different dialect and have different ideas and notions, different mores and moral principles, a different religion and different politics from the bourgeoisie." On the basis of this quotation certain comrades have concluded that Engels denied the need for a national language common to the whole people, that he consequently advocated the "class nature" of language. It is true that Engels is here speaking not of a language but of a dialect, fully comprehending that a dialect, as a ramification of the national language, cannot replace the national language. But evidently these comrades are not very sympathetic to the existence of a difference between language and dialects.

It is obvious that this quotation has been inappropriately cited since Engels is here speaking not of "class languages" but principally about class ideas, notions, mores, moral principles, religion and politics. It is perfectly true that the ideas, notions, mores, moral principles, religion and politics of the bourgeois and proletariat are directly opposite. But what has the national language or the "class" nature of language to do with this? Can the presence of class contradictions in society serve as an argument in favor of the "class nature" of language, or against the need for a single national language? Marxism holds that a common language is one of the most important characteristics of a nation, knowing well that there are class contradictions within a nation. Do the aforementioned comrades recognize this Marxist thesis?

They refer to Lafargue and point out that in his pamphlet "Language and Revolution" Lafargue recognizes the "class nature" of language. They allege that he denies the need for a national language common to the whole people. This is not true. In reality Lafargue speaks of a "noble" or "aristocratic language" and of the "jargons" of various strata of society. But these comrades forget that Lafargue, while not interested in the difference between a language and a jargon and calling dialects one moment "artificial speech" and another "jargon," definitely says in his pamphlet that "artificial speech which distinguishes the aristocracy***came from the language of the people as a whole, spoken by the bourgeois, the craftsmen, the city and the country."

Consequently Lafargue recognizes the existence of and need for a language of the whole people, fully aware of the subordinate nature and dependence of the "aristocratic language" and other dialects and jargons upon the language of the whole people.

It turns out that reference to Lafargue misses the point.

Reference is made to the fact that at one time the feudal lords in England "for centuries" spoke French while the English people spoke English, and that this circumstance is allegedly an argument in favor of the "class nature" of language and against the need for a language common to the whole people. This is not an argument, however, but a kind of anecdote. Firstly, all the feudal lords did not speak French at that time, but only a small upper stratum of English feudal lords attached to the court and in the counties. Secondly, it was not some special "class language" they spoke but ordinary French common to the whole people. Third, it is known that the affection of French later disappeared without a trace, yielding to the English language of the whole people. Do these comrades maintain that "for centuries" the English feudal lords communed with the English people through the medium of interpreters, that they did not use English, that an English language did not then exist for the whole people, that at that time the French language was anything more important in England than the language of the salon, current only in a narrow circle of the upper layer of the English aristocracy? How can one deny the existence of and need for a language common to the whole people on the basis of such anecdotal "arguments?"

At one time Russian aristocrats also flirted with French at the Tsar's court and in the salons. It was their boast that while speaking Russian they hiccuped in French, that they could speak Russian only with a French accent. Does this mean that there was no common Russian language in Russia at the time, that a language common to the whole people was a fiction at that time whereas "class languages" were the reality?

Here our comrades make at least two mistakes.

The first mistake is that they confuse language and superstructure. They hold that if superstructure is of a class nature, then language too should be of a class nature and not common to the people as a whole. But I have already remarked above that language and superstructure are two different concepts and that a Marxist cannot admit of their confusion.

The second mistake is that these comrades regard the contradictory nature of the interests of the bourgeoisie and the proletariat, their violent class warfare, as the disintegration of society and the break of all ties between the hostile classes. They maintain that since society has fallen apart and there is no longer a single society but only classes, a single language for society, a national language, is also superfluous. What then remains if society has fallen apart and there is no longer a national language common to the whole people? Classes and "class languages" remain. Every "class language" will, understandably, have its own "class" grammar, —a "proletarian" grammar, a "bourgeois" grammar. True, such grammars do not exist in reality but these comrades are not embarrassed by this. They believe that such grammars will appear.

There were once "Marxists" among us who maintained that the railroads which remained in our country after the October revolution were bourgeois, that we Marxists ought not to use them, that they should be torn up and new "proletarian" railroads built. For this they earned the sobriquet of "troglodytes."

Of course such a primitive anarchistic view of society, classes and language has nothing in common with Marxism. But there can be no doubt whatever that it exists and still lives in the minds of certain of our confused comrades.

It is, of course, wrong to say that because of the existence of a violent class struggle society has allegedly split into classes which are economically no longer associated with each other in one society. On the contrary. As long as capitalism exists the bourgeoisie and the proletariat will be connected with each other by every economic tie as parts of a single capitalist society. The bourgeoisie cannot live and grow rich without having hired workers at its disposal; the proletariat cannot continue its existence without hiring out to the capitalists. The termination of all economic ties between them signifies the end of any production. The end of all production, moreover, leads to the ruin of society, to the ruin of the classes themselves. It is understandable that no class will want to undergo annihilation. Class struggle, therefore, no matter how acute, cannot result in the disintegration of society. Only ignorance in Marxist problems and utter failure to comprehend the nature of language could have suggested to certain of our comrades the fairy tale about the disintegration of society, about "class" languages and "class" grammars.

Furthermore they refer to Lenin and recall that Lenin recognized the existence of two cultures under capitalism, the bourgeois and the proletarian, that the slogan of a national culture under capitalism was a nationalistic slogan. All this is correct and Lenin here was absolutely right. But what has the "class nature" of language to do with this? They cite Lenin's remarks on two cultures under capitalism, evidently desiring to make the reader believe that the presence of two cultures in society, bourgeois and proletarian, means that there must also be two languages, since language is associated with culture; consequently, Lenin was denying the need for a single national language; Lenin was consequently holding a brief for "class" languages. Here these comrades make the error of identifying and confusing language with culture. But culture and language are two different things. Culture may be both bourgeois and socialist whereas language as a means of communication is always common to a whole people and can serve both bourgeois and socialist culture. Is it not true that Russian, Ukrainian and Uzbek are now serving the socialist culture of these nations just as satisfactorily as they served their bourgeois cultures before the October revolution? Thus these comrades are profoundly in error when they declare that the presence of two different cultures leads to the formation of two different languages and to the denial that a single language must exist.

When he spoke of two cultures, Lenin was proceeding from precisely that thesis that the presence of two cultures cannot lead to the denial of a single language and the formation of two languages, that language must be single. When the members of the Bund charged Lenin with denying the need for a national language and treating culture as "nationless," Lenin, as is known, abruptly protested and declared that he was fighting against bourgeois culture and not against a national language, the need for which he considered indisputable. Certain of our comrades have strangely wandered into the footsteps of the Bundists.

As for a single language, the need for which it is alleged that Lenin denied, we ought to heed the following words of Lenin:

"Language is an extremely important means of human communication; the unity of language and its unimpeded development constitute one of the most important conditions for an organization of trade which will be really free and broad corresponding to contemporary capitalism and for a free and broad grouping of population according to all individual classes."

It turns out that the esteemed comrades have distorted Lenin's views.

Finally they refer to Stalin. They cite a quotation from Stalin to the effect that "the bourgeoisie and its nationalistic parties have been and remain the cardinal directing force of these nations in this period." All this is correct. The bourgeoisie and its nationalistic party really do control bourgeois culture just as the proletariat and its internationalist party control proletarian culture. But what does the "class nature" of language have to do with this? Surely these comrades must know that a national language is a form of national culture, that a national language can serve both bourgeois and socialist culture. Can it be that our comrades are not aware of the well-known Marxist formula that contemporary Russian, Ukrainian, Belorussian and other cultures are socialist in content and national in form, that is, in language? Do they agree with this Marxist formula?

The mistake our comrades make here is that they fail to see the difference between culture and language and do not understand that the content of culture changes with each new period in society's development while language remains basically the same language throughout several periods, serving equally both the new culture and the old.

Hence: (a) language as a means of communication has always been and remains one and the same for society and common to its members; (b) the existence of dialects and jargons does not refute but confirms the existence of a language common to the whole people of which they are ramifications and to which they are subordinate; (c) the formula of the "class nature" of language is an erroneous, un-Marxist formula.

QUESTION: What are the characteristic features of a language?

Answer: Language is one of those social phenomena which operate all during society's existence. It is born and develops with the birth and development of society. It dies together with the death of society. There can be no language outside of society. Hence language and the laws of its development can be comprehended only if they are studied in indissoluble connection with the history of society and with the history of the people to which the language under study belongs and which is the creator and the bearer of this language.

Language is a means, a device, by which people communicate with each other, exchange ideas and achieve mutual understanding. Being directly connected with thought, language registers and reinforces in words, and in combinations of words in sentences, the results of thought, the successes of man's cognition, and thus makes it possible to exchange ideas in human society.

The exchange of ideas is a constant and vital necessity since without it it is impossible to organize the joint activity of people in combatting the forces of nature, in striving to produce essential material goods, and it is impossible to achieve success in society's productive activity. Consequently without a language understood by society and common to its members, society ceases to produce, disintegrates and ceases to exist as society. In this sense language, while a means of communication, is at the same time a means of society's struggle and development.

All the words of a language are known to comprise together the vocabulary of a language. The main part of a language's vocabulary is a basic lexical fund which includes all root words as its nucleus. It is far less extensive than the language's vocabulary. It lives very long, for centuries, and gives the language a foundation for the formation of new words. The vocabulary reflects the state of language. The richer and more diversified the vocabulary, the richer and more developed the language.

Vocabulary itself, however, is not yet the language, but rather the building material for the language. Just as on a construction job the building materials do not constitute the building, although the building cannot be built without them, so the vocabulary of a language is not the language itself, although no language is conceivable without it. But a language's vocabulary receives its greatest significance when it comes under the control of the language's grammar, which determines the rules for word changes, the rules for word combinations in sentences and thus gives language a harmonious, intelligent character. Grammar (morphology and syntax) is a collection of rules of word changes and word combinations in the sentence. Consequently it is precisely thanks to grammar that language has a chance to garb human thought in a material linguistic covering. The distinguishing trait of grammar is that it sets rules for word changes, having in mind not specific words but words in general without any specificity. It sets rules for sentence formation having in mind not specific sentences, say, a specific subject, a specific predicate, but all sentences in general, irrespective of the specific form of one sentence or another. Consequently, abstracting from the particular and concrete both in words and in sentences, grammar takes the general element at the basis of word changes and word combinations in sentences and erects grammatical rules and laws from it. Grammar is the result of the prolonged abstractive work of human thinking, an index of the tremendous successes of thought.

In this respect grammar is like geometry, which establishes its laws on the basis of abstractions from specific objects, regarding objects as bodies lacking concreteness and determining relations between them not as the concrete relations of some concrete objects but as the relations of bodies in general lacking specificity.

Unlike the superstructure, which is connected with production not directly but through the medium of the economy, language is directly connected with man's productive activity as well as with every other activity in all spheres of his work without exception. Hence the language's vocabulary, as most sensitive to change, is in almost constant change. Language moreover, unlike the superstructure, does not have to wait for the liquidation of the base but makes changes in its vocabulary before the liquidation of the base and without regard for the state of the base. However, the vocabulary of the language changes, not as the superstructure and not through the abrogation of the old and construction of the new, but by expanding the existing vocabulary to include new words which have developed in response to changes in the social order, along with the development of production, culture, science, etc. Moreover, notwithstanding the fact that usually a certain number of obsolete words disappear from a vocabulary, a far greater number of new words is added to it. As for the basic lexical fund, it is retained in all essentials and used as the foundation for a language's vocabulary.

This is understandable. There is no need to destroy the basic lexical fund if it can be profitably used over a number of historical periods, to say nothing of the fact that the destruction of the basic lexical fund accumulated in the course of centuries, since it is not possible to create a new basic lexical fund within a short period, would lead to the paralysis of language, to the utter disorganization of communication among people.

A language's grammatical structure changes even more slowly than its basic lexical fund. The grammatical structure, worked out in the course of ages and having become the language's flesh and blood, changes even more slowly than the basic lexical fund. Of course it undergoes changes in the course of time. It is perfected, it improves its rules and makes them more precise, it is enriched with new rules, but the bases of grammatical structure are retained for a very long time, since, as history shows, they can successfully serve society for a number of eras.

Thus, the grammatical structure of language and its basic lexical fund are the foundation of a language, the essence of its identity.

History records the great stability of language and its colossal powers of resistance to forced assimilation. Some historians, instead of explaining this phenomenon, go no further than to express surprise, but there are no reasons for surprise here. The stability of a language is explained by the stability of its grammatical structure and basic lexical fund. For hundreds of years Turkish assimilators sought to maim, destroy and annihilate the languages of the Balkan peoples. In this period the vocabulary of the Balkan languages underwent major changes; many Turkish words and expressions were absorbed; there were "similarities" and "divergences," but the Balkan languages held out and survived. Why? Because the grammatical structure and the basic lexical fund of these languages were retained in the essentials.

It follows from all this that language, its structure, cannot be regarded as the product of any one epoch. The structure of language, its grammar and basic lexical fund, is the product of a number of eras.

It is to be assumed that the elements of the contemporary language were formed far back in antiquity before the slave-owning period. This language was not complex; it had a very sparse vocabulary, but did have its own grammar, primitive, it is true, but grammar nonetheless.

Subsequent development of production, the appearance of classes, the appearance of writing, the inception of the state, which had need of a more or less well-organized correspondence in order to govern, the development of trade, which had even greater need for such correspondence, the appearance of printing equipment, the development of literature, all this made great changes in the development of language. In this period tribes and peoples split up and separated, intermingled and intercrossed, and, subsequently, national languages and states appeared, revolutionary upheavals occurred and old social orders gave way to new ones. All this made even greater changes in language and its development.

It would, however, be profoundly erroneous to believe that the development of language proceeded in the same way as the development of the superstructure: through the destruction of the existing and the construction of the new. Actually the development of language occurred not through the destruction of the existing language and the construction of the new, but through the development and improvement of the main elements of the existing language. Moreover, the transition from one qualitative state of a language to another took place not through an explosion, not through the destruction at one blow of the old and the construction of the new but through the gradual and prolonged accumulation of elements of the new quality, of the new structure of the language and through the gradual dying off of the old quality's elements.

They say that the theory of the development of language by stages is a Marxist theory since it recognizes the necessity of sudden explosions as the conditions for the transition of language from the old quality to the new. This is, of course, false, for it is hard to find anything Marxist in this theory. And if the theory of stage development really does recognize sudden explosions in the history of the development of a language, so much the worse for it. Marxism does not recognize sudden explosions in the development of a language, the sudden death of an existing language and the sudden construction of a new language. Lafargue was not correct when he spoke of the "sudden revolution in language which occurred between 1789 and 1794" in France (see Lafargue's pamphlet "Language and Revolution"). There was no language revolution, much less a sudden one, in France at that time. Of course, in that period the vocabulary of the French language was broadened with new words and expressions; a certain number of obsolete words disappeared, the meaning of some words changed, and nothing more. But such changes do not in any measure determine the fate of a language. The main thing in a language is its grammar and basic lexical fund. But the grammar and basic lexical fund of French not only did not disappear during the French bourgeois revolution but remained without essential changes. Not only were they preserved but they continue to this day to live in present-day French. I am saying nothing of the fact that to liquidate an existing language and build a new national language ("sudden language revolution!") a period of five or six years is short to the point of being ridiculous. Centuries are required for this.

Marxism maintains that the transition of a language from an old qualitative state to a new occurs not through an explosion, not through the destruction of the existing language and the creation of a new one, but through the gradual accumulation of elements of the new quality, consequently, through the gradual dying off of the elements of the old quality.

In general it should be drawn to the attention of the comrades who have been attracted by the notion of explosions that the law of the transition from an old quality to a new through an explosion is not only inapplicable to the history of a language's development, but it is not always applicable to other social phenomena of a basic or superstructure nature. It is obligatory for a society divided into hostile classes. But it is not at all obligatory for a society which does not have hostile classes. In eight or ten years' time we made the transition in our country's agriculture from the bourgeois system of individual peasantry to the socialist, collective farm system. This was a revolution which liquidated the old bourgeois economic order in the villages and set up a new socialist order. However, this upheaval was not accomplished through an explosion, that is, not through overthrowing the existing authority and creating a new regime, but through the gradual transition from the old bourgeois system in the villages to the new. And this could be done successfully because it was a revolution from above; the upheaval was accomplished on the initiative of the existing regime with the support of the main masses of the peasantry.

They say that numerous cases of the hybridization of languages which have occurred in history give grounds for the belief that hybridization results in the formation of a new language by means of an explosion, a sudden transition from an old quality to a new quality. This is quite wrong.

The hybridization of languages must not be regarded as a single decisive act which produces results in several years. The hybridization of languages is a prolonged process which goes on for hundreds of years. Hence there can be no question here of any explosions.

To continue. It would be quite wrong to think that as a result of the hybridization of, say, two languages, a third new language is obtained which is not similar to either of the hybridized languages and differs qualitatively from each of them. In actuality, in the process of hybridization, one of the languages usually emerges victorious, preserves its grammar and basic lexical fund and continues to develop by the internal laws of its own development, while the other language gradually loses its quality and dies off.

Consequently, hybridization does not produce a third new language but retains one of the languages, retains its grammar and basic lexical fund and gives it a chance to develop by the internal laws of its own development.

True, in the process the vocabulary of the victorious language is somewhat enriched at the expense of the defeated language, but this does not weaken it, but, on the contrary, strengthens it.

This is what happened, for example, with Russian, with which the languages of a number of other peoples blended in the course of historical development and which always emerged victorious.

Of course, Russian vocabulary was enriched in the process from the vocabulary of the other languages, but this not only did not weaken but on the contrary, enriched and strengthened the Russian language.

As for the national originality of the Russian language, it experienced not the slightest damage, since, preserving its grammatical structure and basic lexical fund, the Russian language continued to move forward and to improve by the internal laws of its own development.

There can be no doubt that the theory of hybridization can give nothing substantial to Soviet linguistics. If it is true that the main task of linguistics is to study the internal laws of a language's development, then it must be recognized that the theory of hybridization not only fails to meet this task, but does not even pose it. It simply does not notice it or fails to understand it.

QUESTION: Was Pravda right in opening a free discussion of linguistic problems?

Answer: It did the right thing. It will become clear at the end of the discussion in what direction problems of linguistics will be resolved. But it can already be said that the discussion has been of great benefit. The discussion has made it clear, first of all, that both in the center and in the republics, a regime has dominated in linguistic bodies not typical of science and men of science. The slightest criticism of the state of affairs in Soviet linguistics, even the most timid attempts to criticize the so-called "new teaching" in linguistics was persecuted and stifled by the directors of linguistic circles. Valuable scholars and research workers in linguistics were removed from their positions and reduced in status for criticism of the heritage of N. Ya. Marr and for the slightest disapproval of his teaching. Linguists were moved up into responsible positions not according to their qualifications in the field but as they gave unconditional recognition to N. Ya. Marr's teaching.

It is universally recognized that no science can develop and flourish without a struggle of opinions, without free criticism. But this universally recognized rule has been ignored and trampled upon most unceremoniously. A self-contained group of infallible leaders has developed which has begun to ride rough-shod and behave in the most arbitrary manner after guaranteeing itself against any possible criticism.

An example: the so-called "Baku course" (lectures which N. Ya. Marr delivered in Baku) which the author himself rejected and forbade to be republished was, however, at the orders of the caste of leaders (Comrade Meshchaninov calls them "pupils" of N. Ya. Marr) republished and included without any reservations among the textual aids recommended for students. This means that the students were cheated by being given the rejected "course" as a worthy text. Were I not convinced of the honesty of Comrade Meshchaninov and other linguists I should say that such behavior was equivalent to wrecking.

How could this have happened? This happened because the Arakcheyev-like regime established in linguistics cultivates irresponsibility and encourages such disorders.

The discussion has proved extremely useful mainly because it has brought to light this Arakcheyev-like regime and smashed it to bits.

But the usefulness of the discussion does not end here. The discussion has not only smashed the old regime in linguistics. It has also brought to light the incredible confusion in views on the most important problems of linguistics which reigns among leading circles in this branch of science. Before the discussion began, they were silent and ignored the unwholesome situation in linguistics. But after the discussion began, it became impossible for them to keep silent and they were compelled to stand forth in the pages of the press. Well? It turned out that N. Ya. Marr's teaching contained a whole series of gaps, mistakes, inaccurately formulated problems, incompletely elaborated theses. One may ask why is it that the "pupils" of N. Ya. Marr have spoken up on this score only now, after the discussion has begun? Why did they show no concern for this earlier? Why is it that they did not speak openly and honestly on the subject earlier, as befits scientists? Recognizing "certain" errors of N. Ya. Marr, the "pupils" of N. Ya. Marr, it appears, think that Soviet linguistics can be further developed only on the basis of the "refined" theory of N. Ya. Marr which they consider Marxist. Please preserve us from the "Marxism" of N. Ya. Marr. N. Ya. Marr really did want to and tried to be a Marxist, but he did not succeed in becoming a Marxist. He was merely a simplifier and vulgarizer of Marxism, like the followers of the "Proletkult" or "RAPP."

N. Ya. Marr introduced into linguistics an erroneous, un-Marxist formula of language as a superstructure. He confused himself; he confused linguistics. It is impossible to develop Soviet linguistics on the basis of an incorrect formula.

N. Ya. Marr introduced into linguistics another formula, also wrong and un-Marxist, regarding the "class nature" of language. He confused himself; he confused linguistics. It is impossible to develop linguistics on the basis of a wrong formula which contradicts the entire history of peoples and languages.

N. Ya. Marr introduced into linguistics an immodest, boastful, arrogant tone, not characteristic of Marxism and leading to the wholesale and irresponsible rejection of everything in linguistics before N. Ya. Marr.

N. Ya. Marr noisily fulminated against the method of comparative historical analysis as "idealist." Nonetheless it must be said that, notwithstanding its substantial shortcomings, the method of comparative historical analysis is still better than the really idealist four-element analysis of N. Ya. Marr. Since the former is an impetus to work, to study languages, and the second is an impetus to lying on top of the oven and reading teacups about the notorious four elements.

N. Ya. Marr arrogantly dismissed any attempt to study groups (families) of languages as a manifestation of the theory of the "protolanguage." It cannot be denied, however, that language kinship, for example, of such nations as the Slavs is beyond dispute, that the study of the linguistic kinship of these nations could be of great benefit to linguistics in studying the laws of the development of language. Understandably, the "protolanguage" theory has nothing to do with this matter.

To listen to N. Ya. Marr, and particularly his "pupils," one might think that there was no linguistics before N. Ya. Marr, that linguistics began with the appearance of N. Ya. Marr's "new teaching." Marx and Engels were considerably more modest. They believed that their dialectical materialism was the product of the development of sciences, philosophy included, over preceding periods.

Thus, the discussion was also of benefit to the extent that it brought to light ideological lacunae in Soviet linguistics

It is my belief that the sooner our linguistics frees itself of N. Ya. Marr's errors, the sooner it can emerge from the crisis in which it now finds itself.

The liquidation of the Arakcheyev-like regime in linguistics, the repudiation of N. Ya. Marr's mistakes and the inculcation of Marxism in linguistics—such is, in my opinion, the way which would make it possible to instill new health in Soviet linguistics.

A Fighting Program for the Elaboration of Marxist Linguistics*

By Professor T. LOMTEV

In J. V. Stalin's article "On Marxism in Linguistics" the most important problems of linguistics are stated and settled in wise Stalinist fashion, with exhaustive thoroughness: problems which through the discussion on Pravda's pages have excited not only scientific circles but also wide areas of Soviet public opinion.

Comrade Stalin's article is a most valuable contribution to linguistics, a concrete program for the elaboration of Marxist linguistics, a classic model of how to solve the most complex problems of linguistics. J. V. Stalin's article marks a new period in the development of the science of language; like a powerful beam it illuminates the paths of further development in Soviet linguistics.

J. V. Stalin's new work will join the precious body of the most outstanding classics of Marxism-Leninism. It is a brilliant example of creative development of Marxism-Leninism in linguistics.

Questions of language and superstructure, language and classes, vocabulary and grammar, development of language in different periods of society's history, which frequently were topics of discussion among linguists, were extremely muddled and overgrown with a large number of incorrect theses. J. V. Stalin's disclosure that language is not an ideological superstructure, that it is not a class phenomenon, introduces radical changes in the theory and method of linguistic science, creatively develops Soviet linguistics and raises it to a higher level.

Questions of Theory in Linguistics.

Starting from a non-Marxist formula of language as superstructure, N. Ya. Marr advanced a series of hypotheses for the theory of linguistic science which were erroneous in principle.

If language is an ideological superstructure it must correspond to each given [socio-economic] base and meet its needs. If in the development of society one base is replaced by another, then the given language or languages with their characteristic peculiarities corresponding to the given base are also liable to be replaced by a different language or languages with characteristic peculiarities corresponding to the different base. The development of language is a single process on a worldwide scale.

The incorrect general theses, which are a vulgarization of the idea of a materialist explanation of the development of language, naturally turned out to be in obvious contradiction to well-known and long-established facts, testifying to a multiplicity of languages, each of which had its own grammatical peculiarities and its own vocabulary—a multiplicity which could not be reduced to the scientifically established [socio-economic] bases. This patent contradiction was resolved by N. Ya. Marr not by rejecting his initial vulgar

*Pravda, June 27, 1950, p. 3.

materialist position on language as superstructure, but by piling up on this foundation new constructs which turned out to be thoroughly formalist and idealist.

1. It is generally known that N. Ya. Marr proposed a chart of the development of languages, pyramidally drawn, with its base line down. According to N. Ya. Marr's theory, originally there were numerous mollusc-languages whose further development consists in convergence and generalization through hybridization. Convergence of languages must conclude with the creation of a single world language. Common features of related languages are the result not of genealogic separation along the pure lines of what was initially a single protolanguage, but the result of convergence and hybridization of initially distinct languages.

N. Ya. Marr affirmed that each separate language was not a massive whole which appeared in its entirety by burgeoning off from a single original language which had also given life to other related languages. Each language is formed as a result of the blending of various languages and contains traces and deposits of all the world's languages. The grammatical and lexical data of each given language are the aggregate of strata, the layers of data from all preceding languages, whose hybridization and mixing took place on a world scale.

The definition of those elements in every language which testify to the unity of the given language with all the world's languages makes up the main content and purpose of linguistic theory. N. Ya. Marr considered SAL, BER, YON, ROШ and all their phonetic variations to be such elements.

Clearly, the vulgar materialist premise that language is in the superstructure led to an antihistorical, universal scheme of pyramidal development from multiplicity to unity independent of the actual course of society's development, and to the assertion that antihistorical, universal elements existed in all languages of the world.

Marxist-Leninist science, which examines language not as an isolated realm, but in indissoluble relation with the development of society's life cannot fail to recognize certain regularities in the development of language in different periods of development of society's life. The formulation of any one universal scheme of language development for all times and peoples inevitably leads to deviation from Marxism and essentially becomes an expression of formalism and idealism in linguistics.

Language goes where social life goes, and the same way. If the material and socio-political conditions of a tribe's life lead to its breakup into two new tribes, the two dialects can emerge from one. Engels wrote that in primitive communist society each tribe was characterized by a separate dialect peculiar only to this tribe. "Actually tribe and dialect essentially coincide; the formation of new tribes and dialects through fission took place in America only recently and has hardly stopped even now."*

If the material and social conditions of a society's life lead to the unification of several tribes into a whole, then the dialects of these tribes will also be unified in a single language.

In characterizing the transition of primitive communist society to class society, Engels wrote: "Let us look now at what happened to clan structure with this social upheaval. It turned out to be impotent when confronted with the new elements which had grown up without its cooperation. Its premise was the communal existence of the members of a single clan or tribe on the same territory, populated by them exclusively. This had long since ceased. Everywhere clans and tribes were mixed together; everywhere among free citizens there lived slaves, clients, foreigners." Clan elements, says Engels, "were joined by masses of new populations, alien to the clans; they could become a power in the land, as happened in Rome, and they were too numerous to permit gradual incorporation into the consanguine clans and tribes."*

It follows from Engels' remarks that if for given reasons the socio-economic development of a people proceeds along the line of its breakup into two peoples, then two languages will develop in these circumstances; if a people's socio-economic development follows the course of its merging with another to form a single people, then one language will be formed from two. And, "in the process of hybridization, one of the languages usually emerges victorious, preserves its grammar and basic lexical fund and continues to develop by the internal laws of its own development, while the other language gradually loses its quality and dies off," and that "consequently, hybridization does not produce a third new language but retains one of the languages, retains its grammar and basic lexical fund and gives it a chance to develop by the internal laws of its own development" (J. V. Stalin).†

A theory of pyramidal convergence of languages designed to account for all times and peoples is false. It leads to a view of language development independent of social development and is a reflection of formalism in linguistic theory, a departure from the principles of Marxist materialist theory in favor of idealism. Formalism, deviation from dialectical materialism towards idealism consists in ascribing a single schematic direction to the development of language, while the development of society's life is in actuality characterized by different regularities in different periods in the life of human society. During its historical development tribes and nationalities broke up and separated, mixed and hybridized.

2. It is generally known that N. Ya. Marr proposed the idea that language develops by skips. According to N. Ya. Marr's theory development takes place through quantitative accumulation in language, which must end in an explosion and the transition to a new, higher quality, to new, higher languages in skip fashion. In N. Ya. Marr's opinion each given language is a definite quality corresponding to a given base and represents a level in the development from lower to higher; determination of the stage characteristics of a language is the first task of the investigator, while the distribution of languages by stages as steps in the movement from lower to higher is the main content of linguistic theory.

From N. Ya. Marr's point of view, the multiplicity of languages is explained by the fact that some linguistic blocs break away from the single, worldwide process of convergence of languages in the process of their skip-like transition to a higher level in the direction of forming a single universal language.

Thus emerges the need to define the grammatical structure of individual languages and their groups as the unavoidable product of a given level in the progressive development of languages towards a single world language. The amorphousness of the Chinese language corresponds to a primitive communist society and is proof that this language halted at the primary stage of the language-forming process, while inflection in Indo-European languages corresponds to class society and testifies to their being the latest product in time of the world language-forming process headed toward the creation of a single world language.

It is perfectly clear that such a statement of the problem is inseparably and indissolubly tied to the admission that the grammatical structure of individual languages and their groups are of different value, no matter how the adherents to this view may disclaim the charge and no matter what noble quotations from N. Ya. Marr's works they use in justification.

The scheme itself of distributing grammatical indices of all the world's languages which also reflect their national

*F. Engels, The Origin of the Family, Private Property and the State, 1949, p. 93.

*Ibid., pp. 174-5.

†J. V. Stalin, "On Marxism in Linguistics," Pravda, June 20, 1950.

form in a sequence by stages from archaic to modern or from lower to higher is incorrect. It presupposes only one universal explanation of the different national forms in all the world's languages—the different times at which they broke off from the process of the converging of languages in the direction of the creation of a single world language and the different stages at which they took shape from the standpoint of progress in the skip-line replacement of some languages by others. It cannot be denied that particular grammatical indices did not form simultaneously. But to distribute the world's languages according to the various rungs of a sequence by stages is to deny that national forms of language come into being depending on the specific material and social conditions in the life of peoples. The idea of classifying all the world's languages according to a sequence by stages is inseparably connected with the non-Marxist premise of language as ideological superstructure, and is a scheme torn from life, from the specific history of individual peoples.

Dialectical materialism, which examines the development of language in inseparable connection with the development of social life, requires that a periodization of the language-forming process be worked out which would conform with the Marxist periodization of the development of man's productive activity and similarly with activities in all other aspects of his work. If in the process it turns out that the amorphous character of Chinese or the inflection of Russian are present in all formations undergone by these people in their primordial habitat beginning with the primitive commune and ending with the socialist, then this is proof not that the Marxist periodization of the language-forming process is false, but that amorphousness or inflection or any other purely grammatical characterization is not the inevitable product of a given stage of the language-forming process and cannot serve to indicate that a given language belongs to a given stage, but is a product of the specific historical conditions of society's life on a given territory and indicates the peculiarities in the development of languages under various specific historical conditions.

If language, as Comrade Stalin teaches, "is directly linked to man's productive activity and not only to his productive activity but to every other activity in all aspects of man's work," then it cannot be the representative of any one stage because, not being an ideological superstructure, it is not the offspring of any one base. "***Language, its structure," says Comrade Stalin, "cannot be regarded as the product of any one epoch. The structure of language, its grammar and basic lexical fund, is the product of a number of eras."*

The universal scheme according to which the grammatical structures of particular languages rise from an archaic, lower state, be it the amorphousness of Chinese or some other grammatical peculiarity of a given language, to a new, progressive state, be it the inflection of Indo-European or the nominative-active grammatical structure of these and other languages, contradicts the principles of the theory of Marxist materialism and is one of the errors in principle of N. Ya. Marr's theory.

Academician I. I. Meshchaninov admits that "the problem of language classification by stages and the temporal arrangement of these stages still remains unsolved. Still this refers only to the plan itself and not to the basic proposition" (Pravda, May 16, 1950).†

The admission that the numerous schemes for arranging the grammatical structure of individual languages in a sequence by stages proposed by our linguists turned out to be useless does not convince Academician I. I. Meshchaninov that the very phrasing of the question is erroneous. Academician I. I. Meshchaninov does not lose hope that in the future he or somebody else will be able correctly to classify the existing living languages on the rungs of a ladder by stages, failing to observe that the task may not legitimately be stated in this way.

Thus, to state the problem of development by stages as a problem of placing languages in a sequence by stages leads to a formulation of language development divorced from the specific histories of the societies speaking these languages and is a reflection of formalism and idealism in N. Ya. Marr's linguistic theory. Such a statement of the problem must be discarded and not maintained, as Academician I. I. Meshchaninov attempts.

3. If language is a superstructure on a base, as incorrectly affirmed by Marr, then a common national language cannot be inherited; it is created anew by the bourgeoisie in the capitalist period and is limited only to the confines of the ruling class, the bourgeoisie.

The bourgeoisie as a ruling class consolidates its language in literature; the literary language emerging in the capitalist period, bourgeois in origin, becomes national, that is general for all social functions including the function of communication between the various classes while the popular language inherited from previous periods is not national because it allegedly is not uniform: it consists of dialects.

This point of view is also shared to some degree by Academician V. V. Vinogradov. In his article for the discussion he writes: "The teaching of Lenin and Stalin on national languages defines the fundamental historical varieties or types of national language formation*** Essentially the national literary language is a literary language of a qualitatively new system, deeply rooted in the popular soil."* It is clear from this statement that the national language is not inherited but is formed, that it is a literary language since the latter is a common language and not a popular one, since the latter contains dialects.

If language, as Marxism teaches, is not an ideological superstructure on a base, then the common national language is not a product of capitalist formation, but is an inherited community; this mutual intelligibility is a product of the people as a whole and not of a class. In the period of capitalism's victory over feudalism the native speech of a people becomes consolidated in literature and science and becomes national. The national language is the native language of a people which has become the instrument not only of local communication but also of communication in a nation's literary, scientific and political life.

Lenin teaches that "for the complete victory of commodity production, the bourgeoisie must conquer the internal market, territories with a population speaking a single language must be united into a state while eliminating all obstacles for the development of this language and its consolidation in literature."†

Thus, the basic premises of N. Ya. Marr's linguistic theories have nothing to do with the theory of Marxist materialism. Comrade Stalin's brilliant work "On Marxism in Linguistics" creatively enriches the Marxist-Leninist science of language and is a fighting program for the scientific activity of all Soviet linguists.

It contains a Bolshevist evaluation of Marr's doctrine, whose role in Soviet linguistics was overestimated by the author of these lines, even though he did criticize its basic errors.

Questions of Method in the Science of Language.

If linguistics is more than mere empirical knowledge and is a science, a scientific discipline, it must have its theory and its method of investigation. It is said that all sciences have only one method—the method of dialectical materialism and therefore it is not right to raise the question of method in linguistics. However, this is true in one respect only: all sciences have a single method of cog-

*Ibid.

†I. I. Meshchaninov, "For a Creative Development of Academician N. Ya. Marr's Heritage," Pravda, May 16, 1950.

*V. Vinogradov, "Let Us Develop Soviet Linguistics on the Basis of Marxist-Leninist Theory," Pravda, June 6, 1950.

†V. I. Lenin, Works, Vol. 20, p. 368.

nition—the method of dialectical materialism; nevertheless, although all sciences have a single method of cognition, the method of dialectical materialism, they have different methods of investigation. Consequently it is theoretically legitimate to raise the question of method in linguistic science.

If the theory of linguistics defines the subject of this science (that is, the nature of language and its development) and explains the phenomena with which this science deals, then the method of linguistics is an instrument of investigation of linguistic materials.

In the present discussion we are dealing with two methods: the comparative-historical, elaborated by traditional linguistics, and the paleontological, developed by N. Ya. Marr.

The comparative-historical method, as indicated by J. V. Stalin, has serious shortcomings, but it also has its merits.

This method is called historical because it is used in reconstructing the history of languages; it is called comparative because comparison is the technique used in reconstructing the history of languages. If the data of several languages of a single family are the result of distinct evolutions of a body of data initially belonging to a single source, then the technique of reconstructing the histories of these languages can only be the factual comparison of the facts of these languages; the data from other languages, which do not stem from the same source, have nothing to do with the matter. Thus the word "gorod" [city, town] sounds "grad" among Southern Slavs, "grod, grud" among the Western and "gorod" among Eastern Slavs. These words are the result of different phonetic evolutions of one and the same word, which initially had the form "gord" and meant fence, which is proven by the Lithuanian word "gardas" having the same meaning.

The reference to Lithuanian serves to confirm the reconstruction of this word's history in Slavic languages, because Lithuanian and the Slavic languages are the result of distinct evolutions of what initially was a single source.

The data of a given language which has no parallels in related languages cannot be utilized by the comparative-historical method as a source for the historical study of the language. For example, the word "kon" [horse] exists in Slavic languages but cannot be found in other Indo-European ones. It disappears from the body of data which can be utilized by the comparative-historical method for the reconstruction of the history of Slavic languages. The comparative-historical method cannot be used in reconstructing the history of a language which has no kin among languages. Such a language offers no data for use by the comparative-historical method.

The limitations of the comparative-historical method consist in its permitting the comparison of that factual evidence of related languages which stems from one basic source, the existence of which is beyond doubt. However, the theory of science has established that within related languages there is factual material which, although an inseparable part of the basic lexical fund and the morphological inventory of the language, can be remnants of some other source which took part in the formation of a group of related languages. Thus, if the data of related languages stem not from one source but from several, of which only one is basic, then the linguistic evidence of the given language can and must be studied by comparing it with the data of those languages which preserve the remnants of the same sources. It follows from this that the linguistic data of each given language must be studied through comparison with data from various languages, not only related ones, but also unrelated.

The comparative-historical method investigated scientifically only whole sense units in language (words, morphemes). Such elaboration of linguistic data is quite legitimate, but it is not enough. It cannot be denied that certain words which today are viewed as whole, indivisible sense units could have arisen from several sense units (words). This has long been known; for example, it was established long ago that the Russian word "berloga" [lair] is made up of "ber" which originally meant sheep and goats and "log" (cf. "logove" [lair]).

The conclusion follows from this that through comparison one can study not only the data of whole sense units (words) in the contemporary language system but also their parts, if at an older stage in the development of the language they functioned as separate meaning units.

Meanwhile the techniques of the comparative-historical method are not prepared to handle the linguistic material. This does not mean, however, that the techniques of comparative historical analysis of whole sense units and their connections in language must be simply rejected. They must be reorganized, enriched and developed.

The comparative-historical method subjects to comparative study data of the same meaning from related languages; one can juxtapose the Russian word "mat" [mother] with Greek and Latin "mater," Armenian "mair" and so on and make certain deductions, but one cannot juxtapose the Russian word "kon" (horse) with Latin "canis" (dog) as these are words of distinct meanings and have no relation to each other. However, scientific theory has established that the content of comparable data can change historically. Those sense units which to modern thinking seem not to have any mutual relation could have had the closest ties in most ancient times.

It follows from this that one can compare data not only of relatively similar meaning, that is, data having the same sense content, but also data with different meanings, because one must consider the peculiarities of primitive thought and opinion. Remembering that names changed from object to object because of similarities in their functions in social production (cf. "pero"—goose feather and "pero"—pen), one can also compare those words which today have different meanings, but which could have had similar meanings at an earlier stage. If the horse fulfilled originally the same domestic function as the dog, then the dog's name could have been transferred to the horse. This makes it possible, while taking into account the irregularity of the correspondence of Latin k and Slavic s, to establish a close connection between the Russian word "kon" [horse] and Latin "canis"—"dog," whose origin has not yet been clarified by the comparative-historical method.

Thus the traditional comparative-historical method has serious shortcomings as a research tool and does not correspond to the present state of linguistic theory. However, it also has merits which must not be underestimated, since there can be no doubt that a good deal of positive knowledge has been acquired precisely through this method of investigation.

Some Conclusions.

The traditional comparative-historical method of research must not be rejected but reorganized and perfected, while preserving all the valuable techniques and approaches for the study of linguistic data which have been created through the application of this method.

N. Ya. Marr did not follow this path; "N. Ya. Marr introduced into linguistics an immodest, boastful, arrogant tone, not characteristic of Marxism and leading to the wholesale and irresponsible rejection of everything in linguistics before N. Ya. Marr" (J. Stalin).*

He began to reject completely the comparative-historical method with all its achievements in the technique of handling linguistic data. He began to fulminate bombastically against the comparative-historical method as "idealist" and began to advertise the paleontologic method, which he had formulated, as the only correct application of

*J. V. Stalin, "On Marxism in Linguistics," Pravda, June 20, 1950.

Marxist dialectical method to the data of speech and related social culture.

In contrasting his paleontologic method with the comparative-historical one, N. Ya. Marr began to search also for fundamental differences in the techniques of comparative study of linguistic data. He reached the conclusion that words or forms as complete meaningful units in systems of contemporary languages could not be the object of comparative study, because such handling of the data would allegedly lead inevitably to the re-establishment of a protolanguage. For example, the comparison of the Russian word "ruka" [hand] with Polish "renka," Old Slavic "ronka," Lithuanian "ranka" must lead to the conclusion that the initial form for these now different words was the same for all Slavs—"ronka." In each such particular fact, N. Ya. Marr saw the reflection of the protolanguage theory of divergence. And yet in reality these facts testify not to a single protolanguage for all Slavic languages but to one source (along with other sources), which has left traces in the Slavic languages and which, as a result of differences in the development of these languages, underwent various changes. Similar processes are at work even now.

The French word "partia," [party] is in Russian "partia," in Belorussian "partyya;" the French word "dictature" [dictatorship] becomes "diktatura" in Russian, "dyktatura" in Belorussian, etc.

Nobody will draw the conclusion from such facts that French, Russian and Belorussian stem at the same time from one protolanguage, but one cannot avoid the conclusion that a word from one source can acquire different meanings and forms in different languages.

Having incorrectly diagnosed the juxtaposition of whole sense units of related languages as a reflection of the protolanguage conception of the development of language, N. Ya. Marr rejected in principle the juxtaposition of whole sense units in contemporary languages and proceeded to four-element analysis of the data of all the world's languages independent of their actual historical connections.

And yet we juxtapose the linguistic data of a given stratum of any language with the linguistic data of a different stratum of the same language or of any other language only when it has undergone historical study and its meaning and evolution have been clarified in a given layer of given languages. The Russian word "kon" [horse] and the Ukrainian "kin" originally had only one form—"kon." To ignore this is to reject firmly established facts, to deny the incontrovertible possibility of distinct evolutions of the data of one stratum in different languages.

It follows from this that the Ukrainian word "kin" [horse] cannot be separated from Russian "kon" nor its identity suggested with Breton (in France) "ki"—dog, as is done by N. Ya. Marr.

Such antihistorical juxtapositions of N. Ya. Marr were taken up by bourgeois Ukrainian nationalists as proof of the absence of any closer relationship of Ukrainian to Russian and its orientation toward the languages of the West.

N. Ya. Marr did not take into account the different evolutions of whole meaning units in the data of the same level of different languages and described the results of these evolutions as independent facts. Thus N. Ya. Marr placed together Russian "ruka" [hand] with Russian "rok" [fate], ignoring the fact that the form "ruka" is the result of very late changes and that in ancient times it sounded differently. In every language N. Ya. Marr took ready-made words and broke them up into elements, ignoring the changes they had undergone in the corresponding stratum of a given language. This leads to the numerous errors in etymologies of individual words which we find in the works of N. Ya. Marr.

All these distortions in the method of N. Ya. Marr's linguistic doctrine are explained and predetermined by the distortions in the theory of N. Ya. Marr's linguistic doctrine.

The essentially correct principles of comparative study of data, not only from related but also unrelated languages, not only of entire words as separate sense units but also of their parts, if at an older stage of the language's development they were whole sense units, were distorted by N. Ya. Marr due to the antihistorical nature of the very universal scheme of pyramidal convergence of all the world's languages through hybridization and blending and due to the insistence that universal elements are present in all languages.

The result of the distortion of principles of the comparative-historical study of linguistic data is the so-called four-element analysis. It is not something accidental or marginal in N. Ya. Marr's method.

According to Marr the data of contemporary languages can be studied comparatively only after the primary sense units, the four elements, have been first established in each contemporary sense unit. As a result of this, there emerged the technique of four-element analysis which resulted in utter rejection of historical analysis of whole sense units.

The technique of paleontologic analysis was placed into a mutually exclusive relationship with the tecnhique of comparative-historical analysis.

Four-element analysis became the universal means of interpreting the linguistic data of languages of all peoples and times. If the comparative-historical method with all its shortcomings "is an impetus to work, to study languages," the paleontologic method "is an impetus to lying on top of the oven and reading teacups about the notorious four elements" (J. Stalin). *

No breakup of a contemporary sense unit into more primary sense units is correct unless the history of its development and changes is considered. If the history of such a word as "ruka" [hand], according to the data of those languages in which it functions as a whole sense unit, indicates that this word originally had the form "ronka" meant "to gather," then it cannot be broken up into more primary elements "ru" and "ka" and on this ground to insist that "ru" in the word "ruka" and "ru" in the word "ruslo" [river bed] are the same. This is not science but playing games.

Nevertheless, Soviet linguistics cannot reject the very principle of determining some particles in contemporary sense units which represent traces of more ancient sense units. But the technique for determining such particles must rest on the historical data of the meaning unit in which the particles are located. This means that Soviet linguistics cannot reject the principle of reconstructing the history of the sense unit as a self-sufficient unit of contemporary language.

The primary form of a given word as an integral unit of meaning can and must be reconstructed if its initial form differs from the contemporary. There is no retreat from Marxism in this, no return of any kind to Indo-Europeanism or to a rebirth of bourgeois linguistics as the Marrists tried to scare us [into believing]. The disclosure in a contemporary sense unit of its component parts as sense units of older periods, can and must be made, if they actually exist in it. At the same time it must be regarded historically as an integral sense unit. There is here no retreat from Marxism, no return to element analysis, to the formal mechanistic vulgarizing method of N. Ya. Marr.

Following strictly the method of Marxist dialectics and the theory of Marxist materialism, Soviet linguistics must reorganize, refine, enrich, create new approaches and techniques of studying linguistic data and follow daringly the path of innovation and creativity, widen the topics of scientific research work, raise new questions in science, study the questions sharply raised by life.

As a rank-and-file linguist I can find no words to express those feelings of gratitude toward Comrade Stalin which fill me. J. V. Stalin has offered extremely profound generalizations in the area of linguistic science which lead to new understandings of all individual questions on which we are

*Ibid.

working.

With a feeling of deep gratitude to Comrade Stalin we will give all our forces and knowledge to the cause of creating scientific research works needed by Soviet science and Soviet public opinion; following unswervingly Stalin's guiding indications is the only basis for the emergence of Soviet linguistics from stagnation, the foundation of further successes of the Marxist science of language, the durability and viability of its conclusion, its connection with the work and struggle of the Soviet people for the victory of communism.

For a Leninist-Stalinist Path of Development in Soviet Linguistics*

By Professor G. AKHVLEDIANI

The Causes of Stagnation in Soviet Linguistics.

The free discussion which has developed in the pages of Pravda on the questions of Soviet linguistics, which has matured and even become urgent, meets perfectly the desires of all Soviet linguists. In this field of science questions of theory and practice concern deeply not only the linguistic scholars, but also the wide masses of our intelligentsia—particularly the artists of the word and the many millions of teachers and students.

This remarkable discussion acquired truly international significance when J. V. Stalin submitted his article "On Marxism in Linguistics" which initiated a new era in the history of Soviet linguistics.

The importance of this discussion is enormous. Its development is being followed with intense attention by the entire Soviet public, all the world's linguistic science, and by our friends and foes.

The discussion opened with an article by the major student of the Caucasus, Prof. Arn. Chikobava, who has repeatedly criticized Academician N. Ya. Marr's entire theory. The discussion revealed that a regime not characteristic of science had dominated in linguistics, and that Marr's teaching contained a whole series of serious mistakes and blunders.

All of N. Ya. Marr's students (with few exceptions) busied themselves only with chorusing their teacher's declarative statements which were inadequately grounded and thus useless in linguists' research or living practical activity.

At each step his followers referred to Marr, frequently without any need. At best, knowledge of Marr's works written after 1924 was considered by his followers to be the acme of linguistic wisdom. As a rule such linguists were the heads of linguistic departments in higher educational institutions. One can imagine what teaching cadres they prepared and what such teachers could teach the school children.

Running riot particularly of late, the Japhetidologists monopolized all Soviet linguistics ("we claim the whole area of linguistics"—they said). They tried to remove from work—sometimes not without success—a number of famous linguists (Endzelin, Vinogradov, Freiman, Peterson, Bulakhovsky, Acharyan, etc.) who had never stopped enriching Soviet linguistics with their works. The remarkable works of Fortunatov, Shakhmatov, Beaudoin de Courtenay, and others which had brought world fame to our science, were forgotten or ignored. Only isolated linguists in one republic or another remained outside the Japhetidologists' reach; only in Georgia were they almost the whole body of linguists.

The Japhetidologists left fallow the enormous linguistic heritage of comparative linguistics, as though the heirs of everything of value created in the past were anybody except us. The old linguistics, however, (both foreign and native) has to its credit enormous achievements, useful for our work as well.

The rejection by Soviet linguistics of a useful heritage (along with the circumstances mentioned above) played a doubly negative role. Our linguistics, our schools and all our language development suffered from this.

The traditions of good Russian grammars came to an end. Special steps had to be taken to raise the level of literacy in schools at all levels. There was no good, stable Russian grammar till 1938, and, when it appeared under Prof. L. V. Shcherba's editorship, it had a portrait of Academician Marr right alonside the portraits of the pillars of Russian grammatical thought (Lomonosov, Vostokov, Buslayev, Potebnya and Shakhmatov). Yet Academician Marr had no relation whatever, beyond a negative one, to the elaboration of Russian grammar.

It seems strange when we read in Prof. Chikobava: "A considerable number of N. Ya. Marr's works are devoted to the struggle to create a materialist linguistics." One might think Marr wrote a number of works intended to establish a materialist linguistics In reality, however, almost since the beginning of the '20s, he rarely wrote a work devoted wholly to the consistent development of any one idea. Frequently the title of a Marr article does not correspond to its content, and particular statements are not connected with each other.

To the deleterious activity of the Japhetidologists were added our own serious errors as well, exposed in Comrade Stalin's wonderful article; the main one was that we, following Academician Marr, mistook language for superstructure and even considered the fact that he raised the problem of the superstructural nature of language to be Marr's incontrovertible merit. The argument that "to confuse language with superstructure is to commit a grave error" (J. Stalin) is deeply convincing. It was also our error that in attempting to prove the non-class nature of language we did not proceed from the fact that "***everywhere, at every stage of development, language, as a means of communication for people in society, was common and single for the society, serving the members of society equally, regardless of social position" (J. Stalin).*

Our hesitancy on the question of the class nature of language could not but contribute to the stagnation in our science. Only now, after it has been explained that "*** people, particular social groups and classes are anything but indifferent to language" and that "language and the laws of its development can be comprehended only if they are studied in indissoluble connection with the history of society and with the history of the people to which the language under study belongs and which is the creator and the bearer of this language" (J. Stalin), † did it become clear why the impression has developed that in various languages and in different periods language could be of class nature.

Comrade Stalin's elucidations shed new light also on other cardinal questions of linguistics, which had remained unclear so far. Our science thereby received unshakeable support for its development through the elaboration of Comrade Stalin's brilliant thoughts on the basis of linguistic data.

*Pravda, June 27, 1950, p. 4.

*J. V. Stalin, "On Marxism in Linguistics," Pravda, June 20, 1950.

† Ibid.

Difficulties in the Development of Soviet Linguistics.

Soviet linguists are being asked to find ways of raising Soviet linguistics to a higher level, a height worthy of the Stalin epoch — as are [men in] other fields of Soviet science and technology. Stagnation in Soviet linguistics is part of its growing pains, not of decay.

What does the peculiar nature of our difficulties consist in and how can they be overcome? Unfortunately, one must note that these difficulties and the means of overcoming them were stated weakly and sometimes even incorrectly in the discussion articles before J. V. Stalin's statement—both by the "opponents" of Marr's linguistic doctrine, as well as and particularly by its "defenders;" and this could not help in overcoming difficulties.

In Marxism-Leninism we have been given the philosophical and ideological bases on which to erect any Soviet science. We have a tremendously rich heritage of comparative-historical linguistics as a great science with almost a century and a half's history of its exceptionally powerful development in which our leading linguists occupy an honorable place (Vostokov, Buslayev, Potebnya, Fortunatov, Beaudoin de Courtenay, Endzelin, Shcherba and others).

Moreover, what at this stage is of decisive significance for the further development of Soviet linguistics, [we have] the foundation-laying and truly programmatic statements of the Lenin-Stalin theory on nations and national languages.

And all this remained inaccessible for Marr, who "really did want to and tried to be a Marxist, but he did not succeed in becoming a Marxist" (J. Stalin).

Under such circumstances, moreover, the greatest and, because of its consequence, the fatal mistake of Academician Marr was his unconditional decision to fence himself off tightly from "Indo-Europeanism" (that is, comparative-historical linguistics) which brought with it the self-expulsion of Japhetidology, as a general science of language, from the great science of linguistics.

"There can be no mention of reconciling the new theory with the old on matters of principle unless the Indo-Europeanist rejects his main tenets," wrote Marr. "I consider the attempt by some very few of my students and particularly my followers to erect a bridge between the two theories more disastrous than the desire of the great majority of Indo-European linguists to ignore entirely Japhetic linguistics."*

Such statements of Marr, frequently repeated, served as a signal to his students inadequately familiar with the "old" school to shun this school not only ideologically, "on questions of principle" as they were taught by their teacher, but also by remaining unfamiliar with it, by not knowing its basic principles. There was no shortage of criticism of "old" linguistics, but of criticism always couched in the teacher's words. The teacher knew what he was rejecting. The students became familiar with the "old" science only through the sharply polemical works of Marr.

The works of Academician Marr in the new period even show that their author broke in his search not only with his own research practice, using the "old" methods of comparative linguistics (and, true enough, he no longer wrote any such works), but abandoned also the trend of the latest accomplishments of the "old" science. And his followers considered this normal and, imitating the teacher, ignored all the classical linguistics of the past.

There is no other way to explain the contempt, so harmful for our science, for something like the remarkable phonetic laws of Werner or Fortunatov, which have enormous significance in etymological exploration.

The less "obedient" of followers, of which unfortunately there were few, trying to assimilate critically the achievements of earlier linguistics on the basis of Marxist methodology, have been achieving significant results.

Even "Indo-Europeanists" who do not share Marr's views but have worked honestly * have given Soviet linguistics a number of most valuable studies. I have in mind, for example, the works of such leading Slavists as Academician V. V. Vinogradov, Prof. L. A. Bulakhovsky and also Prof. Arn. Chikobava and others.

One cannot say the same about some of Marr's followers. Thus, for example, Prof. N. Yakovlev literally dates a phonetic change with a definite year saying that at the present time after the Great Patriotic War (1947) one can notice the loss of guttural quality in the phoneme "k".

The attempt of Comrade B. Serebrennikov to show the superiority of the comparative-historical method to element analysis should in every way be welcomed. In view of the nature of his discussion article he had a chance to show the enormous superiority of the former over the latter. However, although he might have chosen any one of many thousands of terms of social significance and thus demonstrated to the reader the great force of comparative linguistics even in the etymology of words, he limited himself to one insignificant term. And he, almost apologizing, says the following: "Perhaps it sounds paradoxical, but the comparative method is much more useful as proof of the Marxist idea of development than Marr's notorious four-element analysis."†

Is that how one should talk in this decisive moment in the development of Soviet comparative linguistics, thereby subjecting it to doubt or guess as to whether it is "useful or not?"

Let us take Marr's series of words cited by him: [Russian] ogon [fire]—kon [horse]—kon-ura [kennel], Armenian kin (woman) and [Russian] okunat [to dip]. According to the laws of the "amazingly well-developed methodology" of comparative-historical linguistics (Marr), each word leaves the ranks of this "empty" series and lines up in another, meaningful one.

For example, Armenian kin—woman—quite legitimately corresponds to the word zhena [wife], present in all Slavic languages and consequently indicating the community of all Slavic languages, and not only through this word alone but through an enormous number of words and the language structure; moreover, the very different phonetic and morphological versions of this root (zhen) in the Slavic languages reveal such meanings, so indicative of social relations among the speakers of these languages that no other material documents are capable of giving us some idea of them in either historic or prehistoric times. For example: in Old Russian zhena means woman; the name of a person of the male sex zhenikh comes from the root zhen, indicating a person of the female sex; similarly zhenitba (wedding), zhenitsya (to marry), words for male actions are from the same root; Serbian ženka (female), Old Russian and Czech ženima (concubine), Old Slavic zhenimshit (concubine's son), Czech ženikha (bride) and so on. Each of these meanings points to definite social positions of a person of the female sex, about which one could talk at length.

The same root (zhen) can be found, according to all the "amazing" rules, in the Germanic languages, for example: Gothic—kvens, kvino (woman, wife); English queen and quean (dissolute woman), etc. Similarly diverse are the meanings of this root in classical Greek, for example: gyune (from guan)—woman, wife, servant girl, housekeeper, concubine, lady, female mortal, as contrasted with "immortal goddess," and so on. Here too the changes in woman's position are revealed.

An analysis of a word accidentally handled by the comparative-historical method (thanks to Comrade Serebrennikov) gives such a completely real picture of the his-

*N. Ya. Marr, Selected Works, Vol. I, p. 219.

*N. Ya. Marr thought of even A. Maillet, "the head of Indo-Europeanism," as an honest opponent (Selected Works, Vol. IV, p. 226).

†B. Serebrennikov, "On N. Ya. Marr's Research Methods," Pravda, May 23, 1950.

tory of woman's social position that one could write a whole volume and more about it.

Not as rich, but nevertheless an analagous picture is offered by the other words in this series (ogon—kon—konura) in so far as these terms do not have so much social significance. But if one should transcend the limited framework of Comrade Serebrennikov and take any term with social significance (for example the following words recalled at random: trud [work], rabota [labor], pozor [shame], muzhik [peasant], prisyaga [oath], podly [despicable], mat [mother], otets [father], doch [daughter], vdova [widow]), we would then be confronted with an enormous number of meanings reflecting social, class kinship and other relations.

If one were to take only the word trud [work] which in Old Russian had such meanings as pain, illness, sorrow, suffering, concern, effort, exploit, etc., while in a socialist society work is a matter of honor, a matter of glory, a matter of valor and heroism—[we can see that] our life has re-established one of the many meanings of this word. One could write an enormous monograph on the subject "The Socio-Economic Conditions Affecting Changes in the Meaning of the Word Trud [Work]." It is remarkable that the old meaning of this word has survived until today in a verb of the spoken language: natrudit sebe nogu [to hurt one's foot], trudny—sick (for example, trudnaya ruka [an ailing hand], trudny rebyonok [unmanageable child], etc.). The word muzhik or podly [peasant or despicable] may be used to reveal a no less grandiose panorama if it is restored through use of the comparative-historical method that the original root meaning of the first was simply man, sometimes hero and in some places servant, member of a household, male (for example, in Serbian), while in Russian and Polish this root gives us muzhestvenni [manly, masculine], etc.; the second word—podly [vile, despicable] which arose recently, in the 18th century, from the root pod [under] meant then of common origin and only later did it acquire on the lips of the ruling class meanings related to morality.

In this way the comparative-historical method reveals within a word a variegated range of meanings determined by social conditions.

Can there be any comparison of this with that which is offered us by element analysis? The answer to this question is not difficult. Therefore the defense of the comparative-historical method can hardly be evaluated as a reactionary position, as some of our opponents think. Even such an historical-etymological analysis, which we have not presented vividly enough here and which does not yet stand high enough in Indo-European studies, can give us an idea of its incomparable superiority in the job of "proving the Marxist idea of development" of language (B. Serebrennikov).

Even Academician Marr frequently indicated "the amazing fine development" of the "old" science, while at the same time prohibiting "any appeasing reconciliation with Indo-European linguistics."

To frighten people away from this "amazingly well-developed methodology" is quite natural for the author of a new theory trying to preserve its purity, natural because he considered his doctrine as the antithesis of the "old."

But his pupils were not interested in whether there was something useful in the "amazing" technique of Indo-European linguistics.

One should again consider, especially because of its extreme importance, the matter of the influence of this doctrine on the Soviet school and thereby on the improvement of the whole Union's speech. To the extent to which the interests of the new doctrine were directed primarily into the past, to that extent they served the cultivation of contemporary speech poorly or not at all. Marr himself and his students talked a lot about developing written languages for the unwritten languages of the Union, but actually they needed this only for the scientific recording of texts.

More than that. The new doctrine, as it stands, acted as a brake on the improvement of speech. It demanded a radical break in the grammatical system. It demanded the elimination of traditional grammatical terminology. Marr used his authoritative voice to shake up school grammar, that foundation of literacy and correct speech.

"The formal idealistic doctrine on which so-called grammar is built is absolutely unfit for connection either with true living speech or with its base, production." And this is written in the journal The Russian Language In the Soviet School (1930, No. 4)! Or in the same place "***Created by such an idealist, formal, scientific ideology, until recently still triumphant, grammar looks like an angry she-wolf at the hundreds, thousands and millions of violators of its paper canons***. It is laughable even to speak of reforming Russian writing or grammar***The matter at issue is not spelling or grammatical reform, but a change in the rules of language" (N. Ya. Marr, "Selected Works," Vol. II, pp. 374-5. Emphasis mine—G. A.).

As is well known, normative grammar, which of course must be kept at a level of scientific standards, can play the role of a foundation for speech development just because it is stable over a definite (usually protracted) period of time. Otherwise it loses its meaning. A scientific grammar can be radically changed even with each edition, but the school [grammars], which are practical (normative) and which, of course, can also be perfected, cannot afford this. Changes even in the terminology alone is pedagogically reflected harmfully on the student's attitude toward grammar, making it lose its authority.

"But is grammar necessary altogether?" asks Academician Marr (Ibid., p. 374).

Here is the first difficulty of Soviet linguistic science: lagging behind the great linguistic science which was "amazingly" developed. Finding itself way ahead of the "old" classical linguistics in ideological methodology, our linguistics lags behind it in a technical-methodological respect due to Marr and particularly his followers; and this technical-methodological aspect has enormous significance at the present and the following stages in the development of our social life. If one should turn linguistics toward the present day (which must be considered a primary task) this cannot be done without its being equipped technico-methodologically. And in this we are lagging for the indicated reasons.

The second difficulty is the difficulty of mastering all of the existing linguistic wealth in the treatment of which our linguists (both Soviet and pre-Soviet) occupy an honorable place. "To listen to N. Ya. Marr and particularly his 'pupils' one might think that there was no linguistics before N. Ya. Marr, that linguistics began with the appearance of N. Ya. Marr's 'new teaching'," says J. V. Stalin in his article.*

The third difficulty consists in the atomization of linguistic cadres, which has lasted now for quite a long time. Absence of unanimity in understanding the tasks confronting linguists, the opposition of the new doctrine to the "old," called forth by Marr's erroneous efforts to fence himself off from the "old," mutual misunderstanding, lack of confidence and such created the condition for the atomization of our forces.

The discussion opened on the pages of Pravda which has taken place, with few exceptions, at a high scientific level has already indicated that it will also eliminate our third difficulty.

Concerning Genealogic Classification and Protolanguage.

In the study of historical, stabilized languages (as all languages now known are—ancient and modern) one can also speak about "a protolanguage linguistic condition" (Academician Meshchaninov) and even about protolanguages

*J. V. Stalin, "On Marxism in Linguistics," Pravda, June 20, 1950.

in the broad meaning of this word, about which "Prof. Chikobava speaks between the lines" (the words are Prof. Chemodanov's, in his discussion article). It should be perfectly clear that Prof. Chikobava would have been correct even if he had had the courage to say so,not only between the lines, but very loudly. (And this should be very well known to Prof. Chemodanov, a student of Germanics, which exists only in so far as it has been well worked out by the Indo-Europeanists.)

For we have before us the Romance languages (French, Italian, Spanish, Rumanian and others) and their protolanguage which has been historically verified—vulgar Latin; all main steps in the development of Iranian languages are also present. And if Prof. Chikobava did not utter the terrible word protolanguage, this is only because, as Prof. Chemodanov puts it, this word has become odious, and that quite unnecessarily. Prof. Chemodanov's correct indication of the complexity of "the process of formation of tribes and peoples" does not hinder the recognition that Romance languages are a development from Latin, that protolanguage of all related Romance languages, even if under very complex circumstances. Facts speak for themselves, and the complexity of processes can demand only a complex explanation of complex facts, nothing more. And should science, and Soviet science at that, fear complexity of facts or complexity in their interpretation and try to avoid them?

The terms protolanguage, Indo-Europeanism, family [of languages] and others have become obnoxious only to the Japhetidologists who heard them pronounced by Marr in the heat of inspired, bitterly polemical battle with bourgeois linguists of doubtful honesty; and his listeners repeated them—true enough, also in bitter polemical battle—but very frequently in a battle with obviously honest Soviet linguists. Soviet linguists should not be afraid of terms, particularly those which excellently express their content. (One may, perhaps, have to replace them, but only because they are offensive). But Prof. Chemodanov (and, I fear, also Prof. Chikobava) forgets that we are not talking about whether stabilized languages differentiate or integrate themselves (both happen in these languages and nobody denies this) but about how a language or systems, families of languages, and "protolanguages" come into being.

Consequently, we have in mind the ways in which a language forms, which eventually could of course break up, differentiate and later reintegrate itself, depending on social and political circumstances. (According to Herodotus, there were about a hundred languages in Europe.)

In a linguistic sense, breakup is naturally preceded by uniformity. Such unity existed in Latin, Iranian, Common Slavic and other languages. Some of them broke up into several parts (for example, Latin, Iranian, Slavic); others did not (for example, Armenian, Albanian); some become more fragmented (Latin, Iranian, Germanic), others less (Greek, Baltic), and all this depending on historical circumstances. Otherwise it would be impossible to explain the numerous, clearly regular correspondences between numerous Indo-European languages obviously scattered since prehistoric times over enormous distances from each other, or to deny them any kind of unity at any time (parallel to Hittite). Of course, this kind of unity, also the notorious protolanguage, is in no way terrifying, but is very complex in the paths of its further development.

"It cannot be denied, however, that language kinship, for example of such nations as the Slavs, is beyond dispute, that the study of the linguistic kinship of these nations could be of great benefit to linguistics in studying the laws of the development of language"—is taught us by Comrade Stalin.* The kinship of languages, however, necessarily presupposes their genealogic classification.

As for the glottogonic periods in the formation of speech, there of course can be no question of any protolanguage. And Academician Meshchaninov is undoubtedly right when he says that "thus, at their source (of tribal languages—G. A.) we find a multiplicity of languages and not one form of speech. One can speak of the protolanguage condition of any language, but not about protolanguage, one and the same for all linguistic multiplicity."*

On the contrary, if the only possibility we admit is of differentiation from the very beginning, which means that we do not deal with "sources," that is, genetic questions—we shall have to be responsible for recognizing [the reality of] eternally and naturally ready-made languages with the processes of their fragmentation and unification. We cannot go so far, since it would mean denying the [historical] beginning of languages. This would mean failure to understand the historical nature of linguistic laws.

In examining the question of development by stages Prof. Chikobava incorrectly comes to the conclusion that it is "***Academician N. Ya. Marr's classification by stages, which denies certain languages the capacity for development, that objectively helps racism." There can be no talk of the natural superiority of one language over another among linguists.

Any language at any stage (or to use more customary terminology, at any level of its historical development) can achieve the greatest perfection—depending on circumstances. It can achieve this, let us say, in slightly over a century, even under bourgeois conditions, and in a decade or two under socialism. Not a few such examples exist in present-day reality. Dozens of languages have developed in our country extremely rapidly which before Soviet power did not even have alphabets; at the present time the classical works of Marxism-Leninism, the writings of Rustaveli, Tolstoy and Shakespeare, are being translated into these languages, not to mention the emergence of superb works of Soviet writers to whom these languages are native.

And all this was achieved not through a shift of stages in the given language, which can occur only over thousands of years. [It took place] even without changing its grammatical structure, but through a conceptual and lexical enrichment of the language, which acquired greater syntactic flexibility.

The development of language is not chained by stages, just as the succession of social formations is not chained once and for all by their fixed sequence.

Thus, there is no superiority of Indo-European and Semitic languages. Let there be no denial of a language's developmental capacity!

Our Tasks.

It has been said above that everything necessary exists for raising Soviet linguistics to the required heights. For us, as for all workers in any branch of science and practice, the most valuable, guiding and directing [idea] is the path of society's development foreseen and traced by the genius of Lenin and Stalin, foreseen on the basis of the thorough analysis they made of the socio-economic factors which also condition language. The thematic material of Leninist-Stalinist science, which encompasses all areas of our economic life, is inexhaustible. The field for workers to operate in the cultural and particularly linguistic development in a socialist state is enormous, as is the role of Soviet linguists in this development. To carry out the tasks set by Comrade Stalin before Soviet linguistics will require the intense work of many generations of scholars. I have in mind particularly Comrade Stalin's directing and guiding remarks contained in his works on the nationality question, the excellent article in Pravda "On Marxism in Linguistics" and the teachings of Lenin and Stalin as a whole.

Comrade Stalin's basic instructions are to serve present-day life, living actuality, to reveal its shortcomings and help correct them, to eliminate the lag and move ahead. Only one formula—"the flourishing of cultures national in form and socialist in

*Ibid.

*I. I. Meshchaninov, The New Science of Language in its Contemporary Stage of Development, 1948, p. 35.

content," which includes all of the program guiding today our cultural development—gives linguistics the richest scientific and practical topics in the study of all the various languages of the Soviet Union with all the methods available to linguistics, and in improvement of these languages for their utilization in creative work in the native tongue. All languages of the Soviet Union need this, even those boasting ancient written languages.

The dictionary-writing, terminological and normative grammatical work on all languages of the U.S.S.R., going on at the present time, and which is unmistakeably lagging behind in some areas of given languages, as shown in the recent all-Union congress on these matters, demands gigantic efforts of Soviet linguistics. To participate in this work one must study the given language and its dialects in all aspects. Only this way is it possible to enrich the language, its vocabulary and syntax and to perfect it stylistically.

Many languages of the peoples of the Soviet Union have a historical past, set down in ancient documents. Their study, as well as the study of the language used by the best contemporary writers and those in the immediate past, is necessary also for the history of the given people, since language is the oldest witness of history.

Moreover, in order to participate in, and particularly to direct particular aspects of this work, one must be on the level of the contemporary state of linguistic science, both in general as well as in the specialized studies of particular languages (modern and ancient, living and dead). Without it one cannot solve the problem of the origin of speech, or what is incomparably more important, carry out the tasks posed by present day life and contained in Comrade Stalin's program remarks.

The field of activities for Soviet linguistics has been enlarged still further and its responsibility increased for fulfillment of the plan of linguistic works in light of the foundation-laying work of Comrade Stalin, "The National Problem and Leninism," in which a new world of ideas was revealed by making the distinction between a bourgeois nation and a socialist one; an extremely broad subject was opened for the scientific study of nations in such a differentiated contest, particularly where language was concerned; a new, inexhaustible scientific and practical set of topics, the like of which was unheard of in history, was opened to Soviet linguistics, which is unavailable to bourgeois linguistics.

To study languages with all their dialects under socialist conditions while taking into account their past in the indicated dimensions, to reveal the new regularities in the development of language which are undoubtedly already present now in the new circumstances and those still to appear in the further development of our social life, to service the linguistic requirements of socialist actuality at each stage of its development—these are the profoundly responsible tasks of Soviet linguistics. The periods of development of Socialist nations are carefully indicated in Comrade Stalin's work.

In Comrade Stalin's article "On Marxism in Linguistics" Soviet linguists have received an extremely clear, purposeful program assignment—to overcome the erroneous theses of Marr's doctrine.

"It is my belief that the sooner our linguistics frees itself of N. Ya. Marr's errors, the sooner it can emerge from the crisis in which it now finds itself."

"The liquidation of the Arakcheyev-like regime in linguistics, the rejection of N. Ya. Marr's errors, the penetration of Marxism into linguistics—this in my opinion is the path along which Soviet linguistics could recover" (J. Stalin).

To outline a concrete list of topics for Soviet linguistics is the most important work for linguists. Major problems which may consist of many hundreds and thousands of topics for each language can be presented schematically in the following way:

—The regularities in the development of the given language under socialist and former bourgeois conditions.

—Conditions and forms for improving the national languages (or a given language) under socialist conditions.

—The fate of the dialects of a given language (their mutual influence, the processes of their merging, as a prototype of the merging of languages in the distant future, the decrease in their numbers, etc.).

—The common language of the state and national languages under bourgeois and socialist conditions.

—The tendency of a given language to develop from a prezonal state to a zonal one, etc.

Or one could jot down problems, also subdivided into many hundreds of topics in the area of changing the psychological make-up of the speakers under socialist conditions reflected in language, dialect, etc., in the area of the relation of language to thought—and thus endlessly and inexhaustibly in the study of the development of language under the most diverse conditions of the gradual transition to a communist society.

Thus do the problems of linguistic development appear to a Soviet linguist, as they are presented to us by the great architect of communist society, Comrade Stalin.

The better part of Soviet linguistics, including even some Japhetidologists, are actually at work on such problems, but perhaps without an adequate knowledge of Marxist-Leninist methodology in linguistics.

Our work is inspired by the majestic perspective of building communist society. All Soviet linguistics will unite [to carry out] these responsible tasks. On the basis of the creative practice in the study of living and "dead" linguistic data, they will solve the cardinal theoretical problems of general linguistics, including the Marrist ones, verifying them through rich research practice.

Consolidation of Soviet linguists around these tasks is essential and possible. The difficulties will be overcome because Stalinist science is all-powerful. Soviet linguistics will supercede bourgeois science also in respect to technical methodology and will raise the former fame of Russian linguistics in the guise of a rejuvenated Soviet comparative-historical linguistics.

On Several Problems of Linguistics*

By J. STALIN

Comrade Krasheninnikova!

Here is my reply to your questions.

1. Question: It is convincingly shown in your article that language is neither a base nor a superstructure. Would it be legitimate to maintain that language is a phenomenon characteristic of both base and superstructure, or would it be correct to regard language as an intermediate phenomenon?

Answer: Of course, that which is common, which is inherent in all social phenomena, base and superstructure among them, is characteristic of language as a social phenomenon, namely: it serves society just as all other social phenomena serve it, base and superstructure included. But strictly speaking this exhausts what is common, what is inherent in all social phenomena. Further on, serious differences among social phenomena begin.

The point is that social phenomena have, in addition to that which is common, their own specific characteristics, which are distinct from each other and which are important, most of all, for science. The specific characteristics of the base consist in the fact that it [the base] serves society economically. The specific characteristics of the superstructure consist in the fact that it serves society with political, juridical, esthetic and other ideas and creates for society the appropriate political, juridical and other institutions. What are the specific characteristics of a language which differentiate it from other social phenomena? They are that language serves society as a means of human communication, as a means for the exchange of thoughts in society, as a means of enabling people to understand each other and to set going joint work in all spheres of human endeavor, in the field of production as well as in the field of economic relations, in the field of politics as in the field of culture, in social life as in everyday life. These characteristics are inherent only in language, and precisely because they are characteristic of language alone, language is the subject of study of an independent science—linguistics. Without these characteristics of language, linguistics would lose its right to exist independently.

Briefly: language must never be placed either in the category of bases or in the category of superstructures.

Likewise, it must not be placed in the category of "intermediate" phenomena between base and superstructure, inasmuch as there are no such "intermediate" phenomena.

But perhaps it would be possible to place language in the category of society's productive forces, in the category, let us say, of tools of production. A certain analogy really does exist between language and tools of production: tools of production, like language itself, manifest a kind of indifference to classes, and they can identically serve diverse classes of society, both old and new. Does this fact provide grounds for placing language in the category of tools of production? No, it does not.

At one time, N. Ya. Marr, seeing that his formula—"language is a superstructure over a base"—was being met with objections, decided to "reorganize" and declared that "language is an instrument of production." Was N. Ya. Marr correct in placing language in the category of instruments of production? No, he was absolutely not right.

The point is that the similarity between language and instruments of production is exhausted by the analogy of which I have just spoken. On the other hand, however, a profound difference exists between language and instruments of production. This difference lies in the fact that tools of production produce material wealth, while language produces either nothing or "produces" nothing more than words. To be more precise, people possessing instruments of production can produce material wealth, but these same people who possess a language but who do not possess instruments of production cannot produce material wealth. It is not difficult to understand that if language could produce material wealth, chatterboxes would be the richest people in the world.

2. Question: Marx and Engels define language as the "immediate reality of thought" as "Practical,***actual consciousness." "Ideas," says Marx, "do not exist in isolation from language." To what extent, in your opinion, must linguistics occupy itself with the sense side of language, semantics and historical semasiology and stylistics, or must the subject of linguistics be form alone?

Answer: Semantics (semasiology) is one of the important parts of linguistics. The sense aspect of words and expressions has serious significance in the matter of language study. Therefore, semantics (semasiology) must be accorded a place in linguistics suitable to it.

However, in the elaboration of questions of semantics and in the employment of its data, its significance should by no means be overestimated, and, more important still, it must not be abused. I am thinking of several linguists who, excessively diverted by semantics, disdain language as the "immediate reality of thought," indissolubly bound up with thinking, and they isolate thinking from language and assert that language has outlived its usefulness, that language can be dispensed with.

Note the following words of N. Ya. Marr:

"Language exists only insofar as it is manifested in sounds; the act of thinking takes place without [this] manifestation*** Language (sound) has now already begun to surrender its functions to the latest inventions, which have totally conquered space, and thinking is making progress by virtue of its unutilized accumulations in the past and [by virtue of] new achievements, and it will displace and fully replace language. The future language is thought, growing into a technique free of natural matter. No language, not even sound, though it be bound up with the norms of nature, can stand in its way " (See Selected Works, N. Ya. Marr).

If you translate this "work-magic" gobbledygook into simple human language, then you may conclude that:

(a) N. Ya. Marr isolates thinking from language;

(b) N. Ya. Marr maintains that human communication is possible without language, with the aid of thought itself, free from the "natural matter" of language, free from the "norms of nature;"

(c) Isolating thought from language and "having freed" it from "natural matter," N. Ya. Marr falls into the swamp of idealism.

It is said that thoughts appear in the head of man before they are expressed in speech, that they emerge without language material, without being garbed in language, naked, as it were. But this is completely erroneous. No matter what thoughts arise in the head of man, they can arise and exist only on the basis of the material of language, on the basis of terms and phrases. Bare thoughts, free of language material, free of the "natural matter" of language, do not exist. "Language is the immediate reality of thought" (Marx). The reality of thought manifests itself in language. Only idealists can talk about thought not connected with the "natural matter" of language, about thought

*Pravda, July 4, 1950, p. 3.

without language.

Briefly: the overestimation of semantics and the abuse of the latter led N. Ya. Marr into idealism.

Consequently, if you guard semantics (semasiology) from exaggerations and abuses, like those which N. Ya. Marr and several of his "students" permitted, then it [semantics] can be of great use to linguistics.

3. Question: You quite rightly say that ideas, notions, mores and ethical principles of the bourgeois are in direct opposition to those of the proletariat. The class character of these phenomena is undoubtedly reflected in the semantic side of language (and sometimes in its form—in vocabulary—as you correctly point out in your article). Is it possible by analyzing the concrete material of language and, first of all, the sense aspect of language, to speak of the class essence of ideas expressed by it, particularly in those cases when you are speaking of the expression in language, not only of man's thought, but of his relationship to actuality, where his class affiliation is displayed with particular vividness?

Answer: Briefly speaking, you want to know whether classes influence language, whether they introduce into language their specific words and expressions, whether there are instances where people attribute to one and the same words and expressions different sense signification, depending on class affiliation.

Yes, classes influence language, introduce into language their specific words and expressions and sometimes understand differently the very same words and expressions. There is no doubt about it.

However, it does not follow from this that specific words and expressions, as well as difference in semantics, can have serious significance for the development of a single language common to an entire people, that they are capable of attenuating its significance or changing its character.

In the first place, there are so few such specific words and expressions in language, as well as cases of semantic differences, that they scarcely comprise one percent of all the material of language. Consequently, all the remaining overwhelming mass of words and expressions, as well as their semantics, are common for all classes of society.

In the second place, specific words and expressions which have class overtones, are employed in speech, not according to the rules of some "class" grammar, which does not exist in nature, but according to grammatical rules of an existing language common to an entire people.

Consequently, the presence of specific words and expressions and facts of difference in the semantics of language do not refute, but, on the contrary, support the presence and the necessity for a single language common to an entire people.

4. Question: In your article, you quite correctly adjudge Marr a vulgarizer of Marxism. Does this mean that linguists and we, the youth, among them, must discard all the linguistic heritage of Marr, who nonetheless produced a number of valuable pieces of research (these were discussed by Comrades Chikobava, Sanzheyev and others in the discussion)? May we, taking a critical approach to Marr, nevertheless, take from him what is useful and valuable?

Answer: Of course, N. Ya. Marr's works do not consist of errors alone. N. Ya. Marr allowed flagrant mistakes when he introduced in linguistics elements of Marxism in a perverted form, when he tried to create an independent theory of language. But N. Ya. Marr does have to his credit individual, good, talented writings, where he, forgetting about his theoretical claims, conscientiously and, it must be said, skillfully investigates individual languages. In such works more than a little may be gleaned which is valuable and instructive. Of course, what is valuable and instructive must be culled from N. Ya. Marr and utilized.

5. Question: Many linguists consider that one of the fundamental reasons for stagnation in Soviet linguistics is formalism. I would be most grateful for your opinion on what formalism in linguistics is and how it can be overcome?

Answer: N. Ya. Marr and his "students" accuse of formalism all philogists who do not share the "new teaching" of N. Ya. Marr. This, of course, is not serious and is unintelligent.

N. Ya. Marr considered grammar an empty "formality" and people who considered a grammatical system as the basis of language—formalists. This is altogether stupid.

I feel that "formalism" was fabricated by the authors of the "new teaching" for facilitating the struggle with their opponents in linguistics.

The reasons for stagnation in Soviet linguistics is not the "formalism" invented by N. Ya. Marr and his "students," but the Arakcheyev-like regime and the theoretical gaps in linguistics. N. Ya. Marr's "students" created the Arakcheyev-like regime. N. Ya. Marr and his closest colleagues introduced theoretical confusion into linguistics. To do away with stagnation, both [of the above] must be abolished. The liquidation of these ulcers will cure Soviet linguistics, will lead it onto a broad path and will enable Soviet linguistics to occupy first place in world linguistics. (June 29, 1950)

Clear Prospects*

By N. SAURANBAYEV

The unsatisfactory state of linguistics, its stagnation, particularly the confusion and erroneousness of Academician Marr's theories, have had their effect on the development of linguistic thought in the national republics. In many cases linguistics is here a new, young science. Specialists in particular national languages, in investigating a given problem concerning a national language, always have recourse to the works of Academician Marr.

But they did not find in them a definite scientific method to be used in research. As soon as one turns to Academician Marr's works looking for a definite orientation on a question under investigation, one falls into an opaque fog and loses one's bearings: sometimes one stumbles into the field of archeology or ethnography, sometimes into philosophy, folklore, history and other disciplines, but there is little that is specifically on linguistics. All this has retarded the development of theoretical linguistics in the various localities. An utter separation has prevailed between Academician Marr's theory and practice.

Comrade Stalin's article "On Marxism in Linguistics" brought full clarity to the basic problems of linguistic principles and indicated the path of further development. Creative Marxism has always been and remains that majestic and life-giving force which helps overcome any obstacles and illuminate the developmental path of progressive thought. In Comrade Stalin's work, Soviet linguists have received exhaustive answers to many puzzling theoretical problems and a clear outline for their further work.

It is very important for the students of such little known and, in the past, unwritten languages as are many of the Turkic ones, including Kazakh, to have a clear theoretical framework. Having read Comrade Stalin's article, I have become convinced of the extremely mistaken nature of Academician Marr's theses about language as a superstructure, about the "class nature" of language, etc.

Comrade Stalin has clearly and convincingly pointed out the radical difference between language and superstructure by defining the basic regularities in the origin, development and existence of a language common to a whole people.

The theory of the "class nature" of language led to denial of the existence of a language common to a whole nation, to a whole people, while the theory of development by stages incorrectly dealt with the laws of the gradual transition of languages from one condition to another.

It must be said that the "theory" of a break and a sudden transformation of language was frequently reflected unfavorably in the practice of language development. In Kazakhstan, as in other republics whose languages have for the most part only recently been written, there were cases in which many root words were driven from the literature under the influence of the theory of the "class nature" of language. In doing this, many linguists followed the premise that language is superstructure and thus, to correspond to the new socialist base, a new socialist language had to be created through an upheaval.

J. V. Stalin's brilliant work "On Marxism in Linguistics" is a great new contribution to creative Marxism. It lays the groundwork for a new Soviet materialist linguistics; it marks a turning point in the history of linguistics. The great Stalin has opened before Soviet linguistics a bright path, clear prospects.

*Pravda, July 4, 1950, p. 3.

A Program of Marxist Linguistics*

By Academician V. VINOGRADOV

J. V. Stalin's article "On Marxism in Linguistics" gives clear, thorough and precise answers to the most important questions of the general Marxist theory of language. It indicates the direct and true means of overcoming the standstill at which Soviet linguistics has found itself until now.

At the same time, J. V. Stalin's article places before Soviet linguists a number of new problems which did not emerge during the discussion and suggests their correct, Marxist solution (for example, the question of the relationship between the concepts of language and style; an author's style and its relation to the literary language; the nature and means of utilizing language to express the superstructure, that is, the political, juridical, religious, artistic and philosophical views of society at different stages of its development, etc.).

J. V. Stalin's article sets up a sharp dividing line between the past and present in Soviet linguistics, brilliantly illuminating the path and the tasks of its future development.

Imparting nationwide significance to problems of Soviet linguistics, J. V. Stalin's article has made Soviet linguists more profoundly aware of their responsibility for their work and has called forth among them not only a feeling of greatest gratitude but also an ardent desire to make Soviet linguistics worthy of J. V. Stalin's confidence and concern, worthy of his direct leadership.

Before the publication of J. V. Stalin's article "On Marxism in Linguistics" all Soviet linguists, regardless of their various leanings and points of view, shared in their work the premise that language was "a social phenomenon of a superstructural nature." The erroneous estimation of language as a superstructure on a base was most clearly revealed in the errors of Academician N. Ya. Marr (particularly in his doctrine of language development by stages and description of the course of the so-called language-forming process). However, an approach to language as superstructure was reflected in greater or lesser measure in almost all Soviet works related to the history of language. The stable and all-national in language did not attract attention. Linguistic changes were placed in direct and parallel correspondence to changes in the base. The history of the common literary language was organically interwoven with the history of creative writing and was classified along the same class divisions and stages of development as creative writing and journalism. The concepts of language, dialect and artistic style were confused as systems of expressing class ideologies.

*Pravda, July 4, 1950, p. 3.

J. V. Stalin introduces full clarity into this group of central problems of linguistics and directs Soviet linguists onto a truly Marxist path of linguistic research. The area of this research and its tasks are incomparably enlarged. After all, the "field of operations of the superstructure is narrow and limited."

On the contrary, language is "directly linked to man's productive activity and not only to his productive activity but to every other activity in all aspects of man's work, from production to the base, from the base to the superstructure."*

According to J. V. Stalin's definition,the field of operations of language is "virtually unlimited."

The new Stalinist formulation of such problems as the national language at various stages in its development, the relation between local dialects and the common language of a tribe or people, between the common language of a people or nation and class dialects or jargons, the means which given social groups or classes have of utilizing the popular language in their class interests, language and culture—all this breaks radically with the prevailing notions in Soviet linguistics concerning the history of language and requires a full revision of all basic concepts in its historical investigation.

The antihistorical principle of studying the "class nature of language" is replaced by the task of historical-materialist investigation of "class character" in the utilization of language as well as the study of "class" ramifications of the common, popular, all-national language at various stages of the development of class society.

In J. V. Stalin's article we have an orderly program, astonishing in its wealth of ideas, for a Marxist elaboration of the history of language. In this connection one would like to note J. V. Stalin's important statements on two more cardinal questions of linguistics: (1) the laws of internal development of language and (2) the nature of qualitative changes in language.

Emphasizing that "language and the laws of its development can be comprehended only if they are studied in indissoluble connection with the history of society and with the history of the people to which the language under study belongs and which is the creator and the bearer of this language," J. V. Stalin recognizes that the main task of linguistics is "the study of the laws of internal development of language."

The development of language takes place, according to J. V. Stalin,"through the development and improvement of the main elements of the existing language." Marxism considers that the transition from one qualitative state of language to another takes place "through the gradual and prolonged accumulation of elements of the new quality, of the new structure of the language, and through the gradual dying-off of the old quality's elements."

J. V. Stalin brings a new bright light to the understanding of language's structure. He indicates the truly Marxist paths and the tasks of studying the grammatical structure of language "worked out in the course of ages and having become the language's flesh and blood." The educational and philosophical significance of grammar is understood more profoundly in the light of the dialectical theory of cognition and dialectical logic. "Grammar is the result of the prolonged abstractive work of human thinking and an index of the tremendous successes of thought." J. V. Stalin's article puts an end to all formalism in the field of grammatical investigations.

Unusually valuable and fruitful is J. V. Stalin's theory concerning the basic lexical fund and its relation to a language's total lexical reserve. This theory is a shining example of the application of the method of materialist dialectics to the analysis of vocabulary. It is first of all indicated that the vocabulary of a language is the most sensitive to change and "is in almost constant change." "The vocabulary reflects the state of the language" and its development. The basic lexical fund is the most important part of the vocabulary, the most stable, living a very long time, for centuries. It gives the language a base for the formation of new words. It makes up the basis of a language's vocabulary. Although it changes slowly, being the product of the ages, the basic lexical fund changes nevertheless. Thus, in J. V. Stalin's words, "it is to be assumed that the elements of the contemporary language were formed far back in antiquity before the slave-owning period. This language was not complex; it had a very sparse vocabulary."

J. V. Stalin's theory of the basic lexical fund and the vocabulary reserve of a language lays down the Marxist foundations of a historical lexicology and the history of word formation. The enormous importance of this theory for the theory and practice of dictionary composition (lexicography) is self-evident. It seems to me that on the basis of this theory such important problems in the history of literary Russian as the Old Slavic element in Old Russian and the role of Old Slavic factors in the history of the formation and development of literary Russian must receive completely new solutions.

J. V. Stalin's article "On Marxism in Linguistics" gives Soviet linguists a key to a truly Marxist solution of the basic problems of linguistics. The more one studies this profound, lucid and rigorous work, the more one draws from it, as from a magic treasure house of new directions, new ideas, new generalizations which brilliantly illuminate the wide horizons of Marxist linguistics before the eyes of Soviet linguists.

*For this and all following references to Stalin on linguistics, see J. V. Stalin, "On Marxism in Linguistics," Pravda, June 20, 1950.

An Example of Creative Marxism*

By Professor S. TOLSTOV

The importance of J. V. Stalin's article "On Marxism in Linguistics," a major contribution to the treasure house of Marxist-Leninist theory, goes far beyond the confines of linguistics. This work is a magnificent example of the creative development of Marxism-Leninism. It reveals with Stalinist precision and thoroughness those shortcomings in the organization of scientific work which, unfortunately, are characteristic, of course in varying degrees, not of linguistics alone. Comrade Stalin's article places a number of new problems of cardinal importance before our historians, particularly those who are working on the difficult and complex body of problems regarding the origin of given peoples and groups, questions which are inseparable from the history of these peoples' and groups' languages. I, too, am one of these historians.

There is no point in hiding sin—like most of us who are dealing with these questions, be they historians, archeologists, ethnographers, or anthropologists, I was sympathetically inclined to Academician N. Ya. Marr's theory. Behind the noise and crash of Marrist propaganda, behind the formally sharp "criticism" of racism, which had undoubtedly left a strong imprint on foreign linguistic work, behind the "criticism" of the "protolanguage theory," which had long ago been vigorously contradicted by objective historical-archeological and ethonographic facts, we could not perceive the pseudo-Marxist, vulgarizing essence of Marr's theory.

The discussion opened by Pravda convincingly revealed that endless confusion which reigned in linguistics and which had been started by Marr and the adherents of the "new teaching on language." But only Comrade Stalin contributed to this discussion a genuine Marxist-Leninist, Stalinist precision and clarity, giving a definite and incontrovertible diagnosis of the serious illness suffered by our linguistics and indicating the path of linguistic recovery and ascent.

None of the participants in the discussion who preceded Comrade Stalin could see the basic weakness of Marr's theory. What is more, Prof. A. Chikobava, whose incontrovertible merit it is to have stated with full harshness the many utter failures of Marr's theories, evaluated Marr's erroneous doctrine of language as a superstructure on the base as Marr's only positive contribution to Marxist-Leninist linguistics.

Actually, as Comrade Stalin emphasizes, this thesis of Marr's is the main weakness of his theory.

Thanks to Comrade Stalin's work it is now clear that Marr's theory as a whole, based on this incorrect formula, is basically wrong and is not a Marxist but an over-simplified theory. It is clear now that our attempts to utilize the erroneous premises of Marr's theory in the solution of problems in the origins of peoples were a mistake, whose correction is the next task of Soviet historians of all specialties working in this area.

It would, of course, be incorrect to strike out because of this all our works devoted to problems of peoples' origins. In our specifically historical work we started from historical, archeological, ethnographic and anthropological facts, while using in their analysis the methodology of Marxism-Leninism, the Stalinist theory of the nation. But in utilizing in linguistic matters the conclusions of Marrist theory, we did not strengthen but weaken the argumentation of our conclusions drawn from the examination of other materials and on a number of questions reached even incorrect conclusions.

All of us are now intensively studying Comrade Stalin's outstanding work. Like all the works of the great leader of peoples, the great coryphaeus of Marxist-Leninist science, this work arms us to overcome the errors and inadequacies in our work, indicating the only correct path for the further development not only of linguistics but of the departments of historical science connected with it.

*Pravda, July 4, 1950, p. 3.

For a Creative Path in Soviet Science*

By Academician S. OBNORSKY

J. V. Stalin's work "On Marxism in Linguistics," as is always characteristic of J. V. Stalin, states with extreme simplicity and clarity the basic lines of further activity for Soviet linguists. In J. V. Stalin's article nothing is left indefinite; there is no "perhaps," "apparently," "seemingly." One reads here firmly of what is, one sees here a picture of what must be.

"The pupils" of N. Ya. Marr tried in every way to inculcate the idea that one could approach Marxism-Leninism in linguistics only through N. Y. Marr. "N. Ya. Marr really did want to and tried to be a Marxist, but he did not succeed in becoming a Marxist. He was merely a simplifier and vulgarizer of Marxism, like the followers of the 'Proletkult' or 'RAPP.'"

One of the basic theses of the "new science of language" was the theory of language as superstructure. J. V. Stalin has revealed the erroneousness of precisely this thesis first of all, thereby enriching not only our Soviet linguistics, but also the general theory of Marxism-Leninism.

Another leading premise of N. Ya. Marr's theory whose complete erroneousness has also been demonstrated by J. V. Stalin was the thesis of the "class nature" of language, with which N. Ya. Marr "confused himself and confused linguistics."

In the light of the Marxist solution of these problems basic to linguistics, one may as well forget about such unproven and unfounded theses of N. Ya. Marr as the development of languages by stages and the theory of the singleness of the glottogonic (language-forming) process.

The key to N. Ya. Marr's linguistic works is the so-called paleontologic analysis. It rests on the recognition that originally speech consisted only of four elements which in various combinations allegedly gave rise to all the world's languages. These four elements—the keystone thesis of

*Pravda, July 4, 1950, p. 4.

N. Ya. Marr's "new science"—are searched for in different languages. The most diverse languages are brought into discussion, the history of languages is ignored, various sound metamorphoses are allowed arbitrarily, etc.

Obviously such analysis can convince nobody. Those definite accomplishments which we owe to the old comparative-historical linguistics are nullified by N. Ya. Marr. J. V. Stalin indicates that the comparative-historical method "is an impetus to work, to study languages" while N. Ya. Marr's analysis "is an impetus to lying on top of the oven and reading teacups about the notorious four elements." In general, N. Ya. Marr always took up arms against the comparative-historical method. And yet this method cannot be rejected, as was indicated by J. V. Stalin. It is just the comparative-historical method, regardless of its shortcomings, that helped to establish the common historical origin of the languages of the fraternal peoples—Russian, Ukrainian and Belorussian, as well as of all Slavic languages. We must remember J. V. Stalin's indication that "language kinship, for example, of such nations as the Slavs is beyond dispute."

In N. Ya. Marr's opinion the development of language took place only through hybridization. In his brilliant work J. V. Stalin has shown that in the process of hybridization of two languages, we do not get a new, third language, but that "in the process of hybridization, one of the languages usually emerges victorious."

N. Ya. Marr and his pupils unjustly tried to strike out everything accomplished in linguistics before them; they were intolerant with the heterodox. But "no science can develop and flourish without a struggle of opinions, without free criticism" (J. V. Stalin).

After all, Russian linguists did contribute a great deal in the history of world science. How can one strike out the whole heritage of the past as the partisans of the "new science" in linguistics do?

I think that the elimination of the Arakcheyev-like regime in linguistics, the decisive rejection of N. Ya. Marr's "science" and the inculcation of Marxism in linguistics, as told us by J. V. Stalin, will guarantee the flowering of Soviet linguistics.

Let us Correct Mistakes in Our Work*

By Professor N. YAKOVLEV

The appearance in the pages of Pravda of J. V. Stalin's article "On Marxism in Linguistics" is a real triumph for Soviet science and a cause of celebration not only for us Soviet linguists but also for our historians, ethnographers, and philosophers. For the first time in history a work is published which is wholly dedicated to Marxist-Leninist teaching on language and illuminates the basic theoretical problems of linguistics.

At the base of all true science, including linguistics, must stand a correct Marxist-Leninist methodology. Nevertheless many linguists have not devoted enough attention to the mastery of this methodology. Therefore, despite the tremendous assistance which the development of science in the U.S.S.R. has been constantly given and is still given by the Party and the government, we Soviet linguists have to this day not always been able to figure out the basic problem of our science, the problem of what language is. This was particularly true of the works of the author of this article.

In revealing the radical difference between language and superstructure, J. V. Stalin discovered the basic defect in the work of many linguists who incorrectly considered language as an ideological superstructure on an economic base.

J. V. Stalin's exhaustively complete, profound and clear solution of the basic problem of the radical difference between language and superstructure has become the only methodological weapon with whose aid we can now confidently build a Marxist-Leninist linguistics.

One can express confidence that, having mastered Marxism-Leninism, in a very short time Soviet linguists will overcome in their research work the inadequacies of the comparative-historical method and will be able to apply in their field the method of historical materialism.

It was only in the course of the free discussion in the pages of Pravda that the errors of N. Ya. Marr were revealed in all their nakedness and unsightliness. Comrade Stalin has shown that these errors were not accidental but made up a whole system of erroneous, pseudoscientific theses: language as superstructure, the "class nature" of language, the utterly idealist four-element analysis, the wholesale libeling of the comparative-historical method and of all attempts to study related groups (families) of languages and so on.

N. Ya. Marr's grossest errors made up a whole system of incorrect views and fully justify the characterization of N. Ya. Marr drawn by Comrade Stalin: "Marr really did want to and tried to be a Marxist, but he did not succeed in becoming a Marxist. He was merely a simplifier and vulgarizer of Marxism, like the followers of the 'Proletkult' or 'RAPP.'"

As a consequence of the "Arakcheyev-like regime," which began in linguistics while N. Ya. Marr was still alive, many scholars (not only linguists, but ethnographers, archeologists and historians as well) turned out to have lost their common sense and a correct criterion in evaluating N. Ya. Marr's works.

One must admit that the work written by me jointly with Prof. V. K. Nikolsky, "The Basic Theses of N. Ya. Marr's Doctrine of Language" (Voprosy Filosofii, No. 1, 1949), contains in the opinion of both authors excessive praise of obviously erroneous theses of N. Ya. Marr.

Equally erroneous is another one of my articles "Marr as Citizen and Scholar—on the Fifteenth Anniversary of his Death" ("Scholarly Notes of the Kabardin Scientific Institute," Vol. V, 1950). In addition, in a number of my spespecialized works—"Grammar of the Adighe Language" (1941), "Grammar of the Kabardinian-Cherkess Language" (1949), and others—one can find occasional uncritical references to N. Ya. Marr's mistaken theses. All this places upon me the greatest responsibility, having perceived these erroneous parts, to correct them through an accurate methodology and a scientific criticism of Academician N. Ya. Marr's psuedoscientific theses in my future works.

Comrade Stalin says: "Recognizing 'certain' errors of N. Ya. Marr, the 'pupils' of N. Ya. Marr it appears, think that Soviet linguistics can be further developed only on the basis of the 'refined' theory of N. Ya. Marr which they consider Marxist."

I think that all who, like us, erred terribly about Marr's "Marxism," might well remember the old Latin proverb: "All men can make mistakes but only fools persist in their errors." One learns from mistakes. I intend to correct my errors honestly in future work.

Armed with the Stalinist teaching on language, Soviet linguists are now placed in the front ranks of fighters for progressive materialist science. All who prize the success of Soviet linguistics will warmly greet Comrade Stalin's concluding words:

"The liquidation of the Arakcheyev-like regime in linguistics, the repudiation of N. Ya. Marr's mistakes and the inculcation of Marxism in linguistics — such is, in my opinion, the way which would make it possible to instill new health in Soviet linguistics."

*Pravda, July 4, 1950, p. 4.

Letter to the Editors of Pravda*

By Academician I. MESHCHANINOV

In J. V. Stalin's remarkable work "On Marxism in Linguistics" we Soviet linguists have received for the first time an extremely lucid definition of the nature of language and of the further paths of development of the Soviet science of language.

The majority of us Soviet linguists, and especially myself, were so firmly convinced that language was a phenomenon of a superstructural nature that we did not even make any effort to think over those definitions of superstructures and their relation to the base which are contained in the Marxist-Leninist classics. Hence the erroneousness of many of our other theoretical theses.

Our recognition of the superstructural nature of language inevitably led to the incorrect assertion of its class nature, of its development through "upheavals" and consequently of the incorrect evaluation of the role of language hybridization as the basis of language formation and development. Following the same path, we were unable to understand truly the historical process of the formation of peoples and the development of languages. The extremely exaggerated evaluation of Marr's role in the development of Soviet linguistics, his elevation to the position of being almost the only positive figure not only in this field but in a whole series of related disciplines, follows from the above. Hence, also, the contemptuous attitude to the heritage of all Russian linguistics antecedent to Marr.

These and many other errors of Marr himself and of his pupils, particularly myself, actually led to stagnation in Soviet linguistics. We feared like the plague any application of the comparative-historical method, thinking naively that such attempts inevitably would led to a return to the formalist-idealist ideas of the last century's science. We were unable to understand correctly the basis of language, its specific essence. The attempts made to study the grammatical structure of languages were indiscriminantly proclaimed formalistic and met with direct opposition from the representatives of that linguistic regime which Comrade Stalin quite correctly labeled as Arakcheyev-like. Insistently and, unfortunately, not without some "success" the subject matter of linguistics was artificially torn from the urgent requirements of linguistic development and directed into bygone ages.

In his article Comrade Stalin laid a foundation for Soviet linguistics and opened a new era in its history; only after we had carefully thought through the nature of language as disclosed in that article could we who had followed Marr too uncritically see the error of the theoretical path taken by our investigations, a path along which we had led the young generation. The positive aspects of our work directed toward a thorough study of the vocabularies and grammatical structures of the languages of our multinational motherland were drowned in these vulgar errors.

The invaluable aid of Comrade Stalin calls forth deep and sincere gratitude in the hearts of Soviet linguists. He has liberated Soviet linguistics from stagnation and led it onto the broad path of truly scientific creativity.

We are confronted with a difficult but honorable and responsible task—to follow unswervingly Comrade Stalin's indications and to reorganize radically our investigative work on the foundation of a thorough mastery of the methodological and theoretical principles of Marxism-Leninism.

Let us remember firmly and follow unhesitatingly the wise words of our great leader and coryphaeus of science: "The liquidation of the Arakcheyev-like regime in linguistics, the repudiation of N. Ya. Marr's mistakes and the inculcation of Marxism in linguistics — such is, in my opinion, the way that would make it possible to instill new health in Soviet linguistics."

*Pravda, July 4, 1950, p. 4.

Letter to the Editors*

By Professor N. CHEMODANOV

In the light of Comrade Stalin's work "On Marxism in Linguistics" I must admit the utter erroneousness of my article "The Paths of Development of Soviet Linguistics" printed in Pravda of May 23, 1950, which reflected my mistakes in the basic problems of linguistics.

My fundamental error consists in my incorrect, un-Marxist view of language as a social superstructure on the base, in erroneously identifying language with social ideology and considering it to be a class phenomenon. Incorrectly, I considered N. Ya. Marr's theory on language basically Marxist and held that, freed of certain errors, it represented the general line of development of linguistics.

Now, after Comrade Stalin's article, it has become clear to me that this is not at all true. Comrade Stalin's brilliant new work is a tremendous event, a turning point in the development of social sciences. Among Marxist-Leninist classics on linguistics it is the most outstanding, the fullest and most systematic exposition of Marxism in this field of knowledge.

Comrade Stalin's work has created a firm theoretical foundation for Soviet linguistics and has destroyed the confusion in points of view which has existed until now. Soviet linguists can only be grateful to Comrade Stalin for fatherly assistance.

Now, after the publication of Comrade Stalin's work, the task is to realize the errors which were made [and then] to assume decisively and unconditionally the Marxist positions formulated by Comrade Stalin and in our practical scientific and educational work to transform Comrade Stalin's indications into life.

*Pravda, July 4, 1950, p. 4.

A New Stage*

By Professor L. BULAKHOVSKY

J. V. Stalin's article must be evaluated as a new, important stage in the development of science. With extreme persuasiveness J. V. Stalin has established theses of basic significance: that "a Marxist cannot regard language a superstructure over a base," that "to confuse language with superstructure is to commit a grave error," that "the formula of the class nature of languages is an erroneous, un-Marxist formula."

The significance of Comrade Stalin's article for us linguists is enormous both in a general theoretical way and so far as ways of further developing linguistics are concerned. A brilliant, foundation-laying chapter has been written into our science, [a chapter] which had long been lacking, which will be studied by many generations of linguists who, basing themselves on it, will shape their scientific world view.

The precise distinction made in Comrade Stalin's statements between vocabulary and grammar, the first as able to reflect some of the transformations in social consciousness, the second as conserving for a long time, for centuries, in its basic peculiarities the material envelope of human thought, is of exceptional significance not only for the clarification of the nature of national languages, but for the whole theory and practice of scientific linguistics. The comparative-historical method is generally applicable to languages whose historical rarity rests primarily on the presence of close morphological (structural) similarities [sic].

The characterization of the usual results of linguistic hybridization given by Comrade Stalin is profound and fully confirmed by the facts. [These results] consist not in the emergence of some new third language but in the preservation of the grammatical structure and basic lexical fund of one language and its enrichment in greater or lesser measure with elements of the defeated language.

J. V. Stalin's pointing to the internal laws of development of languages is of primary significance as a confirmation of the actual existence of laws which are almost the chief subject in the work of a linguist. It is also a very important methodological requirement whose fruitfulness will probably soon be revealed in full force in the practical work of linguists of the most diverse specialties.

To exhaust the wealth of ideas in Comrade Stalin's article is impossible in a brief note. Of course, as a genuine work of scientific, creative Marxism, it sharpens the thought not only of linguists.

Met with tremendous joy, as a triumph of truly progressive science in an area where, unfortunately, mystic fairy tales reigned too long disguised as alleged Marxist conceptions, Comrade Stalin's article will undoubtedly inspire thousands of Soviet scholars to new, energetic work.

*Pravda, July 4, 1950, p. 4.

For a Science Worthy of Our Epoch*

By Academician V. SHISHMAREV

Everybody to whom the interests of native linguistics are dear and precious read with a feeling of deep satisfaction J. V. Stalin's article "On Marxism in Linguistics." A sharp dividing line has now been drawn in this science between "yesterday" and "tomorrow," and Marrism, to which our linguists were oriented in one way or another, is an obsolete stage.

It would be incorrect, of course, to bury all of Marr's heritage. He did write a number of valuable works on specific topics in linguistics. What he considered his distinctive accomplishment and his premises are just those errors from which Comrade Stalin asks our linguists promptly to free themselves so as to end the crisis. Our most urgent task is to do this.

Comrade Stalin's article has created great enthusiasm among all scientific workers (not only linguists). In an extremely lucid and distinct form Comrade Stalin has illuminated a number of basic linguistic problems, showing that language is not a superstructure and that to talk of the "class nature" of language is a non-Marxist thesis. He submitted Marr's theory of stages and hybridization to exhaustive criticism. By recognizing the usefulness of the comparative-historical method, which was denied by Marr's followers, Comrade Stalin emphasized the importance of a historical study of languages, while Marr's paleontology accustomed people to neglect history and to elaborate theory irrespective of facts. This created a situation in our universities which can no longer be tolerated and has had the result that we have almost no books dealing with the history of languages and that studies in the history of language in connection with the history of the people speaking it are weakly developed. Only history, however, can help us to reveal the internal laws of the development of languages, which is a basic task of linguistics.

In his harsh evaluation of Marr's arrogant manner (Marr lightly dismissed all that went on before him) and in his condemnation of the "Arakcheyev-like regime," unnatural in science but reigning in linguistics, Comrade Stalin emphasized with particular force the importance of criticism and self-criticism in the development of science. "It is universally recognized," he reminds us, "that no science can develop and flourish without a struggle of opinions, without free criticism."

Only along this path indicated by Comrade Stalin can the errors of Marr's conceptions be definitely overcome and Soviet linguistics become a genuine materialist science of language. Linguists are confronted with a glorious path of scientific development worthy of our great epoch.

*Pravda, July 4, 1950, p. 4.

Only Forward*

By Professor YE. GALKINA-FEDORUK

Words cannot express our deep gratitude to our dear teacher, the great and wise Stalin, for his work on questions of linguistics.

A bright feeling of joy permeated everyone after the appearance of J. V. Stalin's classic article on Pravda's discussion page. Those who, while perhaps in error, nevertheless honestly and without preconceptions were searching for a way to solve the complicated problems of linguistics, frequently suffering persecution from the "self-contained group of infallible leaders," breathed easily.

In his amazingly profound, simple and clear new work on linguistics Comrade Stalin gave linguists a correct orientation and led our science from the impasse into which it had been driven by Marr's irresponsible "pupils," to whom the interests of genuine science were alien. J. V. Stalin has shown us how erroneous were the statements that Marr had already created a materialist theory—"the new teaching on language"—which alone, allegedly, could correctly solve all cardinal problems of linguistics: the origin of language, relations between language and thought and language and society, the development of language, etc. All that had been created before Marr was criticized and banished, while the accomplishments of the best linguists in our country (Buslayev, Shakhmatov, Shcherba, Bogoroditsky and Vinogradov) were characterized as "bourgeois idealist trash."

Using his vulgar view of the class nature of language N. Ya. Marr eliminated the historical category of the common national language. But Comrade Stalin teaches us: "*** The national community is unthinkable without a common language***" Consequently, the division of people into classes does not disturb "the common nature of language" or violate "the common nature of the nation." Thus Marr's concept of the class nature of language is incorrect and contradicts Marxist-Leninist theory on nations and classes.

J. V. Stalin has explained brilliantly, with incontrovertible persuasiveness, that "language, as a means of communication among people in society, serves equally all classes in society and in this respect is, in a manner of speaking, indifferent to classes." And Comrade Stalin categorically concludes this chapter with the statement: "The formula of the 'class nature' of language is an erroneous, un-Marxist formula."

We Soviet linguists have dealt insufficiently with grammatical questions. In his work Comrade Stalin indicates that "grammar (morphology and syntax) is a collection of rules of word changes and word combinations in the sentence. Consequently it is precisely thanks to grammar that language has a chance to garb human thought in a material linguistic covering." This is exceptionally important for each of us.

Scientific linguists had abandoned the needs of schools. The schools await new textbooks, new teaching aids. Even those on the college level have been unable to make up good textbooks in the last 30 years. Not only in the secondary schools but even in higher educational institutions we do not know how to reveal the expressive force of our language, its sonority, its peculiar melodic pattern, its rhythmic quality, the variety and richness of our intonation which adds an enchanting musical quality and creates a general impression of beauty. We still do not reveal adequately the strength and greatness of the Russian language; we do not teach how to master it as a "weapon of struggle." We still do not know how to react to the deep-seated interest in the richness of Russian vocabulary; we do not really help the students to forge a style worthy of our epoch. There are those from whom we can learn. Pushkin, Turgenev, Gogol, Chekhov and Gorky have given examples of the profound and original beauty of the Russian language. V. I. Lenin and J. V. Stalin have given us wonderful examples of effective, realistically laconic, simple, precise, clear and truthful Russian.

In his work Comrade Stalin states and solves the vitally essential problems of the study of language as "a weapon of development and struggle." Not "either forward or backward," as Prof. Sanzheyev wrote, but only forward, overcoming errors and difficulties by introducing Marxism into linguistics and utilizing all that Lenin and Stalin have given us in their works and everything positive which has been created by the best scholars of our country.

*Pravda, July 4, 1950, p. 4.

Path to Progress*

By Professor G. TSERETELI

With the publication in the pages of Pravda of J. V. Stalin's article "On Marxism in Linguistics" a new epoch began in the development of Soviet linguistics. Our linguistics, which has rested over a period of years on the erroneous theses of Marr's so-called "new teaching on language," was in crisis. The great coryphaeus of science, Comrade Stalin, has now shown us the way leading to unlimited growth and the flowering of our science.

Language is "a means, a device, by which people communicate with each other, exhange ideas, and achieve mutual understanding" (J. Stalin). It interests mankind from the very first steps in the development of its civilization. In the middle of the first millenium A.D. we already had various systems of descriptive grammar of some ancient languages. Linguistics, as an independent scientific discipline, is over a century old. Over this whole protracted period scholars and investigators, linguists and philosophers, have many times attempted to arrive at the essence of this most important phenomenon in human life.

But only Stalin's genius was able to grasp the true essence of language with the extreme clarity, the exceptional profundity of a great thinker. J. V. Stalin has established the characteristic features of language, its specificity, and has defined the significance of grammar as "the result of the prolonged abstractive work of human thinking." In determining the relation of the basic lexical fund (the root words) to the vocabulary of the language and clarifying the role of grammatical structure in the development of language, Comrade Stalin has for the first time in the history of science defined with exceptional precision the significance and the

*Pravda, July 4, 1950, p. 4.

paths of development of language as well as its great stability and its colossal resistance to coercive assimilations.

Comrade Stalin has given a profound Marxist analysis of the superstructure on the economic structure of society (the base) and has shown that language "is the product of a great many epochs, during which it assumes shape, grows rich and develops, is polished" and cannot be a superstructure since "it lives incomparably longer than any base and any superstructure." Comrade Stalin has established that "language as a means of communication has always been and remains one and the same for society and common to its members" and thus has never been, nor could it be of a "class nature."

Comrade Stalin's teaching about language, its characteristic features and the laws of its development, is a bright example of the creative development of Marxist-Leninist science and will be included in the treasure house of Marxist-Leninist classics. It opens prospects for the development of science, whether it be the science of language or any other branch of human knowledge. It is an inspiration to creative labor and a program of scientific research work for a number of generations. It elicits a feeling of limitless joy and genuine gratitude to Comrade Stalin and obligates us, Soviet linguists, having fully assimilated the meaning of Stalin's wise indications, to place them at the foundation of all our further work in all branches of Soviet linguistics, thereby guaranteeing it the broadest flowering.

An Inspiring Work*

By Professor A. GARIBYAN

Comrade Stalin's article in the discussion of linguistic problems opens a new epoch in our science. With brilliant clarity and precision Comrade Stalin has defined the path of development for Soviet linguistics.

N. Ya. Marr's profound errors, the mistakes of his "new teaching on language," have now been definitively exposed.

Wanting to assume a Marxist position, N. Ya. Marr was unable to do so. He introduced into linguistics the false notions of the superstructural and class nature of language and thus confused himself and Soviet linguistics. N. Ya. Marr also viewed erroneously the history of the development and the paths of qualitative changes in language. N. Ya. Marr's own efforts and those of his followers to create something new, something distinct from bourgeois linguistics, have become fruitless.

All this led to Soviet linguistics' not following the correct, Marxist-Leninist path and thus reaching an impasse. Correction of the situation created was impeded by the actions, untypical of Soviet science, of N. Ya. Marr's followers, which Comrade Stalin characterized as the "Arakcheyev-like regime in linguistics."

In Comrade Stalin's article the essence of language is explained very clearly; with the aid of numerous profoundly scientific facts it is shown that language is not a superstructure on the base, and the roots of the error made in this matter by N. Ya. Marr are definitively revealed. In exposing the errors of the formula of the "class nature" of language Comrade Stalin has shown that "language as a means of communication has always been and remains one and the same for a society and common to its members."

Our leader and teacher has shown us the general path of the historical development of language and the basic stages in its history in the same way as in another classical work ("The National Problem and Leninism") he had already traced with the greatest perspicacity the paths of further development of the national languages and the formation of a universal language. The profound Marxist-Leninist theses elaborated in Comrade Stalin's article "On Marxism in Linguistics" give solutions for many most important problems of the other humanities.

One need not doubt that a broad path has opened from this moment on for the vigorous growth of Soviet linguistics. Guided by the brilliant theses of the great classic of Marxism-Leninism, Comrade Stalin, Soviet linguistics will free itself of those errors which it has committeed under the influence of N. Ya. Marr's mistakes.

As a follower of Marr, I have now thoroughly taken cognizance of the erroneousness of his ways and have equally profoundly recognized the great significance of the new classic work of Comrade Stalin for each Soviet linguist, for the whole of our linguistics. I have begun to prepare a linguistic work in my specialty following Comrade Stalin's brilliant theses.

And there is one thing more I should like to say:

Comrade Stalin's participation in the discussion has given linguists an opportunity to face fully his fatherly concern for our science, for helping it free itself from error and arrive at the correct path. In response to this concern Soviet linguists will exert all their strength and capabilities for the development of our linguistics on the firm foundation of Marxism-Leninism. We are full of gratitude to Comrade Stalin for coming to our assistance at a difficult moment of stagnation in our science.

May he live and flourish for our joy for many long years, our father and teacher, the world's greatest torchbearer in science, Comrade Stalin!

*Pravda, July 4, 1950, p. 4.

Editor's Note*

Today Pravda publishes articles which the editors have received in connection with the discussion of problems in Soviet linguistics.

The discussion initiated in Pravda elicited a very lively response from the Soviet scientific public. The editors received more than 200 articles from scholars, principally linguists working in research institutes and educational institutions of Moscow, Leningrad, the Ukraine, Belorussia, Georgia, Kazakhstan, Armenia, Lithuania, Moldavia, Latvia, Estonia and various cities, districts and provinces of the Soviet Union. The editors have also received a great many letters from Pravda readers testifying that the questions raised in the discussion aroused great interest not only among linguistic specialists but also in the broadest circles of the Soviet intelligentsia.

In the course of the free discussion, the basic problems in the development of Soviet linguistics underwent critical discussion. Almost all the participants in the discussion concluded that our linguistics is in a state of stagnation and needs proper scientific direction.

J. V. Stalin's articles "On Marxism in Linguistics," which Pravda carried June 20, and "On Several Problems of Linguistics," published today, are an outstanding creative contribution to science and mark a new stage in the development of linguistics. At the same time, J. V. Stalin's articles arm our historians, philosophers and economists with new theo-

*Pravda, July 4, 1950, p. 3.

retical theses which advance the science of Marxism-Leninism.

The great and vital principle of the development of all Soviet science is contained in J. V. Stalin's words: "***no science can develop and flourish without a struggle of opinions, without free criticism*** The liquidation of the Arakcheyev-like regime in linguistics, the repudiation of N. Ya. Marr's mistakes and imbuing linguistics with Marxism—such, in my opinion, is the way to make it possible to instill new health in Soviet linguistics."

The creative development of problems of Soviet linguistics on the basis of Marxist-Leninist teaching will lead linguistics "onto the broad highway and give Soviet linguistics a chance to occupy first place in world linguistics" (J. Stalin).

With the publication of the articles in this issue the editors are closing the discussion on problems of Soviet linguistics.

Replies to Comrades*

By J. STALIN

To Comrade Sanzheyev. —Esteemed Comrade Sanzheyev! I am replying to your letter very belatedly, since the offices of the Central Committee referred it to me only yesterday.

You are absolutely correct in your interpretation of my position in the question of dialects.

"Class" dialects, which would be more correctly called jargons, serve not the masses of the people but a narrow social elite. In addition to which, they do not posses their own grammatical system and basic lexical fund. Because of this, they can in no way evolve into independent languages.

Local ("territorial") dialects, on the contrary, serve the masses of the people and possess their own grammatical system and basic lexical fund. Because of this, several local dialects, in the process of the formation of nations, can lie at the base of national languages and evolve into independent national languages. This was the case, for example, with the Kursk-Orel dialect (Kursk-Orel "speech") of the Russian language, which lay at the base of the Russian national language. The same must be said of the Poltava-Kiev dialect of the Ukrainian language, which lay at the base of the Ukrainian national language. As for the remaining dialects of such languages, they lose their originality, coalesce into these languages and disappear in them.

There are also reverse processes where the single language of a people which has not yet become a nation because of the absence of the necessary economic conditons of development, fails because the state [organization] of this people disintegrates, and the local dialects, which have not yet had time to combine in a single language, come to life and give the impetus to the formation of separate, independent languages. This may possibly be the case, for example, with the single Mongolian language.

July 11, 1950.

To Comrades D. Belkin and S. Furer. —I have received your letters.

Your mistake lies in the fact that you have confused two different things and have substituted another subject for the subject treated in my reply to Comrade Krasheninnikova.

1. In this reply I criticize N. Ya. Marr, who, speaking about language (sound) and thinking, divorces language from thinking and thus falls into idealism. Consequently, my reply was concerned with normal people who possess a language. I further maintain that thoughts can emerge in such people only on the basis of language material, that bare thought, not connected with language material, does not exist in people who possess a language.

Instead of accepting or refuting this thesis, you put forward abnormal, mute people, deaf and dumb, who have no language and whose thoughts, of course, cannot emerge on the basis of language material. As you see, this is an entirely different subject, which I did not and could not touch upon, since linguistics deals with normal people who possess a language and not with abnormal deaf-mutes who do not.

You replaced the subject under discussion with another subject which was not being discussed.

2. It is apparent from Comrade Belkin's letter that he does not differentiate between "the language of words" (sound language) and "gesture language" (according to N. Ya. Marr, "hand" language). He thinks, evidently, that gesture language and the language of words are one and the same, that at one time human society did not possess a language of words, that "hand" language then took the place of the language of words which appeared afterwards.

But if Comrade Belkin really thinks this, then he admits a serious error. Sound language or the language of words was always the sole language of human society able to serve as a genuine means of human communication. History knows of not one human society, even the most backward, which did not have its own sound language. Ethnography knows not one backward tribe, as primitive or even more primitive than, let us say, the Australians or the inhabitants of Tierra del Fuego of the last century, which did not possess its own sound language. Sound language in the history of mankind is one of those forces which enabled people to be differentiated from the animal world, to join together in societies, to develop their thinking, to organize social production, to wage a successful battle against the forces of nature, and to attain to that progress which we have at the present time.

In this respect the importance of so-called gesture language, in view of its extreme poverty and limitations, is infinitesimal. This, strictly speaking, is not a language; it is not even a language substitute, able somehow or other to replace sound language, but an auxiliary expedient with extremely limited means, employed at times by a man for emphasizing one factor or another in his speech. Sign language cannot be equated with sound language, just as it is impossible to equate the primitive wooden plough with the modern caterpillar tractor with a five-frame plow and a row tractor drill.

3. It is apparent that you are primarily interested in deaf-mutes and only secondarily with the problems of linguistics. Obviously, it was precisely this circumstance which impelled you to address me with a number of questions. Well, if you insist, I am not averse to satisfying your request. What then is the situation with deaf-mutes? Do they think, do they have thoughts? Yes, they think and they have thoughts. It is clear that as soon as deaf-mutes are deprived of language, their thoughts cannot emerge on the basis of lingual material. Does this not mean that the thoughts of deaf-mutes are bare, not connected with "norms of nature" (N. Ya. Marr's expression)? No, it does not mean this. Thoughts of deaf mutes emerge and can exist only on the basis of those images, perceptions and ideas which are formed in their everyday life about the objects of the external world and their interrelationships through the senses of sight, touch, taste and smell. Beyond these images, perceptions and ideas thought is empty, deprived of all content, i.e. it does not exist.

July 22, 1950.

To Comrade A. Kholopov. —I have received your letter.

My reply is a bit belated in view of my being overburdened with work.

Your letter proceeds tacitly on two hypotheses: on the hypothesis that it is permissible to quote the works of this

*Pravda, August 2, 1950, p. 2. Reprinted from Bolshevik, No. 14, 1950.

or that author in isolation from that historical period with which the quotation deals, and, in the second place, on the hypothesis that these or those conclusions and formulas of Marxism, derived as a result of studying one of the periods of historical development, are correct for all periods of development and therefore must remain immutable.

I must say that both of these hypotheses are profoundly mistaken.

Several examples.

1. In the '40s of the last century, when monopoly capitalism did not yet exist, when capitalism was developing more or less smoothly along an ascendant line, spreading to new territories not yet occupied by it, and the law of uneven development could not yet operate in full force—Marx and Engels reached the conclusion that the socialist revolution could not be victorious in any one country, that it could be victorious only as a result of a general blow in all or in the majority of civilized countries. This conclusion afterwards became the guiding principle for all Marxists.

However, at the beginning of the 20th century, especially in the period of the first world war, when it became evident to all that pre-monopoly capitalism had clearly grown into monopoly capitalism, when ascendant capitalism was transformed into dying capitalism, when war revealed the incurable weaknesses of the world imperialist front, and the law of uneven development predetermined that the proletarian revolution would ripen at different times in different countries, Lenin, proceeding on Marxist theory, reached the conclusion that in the new conditions of development the socialist revolution might very well be fully victorious in one separate country, that the simultaneous victory of the socialist revolution in all countries or in the majority of civilized countries is impossible in view of the uneven ripening of the revolution in these countries, that the old formula of Marx and Engels no longer corresponds to the new historical conditions.

As is obvious, we have here two different conclusions on the question of the victory of socialism which not only contradict but exclude each other.

Some exegetes and Talmudists, who, without probing into the essence of the matter, quote formally, in isolation from historical conditions, may say that one of these conclusions, being absolutely incorrect, must be discarded, and the other conclusion, being absolutely correct, must be extended to all periods of development. But Marxists must know that the exegetes and the Talmudists are mistaken; they must know that both of these conclusions are correct—not categorically so, but each in its time: the conclusion of Marx and Engels for the period of pre-monopoly capitalism and the conclusion of Lenin for the period of monopoly capitalism.

2. In his "Anti-Dühring," Engels said that after the victory of the socialist revolution the state must wither away. On the basis of this, after the victory of the socialist revolution in our country, exegetes and Talmudists of our Party began to demand that the Party adopt measures [directed] toward the immediate withering away of our state, toward the dissolution of government agencies, toward the rejection of a standing army.

However, Soviet Marxists, on the basis of a study of the world situation in our time, reached the conclusion that in the face of capitalist encirclement, when the victory of the socialist revolution has taken place in one country alone while capitalism continues to dominate in all other countries, the country where the revolution has triumphed must not weaken but must strengthen in every way its state, state organs, intelligence agencies and army if it does not want to be destroyed by capitalist encirclement. Russian Marxists reached the conclusion that Engels' formula envisaged the victory of socialism in all countries or in the majority of countries, that it was not applicable when socialism triumphs in one country separately while capitalism holds sway in all others.

As you see, we have here two mutually exclusive different formulas on the question of the destiny of a socialist state.

The exegetes and Talmudists can say that this circumstance creates an intolerable situation, that one of these formulas must be discarded as absolutely wrong while the other is absolutely right and must be extended to every period of development of the socialist state. But Marxists must know that the exegetes and Talmudists are mistaken, for both of these formulas are correct, but not categorically, and each in its own time: the formula of Soviet Marxists for the period of the victory of socialism in one or several countries, and the formula of Engels for that period when the consecutive victory of socialism in separate countries leads to the victory of socialism in the majority of countries and consequently when the necessary conditions for the application of the Engels formula are created.

The number of such examples could be expanded.

The same thing must be said about the two different formulas on the question of language, taken from various works of Stalin and adduced by Comrade Kholopov in his letter.

Comrade Kholopov alludes to Stalin's work "On Marxism in Linguistics," in which the conclusion is drawn that as the result of the hybridization, let us say, of two languages, one of the languages usually emerges triumphant and the other dies; that consequently hybridization does not produce any new, third language, but preserves one of these languages. Further he cites another conclusion, taken from Stalin's report at the 16th Party Congress, where it is said that in the period of the victory of socialism on a worldwide scale, when socialism grows stronger and becomes a part of everyday life, national languages must inevitably coalesce into one general language which, of course, will be neither Great Russian, nor German, but something new. Comparing these two formulas and seeing that they not only do not coincide with each other but exclude each other, Comrade Kholopov is driven to despair. "From your article," he writes in his letter, "I understand that out of the hybridization of languages a new language can never be formed, while before your article I was firmly convinced that, according to your speech before the 16th Party Conference, under Communism languages fuse into one general [language]."

Obviously, Comrade Kholopov, having discovered the contradiction between these two formulas and believing deeply that the contradiction must be eliminated, considers it necessary to discard one of these formulas as erroneous and to catch hold of the other as correct for all times and countries; but precisely what formula to catch hold of, he does not know. The result is something akin to an impasse. Comrade Kholopov did not think of the fact that both formulas can be correct, each for its own time.

This is always the case with exegetes and Talmudists, who, probing into the essence of matter, quote formally, without relevance to those historical conditions with which the quotations deal, and inevitably fall into an intolerable position.

But nevertheless, if you really get to the bottom of the matter, there is no need for such a position. The fact of the matter is that Stalin's pamphlet "On Marxism in Linguistics" and Stalin's speech at the 16th Party Congress have in mind two entirely different epochs, and consequently the resultant formulas are different.

Stalin's formula in the part of his pamphlet relating to the hybridization of languages has in mind the epoch before the world-wide victory of socialism, when the exploiting classes are the dominant force in the world, when the national and colonial yokes are still imposed, when national isolation and mutual distrust are reinforced by state differences, when there is not yet national equality, when the hybridization of languages takes place by way of a struggle for domination by one of the languages, when there are not yet conditions for the peaceful and friendly cooperation of nations and languages, when the agenda is not cooperation and mutual enrichment of languages but the assimilation of some and the victory of other languages. Under these conditions there can, understandably, be only victors and vanquished. It is precisely these conditions which the Stalin formula has in mind when it says that the hybridization, let us say, of two languages results not in the formation of a new language but in the triumph of one of these languages and the defeat of the other.

As for Stalin's other formula, taken from the speech at the 16th Party Congress, particularly as it concerns the fusion of languages into one general language, here we had another epoch in mind, namely the epoch after the victory of socialism on a world-wide scale, when world imperialism will no longer exist, exploiting classes will have been overthrown, the national and colonial yoke will have been abolished, national isolation and mutual distrust of nations will have been replaced by mutual trust and the rapprochement of nations, national equality will be a reality, the policy of suppression and assimilation of languages will be liquidated, the cooperation of nations will be set going, and national languages will have the opportunity freely to enrich each other in an atmosphere of cooperation. Of course, under these conditions there can be no talk of the suppression and defeat of some and the victory of other languages. Here we will have to deal not with two languages, one of which will suffer defeat while the other will emerge victorious from the struggle, but with hundreds of national languages out of which, as the result of long economic, political and cultural cooperation between nations, will be sifted, at the beginning, the richest, most unified zonal languages, which will later coalesce into one general international language; this, of course, will be neither German, nor Russian, nor English, but a new language, which has imbibed the best elements of the national and zonal languages.

Consequently, the two different formulas correspond to two different epochs of society's development, and, precisely because they correspond to them, both are correct, each for its own epoch.

To require that these formulas not contradict and exclude each other is as absurd as to require that the epoch in which capitalism holds sway should not be in contradiction with the epoch in which socialism predominates, that socialism and capitalism should not exclude each other.

The exegetes and Talmudists view Marxism and its individual conclusions and formulas as a collection of dogmas which "never" change, in spite of the changed conditions of society's development. They think that if they learn these conclusions and formulas by heart and begin to quote them here and there, then they will be able to solve any questions whatsoever, figuring that the memorized conclusions and formulas suit them for all times and countries, for all of life's contingencies. But only those people can think this way who see the letter of Marxism but not its essence, who memorize the texts of Marxist conclusions and formulas but do not understand their content.

Marxism is a science of the laws of the development of nature and society, a science of the revolution of the oppressed and exploited masses, a science of the victory of socialism in all countries, a science of the building of communist society. Marxism, as a science, cannot stand still; it develops and perfects itself. In the course of its development Marxism cannot help but be enriched by new experience, by new knowledge; consequently, its individual formulas and conclusions must change with the passing of time, must be replaced by new formulas and conclusions corresponding to new historical tasks. Marxism does not recognize immutable conclusions and formulas obligatory for all epochs and periods. Marxism is the enemy of all kinds of dogmatism.